POPERY

THE

FOE OF THE CHURCH,

AND OF THE

REPUBLIC.

BY

JOSEPH S. VAN DYKE, A. M.

PEOPLES PUBLISHING CO.
PHILADELPHIA, PA.; CINCINNATI, O.; CHICAGO, ILL.; ST. LOUIS, MO.
SPRINGFIELD, MASS.
1871.

Popery: Foe of the Church
ISBN 1-58509-058-1

© 1999
THE BOOK TREE
All Rights Reserved

Entered according to Act of Congress, in the year 1871, by
JOSEPH S. VAN DYKE,
In the Office of the Librarian of Congress, at Washington, D. C.

PHILADELPHIA:
ELECTROTYPED AND PRINTED BY
S. A. GEORGE & CO.

Published by
The Book Tree
Post Office Box 724
Escondido, CA 92033

We provide controversial and educational products to help awaken the public to new ideas and information that would not be available otherwise. We carry over 1100 Books, Booklets, Audio, Video, and other products on Alchemy, Alternative Medicine, Ancient America, Ancient Astronauts, Ancient Civilizations, Ancient Mysteries, Ancient Religion and Worship, Angels, Anthropology, Anti-Gravity, Archaeology, Area 51, Assyria, Astrology, Atlantis, Babylonia, Townsend Brown, Christianity, Cold Fusion, Colloidal Silver, Comparative Religions, Crop Circles, The Dead Sea Scrolls, Early History, Electromagnetics, Electro-Gravity, Egypt, Electromagnetic Smog, Michael Faraday, Fatima, Fluoride, Free Energy, Freemasonry, Global Manipulation, The Gnostics, God, Gravity, The Great Pyramid, Gyroscopic Anti-Gravity, Healing Electromagnetics, Health Issues, Hinduism, Human Origins, Jehovah, Jesus, Jordan Maxwell, John Keely, Lemuria, Lost Cities, Lost Continents, Magic, Masonry, Mercury Poisoning, Metaphysics, Mythology, Occultism, Paganism, Pesticide Pollution, Personal Growth, The Philadelphia Experiement, Philosophy, Powerlines, Prophecy, Psychic Research, Pyramids, Rare Books, Religion, Religious Controversy, Roswell, Walter Russell, Scalar Waves, SDI, John Searle, Secret Societies, Sex Worship, Sitchin Studies, Smart Cards, Joseph Smith, Solar Power, Sovereignty, Space Travel, Spirituality, Stonehenge, Sumeria, Sun Myths, Symbolism, Tachyon Fields, Templars, Tesla, Theology, Time Travel, The Treasury, UFOs, Underground Bases, World Control, The World Grid, Zero Point Energy, and much more. Call **(800) 700-TREE** for our *FREE BOOK TREE CATALOG* or visit our website at www.thebooktree.com for more information.

"Farewell, a long farewell, to all my greatness!
This is the state of man: To-day he puts forth
The tender leaves of hope, to-morrow blossoms,
And bears his blushing honors thick upon him;
The third day comes a frost, a killing frost;
And,—when he thinks, good easy man, full surely
His greatness is a ripening,—nips his root,
And then he falls, as I do. I have ventured,
Like little wanton boys that swim on bladders,
This many summers in a sea of glory;
By far beyond my depth: my high blown pride
At length broke under me; and now has left me,
Weary, and old with service, to the mercy
Of a rude stream, that must forever hide me.
Vain pomp, and glory of this world, I hate ye;
I feel my heart new opened: O, how wretched
Is that poor man, that hangs on princes' favors!
There is, betwixt that smile we would aspire to,
That sweet aspect of princes, and their ruin,
More pangs and fears than wars or women have;
And when he falls, he falls like Lucifer,
Never to hope again."

King Henry VIII., Act iii. Scene 2.

FOREWARD

The main purpose of this book is to bash the living daylights out of Rome and the pope, but in an intelligent, scholarly manner. The author, Van Dyke, was a strong supporter of Protestantism, which has always been at odds with the Roman Catholic Church. Although a religious man, he wastes no time in sharing his knowledge of the various schemes, deceptions, and shortcomings of the Roman Catholic faith and the pope in general.

What makes this book so interesting is that this guy never quits! There's an endless supply of hypocrisy, lies, and double-dealing dirt that's been dug up for your enjoyment. There are many mysteries in Christianity, but the biggest mystery of all would be why anyone would accept the pope as the head of the Church after reading this book (nothing personal against the pope himself, it's his "job" or post that's the issue).

In centuries past, Protestants routinely considered the pope as being the Antichrist, following in the footsteps of Martin Luther himself—the originator of the Protestant movement who had stated this opinion on more than one occasion (verbally and in writing). Van Dyke backs up this claim in *Popery*, stating that the papacy bears unmistakable "marks of the little horn of the fourth beast, " as predicted by Daniel, and lists off countless pagan attributes that were brought into Christianity by the popes themselves, polluting the original faith in an "antichrist" fashion.

We never hear the word "popery" today, but the word seems to be used in the same fashion as "thievery" or "thuggery." Van Dyke makes it clear that after popery began, Christianity became victimized by its influence and was never the same again. After Christianity began it still took a number of centuries before an interloping pope became accepted by the religion—it was in the late 6th Century (C.E. 590) before the supremacy of the pope was accepted. Contrary to what many believe, it did *not* happen with Peter in Rome.

Once this happened, the religion set out on a path of hatred, violence, and persecution (which was no coincidence), at the same time instituting pagan ideas into the religion, which it has aggressively denied to this day. The church also made sure to suppress knowledge and spread ignorance. For more on this suppression of knowledge, see my book *Triumph of the Human Spirit*, which contains a section that outlines exactly how philosophy, science, and knowledge in general was suppressed and destroyed by the early Church. The point is that the pope was the one calling the shots and many of them throughout the years were corrupt, operating with a hidden agenda.

The pope of today might be "a really nice guy." But that doesn't necessarily mean that we need him. The true authority of the position, once examined, is virtually non-existent. The only reason it continues is because people need a figurehead, a leader, who will provide guidance and comfort. However, in reading this book, take careful note of the guidance we were given by this office in the past, and what we are expected to carry out and how we are expected to live our lives because of that "guidance" today. Many of these ideas and practices instituted by the popes have absolutely NOTHING to do with the original teachings of Jesus.

If we decide to make changes in any of our religions in the future, our decisions must be made on solid research and reason. If we've been deceived or led astray, we should be grateful to those who might point this out in an intelligent fashion. This is why this book is so important—more so to good Christians than to those who oppose the faith. Unfortunately, people who are overly strong in faith are often short on reason. They often take the stance of "don't bother me with the facts." This is quite sad. The mind is like a parachute—it won't work unless it's open.

Long standing traditions may not necessarily be right simply because they've been around for so long. This incredible book will provide one with eye-opening information that deserves to be thought about carefully—especially since the papacy continued to engage itself in immense scandals and dirty dealings throughout the entire century that followed the first publication of this book. For reference on this, I direct you to such works as *St. Peter's Banker*, by Luigi DiFonzo, *In God's Name: An Investigation into the Murder of Pope John Paul I*, by David A. Yallop, *Vicars of Christ, The Dark Side of the Papacy*, by Peter DeRosa and *The Vatican Connection: The Astonishing Account of a Billion-Dollar Counterfeit Stock Deal Between the Mafia and the Church*, by Richard Hammer, to name just a few. It's almost certain that similar crimes (as detailed in these books) are happening right now that we are completely unaware of. Recent reports have surfaced revealing that the Vatican has an entire network of spies operating throughout the world, and also functions as a separate country unto itself. A number of private agendas are clearly continuing to be carried out in secret. There is a clear pattern that the Vatican and its popes had established and kept many secrets over the years.

This book is a great place to start, and will provide one with surprising information on exactly how the Vatican ended up the way it is today. So read up on the history and early scandals of this clever organization and decide for yourself how useful it's really been for us and the world at large.

Paul Tice

PREFACE.

THE deep interest awakened in the hearts of many by the present condition and reawakened energies of the Papal Church, is our apology for presuming to call the attention of the public to Popery's inveterate hostility to civil and religious liberty. And this, most assuredly, is a subject which, though lacking novelty, imperatively demands earnest, serious, thoughtful consideration. In this age of maudlin charity for all systems of faith—instead of genuine charity for all men—the Church greatly needs a fearless reassertion of the principles and doctrines essential to the hope of salvation. Souls struggling with sin need to know that Christ, our elder brother, ever accessible, is a mighty Saviour, and that all the ransomed are "kings and priests unto God."

If the aspirations of Romanism were restricted to increased spiritual power, our duty would terminate with proclaiming a free, untrammelled Gospel, hope for every penitent at the foot of Calvary. But Rome has never yielded her right to temporal rule. The unparalleled efforts now made to extend her influence are instigated by the hope of securing control in the political world. We need, therefore, a reaffirmation of the lesson written in the struggles of thirteen centuries, that Romanism is the ally of despotism, Protestantism the friend of constitutional liberty.

This volume, presented to the public with a deep consciousness that it falls far short of meeting the demand of the times, is a feeble effort to prove that Romanism in this nineteenth century is essentially the same that it has always been, the foe of the true Church and of Republicanism, the determined enemy of liberty, civil and ecclesiastical, personal and national. Prepared in the disconnected hours of ministerial life, we crave for it the reader's generous criticism. Firmly convinced, however, that the subject is one claiming earnest attention, we timidly launch our tiny bark in the feeble hope that it may, in some slight measure at least, awaken attention to the danger to be apprehended from a system of despotism, which for fifteen centuries has fettered the limbs of freedom and darkened the way of salvation.

THE AUTHOR.

CRANBURY, N. J.,
    Sept. 1, 1871.

CONTENTS.

INTRODUCTORY.

PAGE

No just cause of alarm—Call for exertion—Hostility to Republicanism—Present activity—Growth in the United States—Relative gain—Control of irreligious masses—Summary of Evangelism—Converts to Romanism—Unity of purpose—Efforts in the West—Power shrewdly exerted—Choice locations—Designs—Efforts in the South, among the Freedmen—Measures adopted at Baltimore—Reference to Pope—Contribution from Rome—Landing of priests—Establishment of schools—Popery's displays captivate the ignorant—South a second Ireland—Efforts in the East; in large cities—Effectiveness of their agencies—Their schools teach Catholicism—Seeking ascendency—Advantages over Protestants; one will, designs masked, unscrupulous—Their boast—Assertions of bishops and papers—What has been may be—Testimony of Desraeli—The struggle inevitable.. 11

PART I.

POPERY THE PREDICTED ENEMY OF CHRIST'S KINGDOM.

CHAPTER I.

THE ROMAN POWER FORETOLD.

Popery's seemingly charmed life—Claims divine origin—Outgrowth of depraved nature—Prophecies panoramic; the picture incomplete but accurate—Difficulties of interpretation—Prominence of Romanism—Nebuchadnezzar's dream—Two objects; despotism and Christianity—The four kingdoms—Form of government of the last—Unnatural union of despotism and Republicanism—Daniel's interpretation—Rome's conquests—Her policy in later times—Never firmly consolidated—The empire divided—Kept asunder—Christ's kingdom as Rome's foe—Two states foretold—Time of rise—Predicted foe of Republicanism—The struggle through centuries—Some of the kingdoms still lending power to Rome—The Christian's hope.. 24

CHAPTER II.

THE PAPACY PREDICTED AS THE FOE OF THE TRUE CHURCH.

Rome's ecclesiastical power foretold—Nebuchadnezzar's dream and Daniel's vision—Origin of the four beasts—Character of each symbolized—The angel's interpretation—Roman power diverse—Its extended dominion—Its policy—Rise of the papacy—The Little Horn—Date of rise—Three kingdoms plucked up—Unlimited authority predicted—Origin of supremacy—Arrogance foretold—Claiming the keys—Opens heaven, thrusts into hell, retains in purgatory, forgives sin—Assertion of London Vatican; Pope reigns in both worlds—Rebels to the Pope are rebels against God—Infallibility dogma—Warring against the saints—Rome's slaughters—Changing times—Continuance of temporal power—Last act in the drama—Continuance of spiritual power—Her claim to be the true Church and the friend of Republicanism..................... 36

CHAPTER III.
FORMALISM AN OLD ENEMY OF CHRISTIANITY.

Papal claim to antiquity—A hackneyed quotation—Lord Macaulay's testimony—Protestantism as old as the Bible—Popery a novelty—Primacy of Peter a recent dogma—Supremacy of the Pope resisted, by councils, by fathers, by popes—Invocation of the dead a recent dogma—Masses not established till 9th century; purgatory not till 1430; celibacy not till 11th century; transubstantiation not till 13th—The latter denounced, by fathers, by Lateran Council—Insufficiency of the Bible—Adoration of relics—Withholding cup from laity—Immaculate conception still more recent—Infallibility the last dogma—Love of form ancient—Prevalent among Pagans and Jews—Judaism only ritualism—Supposed destruction of spirituality—Phariseeism denounced by Christ—Its early manifestation in the Church—Denounced by Apostles—Its growth; when complete Antichrist—Romanism is perfected ritualism, the foe of spirituality and Republicanism.. 46

CHAPTER IV.
ROMANISM AN APOSTASY.

Paul's predictions—The "Man of Sin" exalts himself; coming with "lying wonders"—"Strong delusion"—Continuance till Second Advent—Popery the predicted apostasy—If Romanism is not Antichrist, Protestantism must be—Which did Apostles teach?—In first three centuries Christianity pure—No unmeaning rites—Early persecutions—Christianity under popular ban—Purity a result—Rome's ceremonies unknown—No universal bishopric—Testimony of Clemens—Popery's assumptions unheard of—Conversion of Constantine—Effect upon Christian religion—Rapid growth of ceremonies—Boniface III. "universal bishop"—The title not assumed without strenuous opposition—Protest of Ireneus; of Maurus—Councils resist—Testimony of St. Ibar; of Theodoret—Two rival popes—Gregory's protest—Infallibility condemns supremacy—Lewis owned no supremacy—False decretals—Constantine's gift; a base fabrication—Nicholas I. assumes supremacy—Government of the Church entirely changed—Testimony of Mosheim; of Bellarmine. Extracts from Janus—Infallibility declares submission essential to salvation—Assertion of Boniface VIII.; of recent Vatican Council—See of St. Peter free from error—Opposers of infallibility and supremacy anathematized..................... 57

CHAPTER V.
POPERY, PAGANISM.

Boniface merely sanctioned existing rites—The motive for introducing heathen forms—Testimony of Gregory—The policy disastrous—Method of manufacturing dogmas—Pagan rites when imported—Idolaters made Christians—Same ceremonies—Fish listening to preaching—Festival of St. Anthony—A comic scene—The custom borrowed—Catholic legend—Holy water, its spiritual and corporeal usefulness—Use of incense—Original test of faith in Christ—Kneeling before idols—Specimens of prayers to Mary—Images in rows—Priests in robes—Boy in white—Burning candles—Feast of lights—Purgatory stolen—Homer's testimony—Invocation of the dead—Sample of prayers—Cincinnati's new saint—Worshipping bones—Beneath St. Peter's—Temple of Romulus—The Pantheon—Same festivals—Heathen feast-days too few—Prostration before images—Testimony of a traveller—Statue of St. Peter—Ridiculous mistakes; a canonized heathen, sainted mountain, sainted cloak—Prayer to St. Handkerchief—Patron saints—Advice to children—Processions; festival of the Annunciation—Title of Supreme Pontiff—Votive offerings—Scene in Paris—Sacrifice of the mass—Priest handling wafer—Infants—Absurdities—Asceticism—Self-whippers—Seneca's testimony—Edict of Commodius—Kissing the Pope's toe—Suing for forgiveness—Testimony of Dean Waddington; of Aringhus; of Dr. Middleton—Affinity to Buddhism—Two infallibles—Same rites—Similar defences.. 71

PART II.

POPERY ESSENTIALLY HOSTILE TO CHRISTIANITY.

CHAPTER I.
ARROGANCE.

PAGE

Unrivalled assumption—Claim of Fagnani; of Innocent III.; of Bellarmine—Extract from *L'Univers* — Contradictions — Inerrancy erring — Infallibility ignorant of geography—Le Père Lacordaire on immutability—Claim of exclusive right to interpret Scripture—Obedience the people's only right—Even God must speak through the Pope—Publication of Bible anathematized—American Bible Society denounced—Letter of Pius VII.—No version without notes—Bible-reading condemned—Indulgence purchasable—Defended by logic —Opposition to popular education; to freedom of the press—Bull of 1832—Rome's golden age—Priestly forgiveness—Anathema against opposers—Treasury of good works—Every sin its price—Without money no forgiveness —Use of rosary—Continuance in purgatory dependent on liberality—Creation of the world's Creator—Latest assumption—Catholics must yield obedience... 101

CHAPTER II.
INFALLIBILITY.

Pio Nono declares himself infallible—Response of the faithful—The encyclical and syllabus of '64—Protest against the civilization of the age—Anathema against the friends of progress—Suppression of free speech—Protests contemned —Opposition of German Prelates—Assertion of Cardinal Schwarzenberg—Recantation of the Syrian Patriarch—Threat of deposition—The manifesto of French bishops—Argument from antiquity; from silence; of Dr. Newman; from Scripture; of Bishop of Poitiers—Believe or be eternally lost—The contest ended—Refutation unnecessary, done by Catholics—Feeble attempts to answer Janus—How shall we know what Infallibility teaches—Infallible transmission—A cart-load of contradictions—Infallibility useless—An infallible infallibly pronounced a heretic—Earth's revolution condemned—The dogma of political engine; an object of horror; of sadness; of ridicule—Popery becoming more bigoted—Results of the dogma—The wail of despair —Extract from *The Tablet*—Call for a new crusade—Sympathy for Pio Nono.. 118

CHAPTER III.
DESPOTISM.

Popery's assumptions equal those of Brahmanism—Her seven sacraments instruments of tyranny—Doctrine of intention as affecting sacrifice of mass, baptism, extreme unction, marriage—Chance for an adventurer—Without intention no marriage—Confessional an engine of despotism—Catholics disqualified for American citizenship—Pope's claim of right to damn the soul—Bull against Henry VIII.; and Queen Elizabeth—Letter from heaven to king Pepin—Pope becomes temporal sovereign—Pope's denunciation of liberty—Extracts from Pio Nono's letters—Voluntary obedience impossible—Pope supreme in Council; all power emanates from him—Washing pilgrims' feet—The Senegambian negro.. 137

CHAPTER IV.
FRAUD: — RELICS.

Singular objects of veneration—Four heads of John Baptist—Eight arms of St. Matthew—Three of St. Luke—Two heads of St. Paul—Two of St. Peter—The tail of Balaam's ass—Oil from the bones of St. Elizabeth—Five legs of an ass—Pieces of the cross—Table at which Christ supped—Upper chamber—Manna of the wilderness—Blossoms of Aaron's rod—Moses' ark—The dice used in casting lots for Christ's vesture—A piece of the Virgin's petticoat—St. Anthony's toe-nails—A vial of St. Joseph's breath—A little cheese made from Mary's milk—Twelve combs "as good as new"—Rays of a star—The beard of Noah—A step of Jacob's ladder—Adoration of statues and images—Prayers said to them.. 149

CHAPTER V.
FRAUD:—MIRACLES.

Her claim of power to work miracles defended in recent publications—Specimens—Broken back made whole—Sailing on a millstone—Resisting the devil—A dead saint works miracles—Conflicting testimony—Headless woman restored—The enraged image—Liquefaction of St. Januarius' blood—Recent wonders—The wafer-infants—A dying man instantaneously made well—The infant's penance—Prayers in letters of gold—Two hundred in "Glories of Mary"—The suicide—Alexandra's head makes confession—The wooden nun—The fountain of Lourdes—Bernadette's vision—Huge fabrication....................... 155

CHAPTER VI.
IDOLATRY.

Testimony of Origen; of Gibbon—Cunningly introduced—Condemned by Council; by Pope—Controversy between Leo and Gregory II.—Tragical death of Leo IV.—Bloody Irene—Image worship established—Decree of Council of Nice—Defence of monstrous wickedness—Road-side images—"Virgin of Pillar"—The crucifix of St. Salvador—Letter of Gregory to Constantina—Filings from Paul's chains—Distinction between absolute and relative worship—Serenading the Virgin—Kissing stones—The papist's apology—The Virgin's titles—Mary's cooperation in redemption—The only fountain of hope—Appearance to St. Bridget—All mercy through Mary—The door of heaven—Dispenser of all grace—Omnipotent—God under obligations—Commands Deity—Specimen prayers from the "Glories of Mary;" from Catholic Manual—With the instructed, semi-political papers powerless—Corrected Psalms—The Prisoner-Pope imploring Mary's intercession........................... 171

CHAPTER VII.
WILL-WORSHIP.

Abstinence from meat characteristic of popery—Meat eaten on Friday eternally damns—Pope grants indulgence—Penance condemned by Paul—Self-torture—St. Simeon—Forbidding to marry characteristic of popery—Marriage more sinful than concubinage—Celibacy disastrous to morals—Testimony from Gavin; from confessions of priests; from St. Liguori—Extracts from "Master Key to Popery"—Licentiousness... 189

CHAPTER VIII.
CREDULITY.

Strong delusion—Popery worse than Paganism—Priest in the place of Christ—Disgusting exhibitions—A delusion or a falsehood—Purgatory a gross swindle—All papists enter purgatory—Supererogation—Insurance policies against hell-fire—Papal succession—The Apostolic office abrogated—No vestige of papal authority—The paramours of abandoned women in the papal chair—Two infallible pontiffs—Three infallibles, all perjured—Rejection of the fundamental doctrines of salvation—Use of incense—Form of priestly tonsure—Frauds to induce belief in miracles—Falsehood justified—Appeals to ignorance—Immutability—Bossuet's testimony—Pathetic appeal to antiquity; its absurdity—Crimes of Pope John XII.; of John XXII.; of Alexander VI.; of Julius II.; of Leo X.; of Paul III.; of Julius III.—Testimony of Genebrard; of Baronius—Crimes of Councils; of Constantinople; of Nice; of

CONTENTS.

Lyons; of Constance—John Huss burned in violation of pledges—Wyckliffe's bones disinterred—Infallibility a delusion—Misquotation of Scripture by Pius IX.—Monks proved angels.. 195

PART III.

POPERY THE FOE OF LIBERTY.

CHAPTER I.

PERSECUTION.

Tyrants' professions—The Gospel seized upon—Persecution adopted—Heretics denied the right of inheritance—Decree of the Council of Constance—The Inquisition—Persecution a dogma—Defended by theologians and emperors—Declared reasonable—Popes defend it—Bull of Urban II.—Plenary Indulgence—Councils enjoin extermination—Bishop's oath to persecute—Kings forced to destroy heretics—Scriptural prophecy—An engine of terror—Trivial pretexts for arrest—Mode of arrest—Heartlessness—Confession or torture—Methods of cruelty—Auto-da-fè—Holy wars—Preaching a crusade—Papal apology—Slaughter of Albigenses; of Waldenses—Whipping Count Raimond—Cruelty in Beziers; in Menerba; in valleys of Loyse and Frassiniere; in Calabria; in Ireland—St. Bartholomew's day—Charles IX. rejoicing—The scarlet robe put on—Te Deum in Rome—Attempt at white-washing.............. 215

CHAPTER II.

POPERY THE ENEMY OF CIVIL LIBERTY.

Opposed to every safeguard of freedom—Same in the United States as formerly in Europe—The enemy of Public School system—Charge of sectarianism—Hostility to the Bible—Their own version uncirculated—Call for expulsion—Council in Baltimore—The School Fund—Pits of destruction—One policy in Austria, another in U. S.—Unfounded assertions—Fatal results—Not content with expulsion of Bible—Divine right of education—No ground of complaint—Yield all or resist—Defence in Constitution—Liberty used to overturn liberty—Legislative assistance—India-rubber consciences—School Bill—Their schools sectarian—School books—Allegiance to Pius IX.—Pope's jurisdiction in U. S.—Protest against civilization—Denial of Jesuits—Father Hecker's address—Mistimed assertion—Priests above law—Murderer shielded—Catholics in recent war—Visit to Pope—Recognition of southern Government—Benediction to Davis—Assassination of Lincoln—Papal admission—Vote as directed from Rome—Popery established by ballot—Orange riots—Political cowardice—Spirit of Catholic press—Singular devotion—Wail of despair—Protests—Americans oppose Italian unity—Call for crusade—Catholics in Zouave dress—Raising funds—Raffle for Pope's snuff-box—No cause of alarm—Catholics despairing—Church and State... 231

CHAPTER III.

THE PAPACY A FOE TO RELIGIOUS LIBERTY.

Right of private judgment condemned—Bible reading condemned—Decision of the Trent Council—No society for distributing Bibles—Recent Bible-burning—Liguori's regret—Freedom of conscience—Declaration of Pope; of bishop; of New York *Tablet*—Persecution in 1870—Opposition to freedom of press—Sign of weakness—Education of the masses—Comparison of papal lands with Protestant—Claim of the *Catholic World*—Strange idea of liberty—Civil liberty without religious impossible—Testimony of Gattini; of Father Hyacinthe.. 265

CHAPTER IV.

POPERY AND MORALITY.

PAGE

Though many papists are rigid moralists the system immoral—Comparison of papal lands with Protestant—The immoral masses in Chicago; in London; in Rome—Entertainment in the Vatican—Estimate of priests in Rome—Morality scarcely expected—Profanity—Specimen of Pope's cursing—Anathema against all Non-Catholics; against readers of condemned books; against members of secret societies; against opposers of the Church—Four-fifths of human race under anathema—Character of Jesuits—Testimony of Macaulay—Immoralities a result of teaching—Influence of the confessional—Rules for confessors—Theft justified—Every sin lawful—Infallibility condemns speculative beliefs and sanctions impurities—Dispensing with oaths—Conduct correspondent—Infidelity and atheism fruit of popery—Testimony of Coleridge..... 274

CHAPTER V.

POPERY UNCHANGED.

Greatness departed—Methods changed; spirit the same—No dogma revoked—No superstition abandoned—Growling and waiting—No less eager for power—No less avaricious—No less intolerant—Threats of coming vengeance—Rome's worst acts defended in U. S.—Protestantism an intruder—Unrivalled audacity—Extracts from Catholic papers—Unexpected candor—Text-books—Anathema of Pius IX. against those who deny his right to persecute—The stolen child—Buried in a monastery—Persecutions in Switzerland—Imprisonment of a physician—Sentence of death against a convert—A suffering family—Convert in dungeon—American bishop in the power of the Inquisition—Protestant worship prohibited in Rome—Ingratitude—Papal Zouaves from America—Archbishop's address—Opposition to Italian republic—Popery supreme over Republicanism—No vacillation in hating liberty—Continuance of popery—Overthrow gradual—Many complications—Labor and wait.......... 288

INTRODUCTORY.

WITH those who prophesy the speedy triumph of Romanism in this country we have little sympathy; with those who counsel supreme indifference to her increased activity, less still. Whilst —as a comparison of statistics clearly proves—there is no just cause for alarm on the part of the friends of civil liberty, there are reasons many and cogent why Protestants should put forth their most strenuous efforts to defeat the wily machinations of their arch-enemy, and to give the masses the only true antidote to Popery, the simple, unadulterated Gospel. This call to redoubled exertion is found not simply in the fact that the Papacy is by necessity bitterly hostile to the true Church and to Republicanism, but especially in its recent energy and growth. Earnest effort and unwearied vigilance are duties we owe alike to ourselves and to God. If activity is essential to healthful piety; if the truth as taught by Christ is in its very nature aggressive; if the true Church of God can fulfil its mission in the world only by conscientiously endeavoring to obey the commands of its ascended Lord; if, as every well instructed Protestant firmly believes, Popery is the uncompromising enemy of genuine Christianity, and of

INTRODUCTORY.

Republican forms of government, then most assuredly Protestants should exert themselves to counteract the unparalleled efforts now made to extend Rome's baneful system of spiritual despotism over a country dedicated to Protestantism and civil liberty.

The subjoined figures show a remarkable growth of Romanism in the last thirty years. There were in the United States in

	1840	1870
Dioceses................	13	53
Vicariates-Apostolic.....	0	9
Bishops................	12	62
Priests................	373	3483
Churches and Stations..	300	5219
Catholic Population....	1,500,000	5,000,000 *

This condensed view fails in giving an adequate idea of the full strength of the Papal Church in the United States. In several of the dioceses the numbers are not given. Moreover, in addition to their regular priests, they have about 2000 seculars, and nearly 1000 clerical students. To these cohorts of Rome must be added several thousand "religious" in 286 nunneries and 128 monasteries. Imperfect as the figures are, however, they show a remarkable increase in the last three decades. Their dioceses have more than quadrupled; their bishops quintupled. Their churches are now seventeen times more numerous than in 1840; their priests nine times.†

---

* See "Catholic Directory and Ordo."

† At their present rate of increase—without supposing that numbers shall give them greater efficiency, and correspondingly more rapid

INTRODUCTORY. 13

It is indeed true that during the same period Protestantism has greatly added to its numbers. And if it had kept pace with its adversary, there would be little, if indeed any, ground for fear. But what are the facts? Is the Catholic increase only absolute, or is it an increase relative to Protestants? In 1840, of the entire population, one-twelfth was Catholic; now about one-seventh is. And of the large number belonging to no creed, the Papal Church, which is to an alarming extent a political organization, can effectually control at least its proportion. It is the constant boast of their papers that if our nation is "Non-Catholic," it is certainly "Non-Protestant;" that they are as numerous as the members of the dissevered branches of the "damnable heresy," and are therefore—even in point of numbers, to say nothing of divine right—entitled to control the future destinies of this country.*

The number of their priests is indeed small when

---

growth—they will have in 1900, Dioceses and Vicariates-Apostolic 295; Bishops 320; Priests 32,497; Churches and Preaching Stations 903,322; Catholic Population 16,666,666.

* SUMMARY OF EVANGELICISM IN THE UNITED STATES:

Denominations.	Churches.	Clergymen.	Communicants.
Baptists (Regular and Free Will)...	16,422	9,948	1,282,593
Congregationalists...............	3,043	3,168	300,362
Episcopalians....................	2,512	2,762	176,686
Lutherans.......................	3,392	1,926	388,538
Methodists (all branches).........	15,509	25,021	2,447,993
Presbyterians (all branches)......	7,262	6,833	687,373
Reformed (Dutch and German)....	1,633	1,019	279,354
Moravians......................	3,663	1,647	108,122
Total.....................	53,436	52,324	5,671,021

compared with the number of Protestant ministers; they are sufficient, however, to manage the affairs of the Church with energy and zeal. And an alarming feature in their rapidly increasing number is that many —and among these the most intelligent, zealous, efficient and intolerant—are American born: Bronson, Doane, Hecker, and a long list of others, sons of Methodists, Episcopalians, Congregationalists, and Presbyterians.

And all, from the highest to the lowest, archbishops, bishops, priests, Jesuits, monks and nuns, are assiduously engaged in advancing the interests of Rome. One will controls all. The entire country, from Maine to California, from Oregon to Florida, is comprised in the field of their operations. Divided into seven provinces, embracing fifty-three dioceses and nine vicariates-apostolic, each under the watchful eye of a bishop, there is no section of this broad land but Rome claims as her own. Wherever the interests of Popery can be subserved, a preaching station is established, an academy founded, or schools opened. As the tide of emigration rolls westward, Romanism is always the first to erect hospitals, to build churches, and to open institutions for the instruction of the young. We are learning by experience the truth of the European proverb:—" Discover a desert island, and the priest is waiting for you on the shore."

Great shrewdness is also shown in the disposition of the men and means at their disposal. Points are selected which may become centres of influence. Their strength is not frittered away in sparsely settled rural districts; but establishing themselves in state capitals, county towns, and rapidly growing cities, they effectually guard the interests of Rome in all the surrounding country, moulding public opinion, securing influence with those who control legislation, and in many instances—to the burning shame of Protestantism—educating the children of those in the communion of the true Church.

The design of the efforts so persistently made in all parts of the west, is clearly announced in a Catholic paper in Boston:—" Catholics should control and sway the west. The Church has the right to claim the immense Valley of the Mississippi, of which the Jesuit missionaries were the first explorers."

And in the south they are no less active. Organized efforts are made, on an extensive scale and with a lavish outlay of funds, to bring the freedmen over to Popery. At a convention of bishops held a few years since in Baltimore, measures to secure this end were adopted. The precaution required by the Papal Church, of conducting their proceedings with closed doors, renders it impossible for us heretics to learn all that was done by these assembled dignitaries. That agencies were inaugurated to proselyte the colored race on this continent is beyond question. And that the measures adopted and referred to the Pope for confirmation—whatever they were—received his approval, may be confidently inferred from the fact that the "Society for Propagating the Faith," whose office is at Rome, straightway contributed $600,000 in gold for one year's missionary work among the freedmen in our country. Is it not fair to assume that a contribution so large presupposes effective agencies for carrying forward the work on a scale corresponding with the cost? Jesuits—who, in worldly wisdom, if not in purity of purpose, have always been pre-eminent—seldom invest without securing large dividends, munificent returns, in blind attachment to the interests of Rome.

Lavish expenditure is immediately succeeded by organized effort. With a celerity evincing great earnestness, sixty-six Romish priests were landed in New Orleans to commence missionary efforts. And these, we are informed, are only the pioneers, whose business it is to examine the field of operations, and report to their superiors the force needed, and the points where labor can be most advantageously prosecuted. Already they have opened large, well-equipped schools for the blacks at Raleigh, at Mobile, at New Orleans, and at many other important centres of influence. And most of these institutions are successful to an extent quite disheartening to the friends of Protestantism. They have drawn largely from the schools opened by the benevolence of the northern Church, and in some instances have driven their rivals from the field.

To most Protestants, we presume, it is but too painfully evident that the Romish Church, by its gorgeous displays, is well fitted to secure a powerful influence over the hearts of a half-civilized people. Enslaved by ignorance, naturally fond of show, and taught by long years of servitude to yield an unquestioning obedience, they are quite as likely to accept the religion presented them by Rome as the simple unostentatious Gospel of Christ. A future not very remote may, therefore, possibly witness a control maintained by the Romish Church over this helpless race as complete as that now exercised over the Irish—a spiritual despotism more debasing in its character and more permanent in its nature than the slavery from which they have so recently emerged.

Not alone in the west and south, but in the east as well, especially in our large cities, Rome is laboring untiringly to acquire power. Magnificent churches are built, hospitals founded, nunneries and monasteries established, schools opened, tracts and pamphlets distributed gratuitously, and popular lectures—designed to prove that Popery is the guardian of morals, the friend of civil liberty, the educator of the masses, the dispenser of charities to the poor, the inspirer of true devotion, and the only gateway to heaven—are frequently and unblushingly delivered in the very heart of cities which owe all their greatness to the principles of the Protestant religion. Nor have these efforts proved abortive, as New York, alas, can clearly testify. In the centres of wealth and culture, which invited those possessing a religion intensely hostile to our free institutions, Romanism has proved a Grecian horse, disgorging a legion of enemies. Lawlessness, excessive taxation, political corruption, and utter contempt for the interests and wishes of the people, have followed as naturally as darkness succeeds sunset.

In Rome's list of agencies, schools occupy a prominent place. If these imparted only secular knowledge, the principles of morality and a system of religious faith free from superstition, all true friends of the rising generation might indeed rejoice. But, alas, the instruction is intensely Popish. Avowedly—except in the case of Protestant children, and there in reality—the primary object is to make the pupils ardent advocates of Romanism. Her seventy ecclesiastical institutions, her hundreds of colleges and boarding schools, her 2500 parochial schools, and her Sunday-schools in connection with almost every church, are so many nurseries of Popery, agencies for riveting the chains of spiritual despotism on the coming generation.

The design of these efforts is plain; Romanists are aiming at power in this country. We need not delude ourselves with the belief that they seek only the eternal welfare of our people. The aspirations of the Papacy in all countries during its entire history of thirteen centuries have been to become dominant in the state. And we can scarcely hope that an infallible Church will change its character at this late day. If the power for which they toil so arduously is acquired, there can be no doubt of the results. Protestantism will be persecuted, perhaps suppressed, as heretofore in Rome, and our free Bible, free schools, and free press will be things of the past. Possibly some Protestants with a smile of contempt may affirm, "Romanism, at least in this country, is a friend of liberty." Let them point, however, to the country or the time in which Popery has not opposed a will of iron to all free institutions. *

In estimating the strength of the organization which seeks our destruction, we should remember that the 5,000,000 of our citizens whose first allegiance is due to Rome are drilled to implicit obedience and directed by one will: that their plans are cunningly masked, while ours—if indeed we have any—are well known: that they are a unit in action, waging an unceasing warfare, resolved on victory; we, disconnected bands, without unity of purpose, carrying on at best but a fitful struggle. Moreover, since they are thoroughly unscrupulous in the use of means, they necessarily wield more power with the irreligious masses than we. Possibly also the tendency to ritualistic forms, so apparent in certain quarters, may prepare the way for Popery by producing a love of meaningless rites and imposing ceremonies.

---

* A Catholic paper of St. Louis said, not many years since: "We are not advocates of religious toleration except in cases of necessity. . . . . We are not going to deny the facts of history, or blame the Church and her saints and doctors, for doing what they have done and sanctioned. . . . . We gain nothing by declaiming against the doctrine of civil punishment for spiritual crimes."

Facts like these, and numerous others which might be adduced, make it but too painfully evident that there is more than an idle boast in the assertion of the *Catholic World*, that "The question put to us a few years since with a smile of mixed incredulity and pity, 'Do you believe that this country will ever become Catholic?' is changed into the question, 'How soon do you think it will come to pass?' Soon, very soon, we reply, if statistics be true, for it appears . . . . that the rate of growth of the Catholic religion has been 75 per cent. greater than the ratio of increase of population; while the rate of the increase of Protestantism has been 11 per cent. less." The Bishop of Cincinnati said, in 1866: "Effectual plans are in operation to give us the complete victory over Protestantism." Another bishop affirms: "Notwithstanding the Government of the United States has thought fit to adopt a complete indifference towards all religions, yet, the time is coming when the Catholics will have the ascendancy." The Bishop of Charleston, in his report to Rome, said: "Within thirty years the Protestant heresy will come to an end." The *Pilot*, a Catholic paper of Boston, recently affirmed: "The man is to-day living who will see a majority of the people of the American continent Roman Catholics." "Let Protestants hate us if they will," says another Catholic paper, "but the time will come when we will compel them to respect us." Should that day ever arrive, we may expect little favor from a Church, all of whose priests, according to the assertion of one of their number, " swear, we will persecute this cursed evangelical doctrine as long as we have a drop of blood in our veins ; and we will eradicate it, *secretly and publicly, violently and deceitfully, with words and deeds, the sword not excluded.*"

Though there may be no just cause for alarm, there certainly is an imperative call to action. Their oft-repeated prophecy, that from twenty-five to thirty years will suffice to give them a clear majority in this country—however absurd it may now seem to many—ought to arouse us to renewed exertion. If Papists conquered Rome, why may they not conquer America? Is it so utterly impossible that the next generation should witness the supremacy of Romanism that we can afford to fold our arms in ease?* Possessing the balance of power between the two political parties, demanding favorable legislation as the condition of support, and wielding political power in some of our largest cities, Popery is a foe whose giant strength it is folly to underestimate. Already it has succeeded in banish-

---

* Speaking of the Papacy, Mr. Disraeli said, in 1835: "What is this power beneath whose sirocco breath the fame of England is fast withering ? Were it the dominion of another Conqueror—another Bold Bastard with his belted sword—we might gnaw the fetters which we cannot burst. Were it the genius of Napoleon with which we were again struggling, we might trust the issue to the God of battles, with a sainted confidence in our good cause and our national energies. But we are sinking beneath a power before which the proudest conquerors have grown pale, and by which the nations most devoted to freedom have become enslaved—the power of a foreign priesthood."

ing the Bible from some of our public schools, and in securing, in some instances in marked degree, the advocacy of its interests in the secular press. A contest between the Papacy and Protestantism seems therefore inevitable. Other names may be substituted—Jesuitism can readily devise those that will better answer its purpose. Under the banner of civil liberty Rome may possibly bind upon us the fetters of spiritual despotism.

PART I.

Popery the Predicted Enemy of Christ's Kingdom.

CHAPTER I.

THE ROMAN POWER FORETOLD.
(Daniel ii. 31–45.)

SOMEWHAT like the fabled Sphinx, who, sitting by the roadside, propounded her riddle to each passer-by, Popery has for centuries demanded an explanation of her seemingly charmed life. And he who has presumed to give an answer not in accordance with her arrogant assumptions, has incurred her lasting enmity; where she had the power, *death*. If she comes forth from God, however, as she claims, how shall we account for the errors, the follies and the crimes that blacken her name? If she is the outgrowth of the depraved heart, or Satan's cunningest workmanship, how explain her continued power, her seemingly deathless life? Unquestionably the explanation is found in the fact that God, for infinitely wise purposes unknown to us, permits the continuance of this organized adversary of the true Church for the express purpose of testing the intelligence, the fidelity, and the zeal of his people.

Should we not expect a prediction of the rise and progress of Popery? This would be in accordance with God's usual mode of dealing with his Church.

Jehovah's purpose of destroying the world by a flood was made known one hundred and twenty years before its execution. The destruction of Babylon, Nineveh, Tyre and Jerusalem, was accurately predicted. So likewise it was declared that the descendants of Abraham should be as numerous as the stars of heaven, when as yet he had no child; and that the land of Palestine should be their possession when the Father of the Faithful owned not even a burial-place for his dead. Not only was the coming of Christ predicted immediately after the transgression of our first parents, but in subsequent ages, and long prior to the incarnation, many circumstances of his birth, mission, life and death—and some apparently the least important—were foretold.

Nor are the prophecies mere isolated predictions of disconnected events. A system dating from the fall, and embracing all the principal changes which have taken place in either the Church or the world, and extending onwards to the final triumph of Christ's cause, may be found in Scripture.

We should not, however, expect predictions respecting minute particulars. The portraiture of the future given by the prophets, is like the vivid description of a landscape viewed from a commanding eminence. Although the eye of the beholder surveys the whole extent, seeing all prominent objects, yet, by describing those which from his standpoint are most conspicuous, he presents a picture, imperfect indeed, yet accurate, of the scene. What description by a master hand is to the landscape, the predictions of the prophets are to the future. To complete the picture the reader must determine the position occupied by the seer in beholding the ceaseless current of events.

Hence, doubtless, arises the difficulty in interpreting prophecy. We are embarrassed not so much by what is said as by what is left unsaid. To unveil the half-hidden meaning of a few sentences in which is compressed the history of centuries is almost or quite impossible. Shall we, therefore, give over all effort to understand the prophetical books? Is so large a portion of the Bible given us merely to confirm the faith of the Church after the events referred to have occurred? This cannot be, otherwise the command, "Search the Scripture," would have read, 'Search the Law, the Psalms, and the fulfilled prophecies.'

In the field of prophecy, co-extensive with time, and earnestly soliciting an unprejudiced examination, we are led naturally to expect some predictions respecting the rise and progress of Popery. It is highly improbable, scarcely possible, that no place should be found for a system of religion which, numbering its adherents by millions, has existed for more than twelve centuries, and while professing to be the only true form of Christian worship, and claiming for its ecclesiastical head the titles of *"Vicar of Christ," and "Vicegerent of God,"* has not hesitated to claim and exercise the right to put to death those who, however devout, humble and Christlike in character and conduct, have denied its spiritual supremacy.

An examination of prophecy, even the most casual, reveals, in the Old Testament, two passages which refer to the Roman Empire; the former chiefly to its civil, the latter to its ecclesiastical power. In Nebuchadnezzar's dream (Dan. ii. 31-45), we have a prediction of the rise of the powerful kingdom of the west, which, during so many centuries, has lent its strength to sustain the Papal Church:

"Thou, O king, sawest, and behold, a great image. This great image, whose brightness was excellent, stood before thee; and the form thereof was terrible. This image's head was of fine gold, his breast and his arms of silver, his belly and his thighs of brass, his legs of iron, his feet part of iron and part of clay. Thou sawest till that a stone was cut out without hands, which smote the image upon his feet that were of iron and clay, and brake them to pieces. Then was the iron, the clay, the brass, the silver, and the gold, broken to pieces together, and became like the chaff of the summer threshing-floors; and the wind carried them away, that no place was found for them: and the stone that smote the image became a great mountain, and filled the whole earth."

Here are presented two, and only two distinct objects—"the great image," and "the stone cut out without hands." Although the image has its several parts—by which four successive kingdoms are represented—these constitute the one great figure symbolizing a form of civil government essentially hostile to the Church, government by brute force, *despotism*. In all the members the same spirit prevails, hostility to the kingdom set up by the God of heaven. Though having "his head of fine gold, his arms of silver, his belly and his thighs of brass, his legs of iron, his feet part of iron and part of clay," yet this image forcibly presents the idea of unity. This, which is set forth by the first symbol of the dream, is still more distinctly represented by the second. The little stone—not separated into members, but one and indivisible—is well fitted to symbolize the one spiritual kingdom, the Church of Jesus Christ, whose unity is preserved by the indwelling of the same spirit. As the invisible atoms of the stone of necessity cohere, so the different members of Christ's Church, however far separated in space or time, constitute one spiritual kingdom.

By the several parts of this figure are represented the four kingdoms, the universal empires of the world. "The head of fine gold" is a symbol of the Assyrio-Babylonian Empire, founded, in the valley of the Euphrates, by Nimrod, the grandson of Noah. Of this kingdom the chief cities were Babylon and Nineveh.* "The breast and arms of silver" represented the Medo-Persian Empire, founded by Cyrus on the ruins of the Assyrio-Babylonian. It is probably not pressing the symbol too far to suppose that by the arms are represented the two nations, the Medes and Persians, which uniting constituted this kingdom. The third

---

* These alternatively held each other in subjection till the year 625 B. C., when Nineveh was finally overthrown by the combined forces of the Medes and of Nabopolassar.

kingdom, symbolized by "the belly and thighs of brass," was the Græco-Macedonian, founded by Alexander the Great. Before this victorious warrior the preceding kingdoms crumbled to pieces, and the kingdom of brass ruled the world. The two thighs may be intended to represent the two most powerful divisions of this kingdom—the Ptolemies in Egypt, and the Seleucidæ in Syria.

The fourth kingdom is the Roman.* In reference to this the prophecy is fuller, both as respects its character and its collision with the little stone. Its form of government, partly despotic and partly republican, combining the strength of iron with the brittleness of clay, is represented by "the legs of iron and the feet part of iron and part of clay." Whereas the former three kingdoms were pure despotisms, this, whilst even more despotic, as symbolized by the harder metal, iron, always contained an element of weakness. Under the form of a republic—which was often little more than a name—it maintained a stronger hold on the affections of its subjects, and, therefore, secured longer continuance. Yet, whilst always endeavoring to convert the fragility of clay into the hardness of iron, it failed in the end, and crumbled to pieces.

"And the fourth kingdom shall be strong as iron: forasmuch as iron breaketh in pieces and subdueth all things: and as iron that breaketh all these, shall it break in pieces and bruise. And

---

* Rome was founded in 753 B. C., about 150 years before the utterance of Daniel's prophecy.

whereas thou sawest the feet and toes part of potter's clay and part of iron, the kingdom shall be divided; but there shall be in it of the strength of the iron, forasmuch as thou sawest the iron mixed with miry clay. And as the toes of the feet were part of iron, and part of clay, so the kingdom shall be partly strong, and partly broken. And whereas thou sawest iron mixed with miry clay, they shall mingle themselves with the seed of men; but they shall not cleave one to another, even as iron is not mixed with clay. And in the days of these kings shall the God of heaven set up a kingdom, which shall never be destroyed: and the kingdom shall not be left to other people, but it shall break in pieces and consume all these kingdoms, and it shall stand for ever. Forasmuch as thou sawest that the stone was cut out of the mountain without hands, and that it brake in pieces the iron, the brass, the clay, the silver, and the gold; the great God hath made known to the king what shall come to pass hereafter: and the dream is certain, and the interpretation thereof sure."—Dan. ii. 40–45.

Here it is expressly said that "the fourth kingdom shall be strong as iron, and break in pieces and bruise." During its existence as a limited monarchy (nearly two hundred and fifty years), it gradually extended its power till all the surrounding nations fell before its victorious arms. The exact date of its succession to the kingdom of brass we cannot fix. Of the fact, however, there can be no doubt. From the year 509 to 48 B. C., during her existence as a republic, Rome extended her conquests over a great part of Asia, Africa and Europe. Britain was twice entered. Cæsar's legions penetrated to the heart of Germany. Macedon, Syria and Egypt were conquered. After the battle of Pharsalia (48 B. C.), in which

Pompey, the commander of the armies of the republic, was utterly defeated by Cæsar, the government was imperial rather than republican. For five hundred and twenty-four years subsequent to this, the emperors, for the most part, were content with retaining those provinces which were conquered under the republic. The advice bequeathed by Augustus, of confining the empire within its natural limits, the Euphrates, the Desert of Africa, the Atlantic Ocean, and the Rhine and Danube, was seldom departed from. A few exceptions there indeed were. Britain was made to submit to the Roman yoke during the reign of Domitian; Dacia, Armenia and Assyria during that of Trajan.

The fourth kingdom was, as Daniel had predicted, strong as iron, enduring in its three forms, of a monarchy, a republic and an empire, for more than twelve centuries, and wielding, for nearly the half of this long period, the sceptre of universal dominion. During all the ages of its existence, however, it was "iron mixed with miry clay." It was never a firmly consolidated empire. It was the unnatural union of despotism and democracy.

Of the Roman state, the fourth section of the image, Daniel declared, "the kingdom shall be divided." The ten toes, like the ten horns of the fourth beast, (Dan. vii. 24, and Rev. xvii. 16,) represent the ten kingdoms established on the fall of the empire. "The fourth beast shall be the fourth kingdom . . . .

And the ten horns out of this kingdom are ten kings that shall arise." By the reasoning of Bishop Newton, it has been successfully established that these ten kingdoms should be looked for in the Western Roman Empire, that portion of the fourth kingdom which was no part of the preceding three. As to the powers constituting them, however, diversity of opinion always has, and perhaps always will, exist.

By the words, "they shall not cleave one to another," we have, perhaps, a prediction that the ten kingdoms shall never again be united in one empire. Certain it is, that since 476 (the date of the downfall of the Roman Empire generally received) they have, with very slight changes, remained territorially the same.

By "the stone cut out of the mountain without hands" is symbolized the kingdom of Christ, which "the God of heaven shall set up," and "which shall never be destroyed." These expressions, and especially the latter, are evidently inapplicable to any form of civil government. "Cut out without hands" indicates God's agency, and not man's. Of the "kingdom not of this world," all the benefits, blessings and privileges are heaven's free gift to the human race. And of what earthly kingdom could perpetuity be predicated? Is not decay written on all?

Of this kingdom two states are here prefigured; one of comparative insignificance, represented by the stone; one of widely extended and powerful influence, symbolized by the mountain. The same gradual growth is alluded to in Christ's parable of the Mustard Seed.

We are also told when this kingdom shall arise: "In the days of these kings." It was during the existence of the last of the four, when the entire world humbly bowed at the throne of the proud Cæsars, that God, by the incarnation of his Son, set up, or perhaps more properly, as the Latin Vulgate has it, "*resuscitated*" a kingdom. Having existed since the Fall, it was now strengthened, enlarged, and its privileges extended to the Gentiles.

In this entire prophecy reference is evidently had to the rise and progress of that empire which, divided into ten kingdoms, has given its power and strength to Popery. It makes war with the Lamb. It is the enemy of the Church and of Republicanism, the deadly foe of liberty, civil and religious, personal and national. With democracy it can form no alliance, and will make no compromise. The iron will not mix with the clay. With Protestantism, the parent and champion of constitutional government, it wages unceasing warfare. Deriving moral support from Popery, its natural ally, it is antagonistic to the kingdom of the little stone, so far at least as this is hostile to despotism.

The warfare, desperate and deadly, is not carried on, however, with carnal weapons. Noiselessly, but with terrible earnestness, the struggle is prolonged through centuries. Kingdoms rise, grow hoary with age and crumble to decay, still the contest is undecided. The

ORIENTAL PATRIARCH FORCED TO RESIGN HIS RIGHTS. *Page* 122.

three kingdoms, of gold, of silver and of brass, have become as "chaff of the summer threshing-floors," but the stone has not yet become a great mountain filling the whole earth. Nebuchadnezzar, Cyrus, Alexander and Cæsar, sleep in their unknown graves, but not as yet have the feet and the toes of the great image, revealed in the palace of Shushan, crumbled to pieces.

Of the ten kingdoms which, "with one mind gave their power and strength unto the beast," some are yielding to the rule of Immanuel; others, in still lending their strength to the papal Antichrist, are filling to the full the cup of wrath. In their adulterous alliance with the Mother of Harlots they are aiding in sustaining a system which, "composed of specious truth and solid falsehood," is at war with the fundamental doctrines of the Gospel. The Christian's hope is sustained, however, by the assurance, "The ten horns which thou sawest upon the beast, these shall hate the whore, and shall make her desolate and naked, and shall eat her flesh, and burn her with fire."* Of Christ's kingdom it is said, "It shall break in pieces and consume all these kingdoms, and it shall stand for ever."

---
* Rev. xvii. 16.

CHAPTER II.

THE PAPACY PREDICTED AS THE FOE OF THE TRUE CHURCH
(Daniel vii. 2-27.)

IT is the assertion of Protestants not only that Rome's civil power, but that the Papacy itself, was predicted twelve centuries before its rise. Of this affirmation the truth becomes apparent if to a description of Nebuchadnezzar's image be added an examination of Daniel's vision; for by the former is foretold Rome's civil despotism—by the latter, her spiritual. The powers represented to the king as four kingdoms, appeared in vision to the prophet as four wild beasts trampling upon Christianity. To the monarch even the Church is "a kingdom which the God of heaven should set up," small indeed in its origin, but destined to fill the whole earth; to the prophet it is a feeble band of struggling martyrs, "the saints of the Most High," oppressed by the little horn of the fourth beast. It is a small and scattered company of faithful witnesses, ground down by the Papal hierarchy for the term of 1260 years, yet, inspired with faith in God's promises, suffering in the assured hope of ultimate triumph. Daniel says:

"I saw in my vision by night, and behold, the four winds of the heaven strove upon the great sea. And four great beasts came up from the sea, diverse one from another. The first was like a lion, and had eagle's wings: I beheld till the wings thereof were plucked, and it was lifted up from the earth, and made stand upon the feet as a man, and a man's heart was given to it. And, behold, another beast, a second, like to a bear, and it raised up itself on one side, and it had three ribs in the mouth of it between the teeth of it: and they said thus unto it, Arise, devour much flesh. After this, I beheld, and lo, another, like a leopard, which had upon the back of it four wings of a fowl; the beast had also four heads; and dominion was given to it. After this I saw in the night visions, and behold, a fourth beast, dreadful and terrible, and strong exceedingly; and it had great iron teeth: it devoured and brake in pieces, and stamped the residue with the feet of it: and it was diverse from all the beasts that were before it; and it had ten horns. I considered the horns, and behold, there came up among them another little horn, before whom there were three of the first horns plucked up by the roots: and behold, in this horn were eyes like the eyes of man, and a mouth speaking great things."—Dan. vii. 2-8.

These four beasts arise out of the troubled sea of human society. "The first, like a lion," symbolizes the Babylonian Empire, the characteristics of which were boldness, consciousness of power, cunning and cruelty. "The wings of an eagle" represent its rapid conquests. In the later years of the empire these were plucked. Its victorious arms no longer struck terror. By the expression "a man's heart was given unto it," we are to understand that the rigors of despotism were somewhat abated.

By the "second beast, like to a bear," is symbolized the kingdom of the Medes and Persians. In the expression, "it raised up itself on one side," we find a prophecy of the superior enegy and efficiency of one of the nations constituting this kingdom. The three ribs in the mouth of it denote a partially civilized people in the act of devouring kingdoms to increase their own strength. The command, "Arise, devour much flesh," was fulfilled by Cyrus.

"The third beast, like a leopard," represents the Græco-Macedonian empire. The rapidity of Alexander's conquests, by the aid of his four distinguished generals, is denoted by "the four wings of a fowl," and the division of the kingdom on his death, *by four heads*.

Having premised this much—which seemed necessary to an understanding of the scope of this famous prophecy—we hasten to consider the fourth beast. As this represents a power still in existence, and bitterly hostile to Christianity, it is, to us, more deeply interesting than its predecessors. Of it the interpreting angel says:

"The fourth beast shall be the fourth kingdom upon earth, which shall be diverse from all kingdoms, and shall devour the whole earth, and shall tread it down, and break it in pieces. And the ten horns out of this kingdom are ten kings that shall arise: and another shall rise after them; and he shall be diverse from the first, and he shall subdue three kings. And he shall speak great words against the Most High, and shall wear out the saints of the Most High, and think to change times and laws: and they shall be given into his hand, until a time and times and the dividing of time. But the judgment shall sit, and they shall take away

PAPACY THE FOE OF THE CHURCH.

his dominion, to consume and to destroy it unto the end. And the kingdom and dominion, and the greatness of the kingdom under the whole heaven, shall be given to the people of the saints of the Most High, whose kingdom is an everlasting kingdom, and all dominions shall serve and obey him."—Dan. vii. 23–27.

Diverse from all others, being the union of monarchical and republican principles, it had the power to repress revolt and the facility of adapting itself to the ever varying phases of human society. Hence, for more than six centuries, half the time between its founding and the division into the ten kingdoms, its very name was a terror. Of her extent and power we need no proof. "Half our learning is her epitaph." She became terrible and strong exceedingly. By her invincible legions all independent nationalities were trampled in pieces. Being first crushed, they were devoured, and became parts of the all-embracing empire. At length, as we have seen (Chapter I.), this kingdom was divided into ten, represented in Daniel's vision by ten horns; in Nebuchadnezzar's by the toes of the image. Thus, on the Roman state are found all the marks of the beast.

Among the ten horns another little horn came up, "before whom there were three of the first horns plucked up by the roots." The belief that this little horn represents the Papal hierarchy is, among Protestants, almost universal. It was to arise after the ten kingdoms. These arose in the interval between 356 and 526 A. D. The Papacy, after gradually acquiring power for three centuries, was perfected as an engine of ecclesiastical despotism in 606 A. D., when Phocas, the murderer and usurper, conferred upon Boniface III. the title of *Universal Bishop*. Then Romanism, as a system of oppression, became complete. The little horn had grown upon the unsightly monster.

The three horns plucked up by the roots were, it is commonly believed, the kingdom of the Goths, of the Ostrogoths, and of the Lombards.

Of this last foe of the true Church, the characteristics are given by Daniel. "And behold, in this horn were eyes like the eyes of a man." "By its eyes," says Sir Isaac Newton, "it was a seer. A seer is a bishop; and this Church claims the universal bishopric." Ecclesiastical power is its most marked characteristic. In this it is "diverse from all the kingdoms that were before it." The mode in which this unlimited authority was acquired, furnishes an instructive chapter in history. On the conversion of Constantine, a golden opportunity was given of evangelizing the world. The bishops of Rome, however, caring more to extend their own authority than to spread a knowledge of the truth, labored zealously to acquire rule over the entire Church. Their stupendous assumptions, favored by the profound ignorance of the people, made the effort comparatively easy. Soon the Pope's authority was believed to be equal, and by some, even superior to that of a General Council. Still, by the more intelligent of the clergy, these claims were stoutly resisted.

Refusing, however, with characteristic effrontery, to yield the assumed right to all authority, secular and religious, they in the end won the victory—the Roman bishop was acknowledged *spiritual and temporal sovereign*. Henceforth the episcopal court occupied the room of the imperial.

Again; it is said, "He shall speak great words against the Most High." The arrogant assumptions of the Popes know no bounds. They claim to be legitimate successors of the Apostle Peter, vicegerents of God, vicars of Christ. In their possession, they gravely tell us, are the keys of heaven and of hell. Sitting in the temple of God, the Pope may deal out glory or damnation, as suits his fancy. Even each priest, according to Roman infallibility, can forgive sins, and sell the most enrapturing bliss of heaven to the highest bidder or the wealthiest knave. Liguori—one of their canonized saints, and whose "Moral Theology," a standard text-book in their theological schools, is declared, by the highest papal authority, to be " sound and according to God "—affirms, " the proper form of absolution is indicative: *I, the priest, absolve thee.*" To the claim of sole right to interpret Scripture, the Pope adds the still more absurd claim of infallibility. This, so recently exalted into a dogma, every true Catholic, according to the *Freeman's Journal* of August 20th, 1870, must *cordially assent to, and believe with the whole heart*. And the *London Vatican* of July 29th, 1870, uses this language: " It was not enough that a mortal should rule over God's kingdom on earth, *unless the keys of heaven were also committed to him.* *He (the Pope) was to reign in both worlds at once. It would seem that God in stooping to become man, had almost made man God.*" Again: " He who lifts up his hand against the Pope resembles, without knowing it, the accursed Jew who smote Jesus in the face." And again: " The Church has told them (the heretics) who and what his Vicar is. Either her message is true, and then *all who refuse obedience to the chair of St. Peter are rebels against the Most High, and without hope of salvation; or it is false, and then the Church of Christ has ceased to exist.*" " Not a few are found," we are told in the fourth chapter of the Constitution lately promulgated, " who resist it," and for this reason, says the Decree, " we deem it altogether necessary solemnly to assert *that prerogative (infallibility) which the only begotten Son of God deigned to annex to the supreme pastoral office.*" Surely Popery has a mouth speaking great things.

Daniel further says, " I beheld, and the same horn made war with the saints, and prevailed against them." And the interpreting angel says, " He shall wear out the saints of the Most High." What language could more fitly characterize the Papacy? It has waged for more than twelve centuries a relentless warfare against the followers of Christ. We may affirm, and without exaggeration, that this little horn of the fourth beast, the Papacy, has put to death millions of Christians. And of thousands of others the lives have been rendered more intolerable than death itself. History proves the appropriateness of the names given to Popery in Revelation, "the scarlet colored beast, drunk with the blood of the saints, and of the martyrs of Jesus;" "the tormentor of the saints of the Most High."

"He shall think to change times and seasons." Who, since the days of Julius Cæsar, save the Popes, has assumed the right of regulating the calendar, and enacting laws for the world?

With the interpretation of Daniel's expression, "a time, and times, and the dividing of time," we have, in this chapter, little to do. It may be, and most probably is, an equivalent of the expression in Revelation, "a thousand two hundred and threescore days." Each, perhaps, may be properly understood as indicating the continuance of Rome's temporal supremacy, 1260 years. Possibly, also, dating the rise of Antichrist in A. D. 606, when Boniface III. was declared universal bishop, we ought to have expected, between the years 1866 and 1872, the overthrow of the Pope's authority. And some, no doubt, will imagine that in the removal of the French troops from Rome, in the overthrow of Napoleon III., and in the Pope's loss of temporal power—following as they did so close on the promulgation of the dogma of Papal infallibility—they discern one of the last acts in the drama of this mystery of arrogance.

Not less foreign to our present purpose is the explanation of the passage, "But the judgment shall sit, and they shall take away his dominion to consume and to destroy it *unto the end.*" That this powerful foe of the true Church is to continue—not in its temporal power, but in its spiritual—till the judgment of the great day, seems highly probable. Paul affirms, "Then shall that Wicked be revealed, whom the Lord shall consume with the spirit of his mouth, *and shall destroy with the brightness of his coming.*"* In the Apocalypse (xiii. 3), where the history of this scourge of Christianity is fully given, we are told "the deadly wound shall be healed, and all the world shall wonder after the beast." It seems probable, and some tell us *certain*, that the system of superstition, known as Popery, shall "*continue unto the end;*" that through all time it is to be the relentless enemy of the Church.

However this may be, certain it is that the Papacy is described in this chapter as during its entire continuance the uncompromising foe of Christ's kingdom. Bearing unmistakably the marks of the little horn of the fourth beast, having an ever-living connection with the despotism from which it sprang, and waging an incessant warfare with the saints of the Most High, it has ever shown itself the tireless enemy of civil and religious liberty, of Christianity, and of Republicanism. As such it was predicted. As such it has ever been known. And yet, either with blindness that deserves pity, or with arrogance that richly merits rebuke, it

---

* 2 Thess. ii. 8.

even now proudly claims to be *the Church, the only Church, Holy Mother infallible, visibly guided by the indwelling of the Holy Ghost, the guardian of morals, the guide of conscience, the most efficient agent of civilization, the friend of freedom.*

CHAPTER III.

FORMALISM AN OLD ENEMY OF CHRISTIANITY.
(2 Thess. ii. 7.)

PAPISTS—we shall seldom honor them with the name of Catholics—greatly pride themselves in the antiquity of their organization. They boastingly ask Protestants, "Where was your so-called Church three centuries ago?" With a frequency and an eagerness which painfully remind one of the struggles of a drowning man, they quote, in proof of Rome's greatness and especially of her perpetuity, a passage from Lord Macaulay's "Review of Ranke's History of the Popes:"

"No other institution (save the Catholic Church) is left standing which carries the mind back to the times when the smoke of sacrifice rose from the Pantheon, and when camelopards and tigers bounded in the Flavian amphitheatre. The proudest royal houses are but of yesterday compared with the line of the supreme Pontiffs. That line we trace back in an unbroken series from the Pope who crowned Napoleon in the nineteenth century to the Pope who crowned Pepin in the eighth; and far beyond the time of Pepin the august dynasty extends, till it is lost in the twilight of fable. . . . .

Nor do we see any sign which indicates that the term of her long dominion is approaching. She saw the commencement of all the governments and all the ecclesiastical establishments that now exist in the world; and we feel no assurance that she is not destined to see the end of them all. She was great and respected before the Saxon had set foot on Britain, before the Frank had passed the Rhine, when Grecian eloquence still flourished in Antioch, when idols were still worshipped in the temple of Mecca. And she may still exist in undiminished vigor when some traveller from New Zealand shall, in the midst of a vast solitude, take his stand on a broken arch of London Bridge to sketch the ruins of St. Paul's."

By the music of this inflated eloquence they have beat many an inglorious retreat. Nay, it has even done service in leading an attack. The Rev. James Kent Stone, a recent pervert to Popery, in his " Invitation Heeded," hurls it against the luckless head of defeated Protestantism. But how much argument is there in it? The devil is as old as the Romish Church, and a little older, and probably has quite as long a lease on life; is he any better for that? If, however, an answer is necessary, or rather possible—bombast is generally unanswerable—it may be found in an appeal from the youthful, "*vealy*" reviewer, to the mature, accurate, learned and elegant historian; from Macaulay, the youth giving promise of future greatness, to Macaulay, the intellectual giant. In his " History of

England," with a sword that cuts the keener for its polished beauty, he lays bare the treacherous heart, pierces the arrogant assumptions, unveils the concealed wickedness, and utterly demolishes many of the absurd claims of the Papacy. One quotation must suffice. This, chosen because of its bearing on our general subject, the hostility of Popery to modern civilization, shall be taken from Vol. I. chap. i. page 37:

"During the last three centuries, to stunt the growth of the human mind has been her (the Church of Rome's) chief object. Throughout Christendom, whatever advance has been made in knowledge, in freedom, in wealth, and in the arts of life, has been made in spite of her, and has everywhere been in inverse proportion to her power. The loveliest and most fertile provinces of Europe have, under her rule, been sunk in poverty, in political servitude, and in intellectual torpor; while Protestant countries, once proverbial for sterility and barbarism, have been turned, by skill and industry, into gardens, and can boast of a long list of heroes and statesmen, philosophers and poets. Whoever, knowing what Italy and Scotland naturally are, and what, four hundred years ago, they actually were, shall now compare the country round Rome with the country round Edinburgh, will be able to form some judgment as to the tendency of Papal domination. The descent of Spain, once the first among monarchies, to the lowest depths of degradation, the elevation of Holland, in spite of many disadvantages, to a position such as no commonwealth so small has ever reached, teach the same lesson."

If by Rome's claim to antiquity is meant that her doctrines antedate those of Protestantism, few things are more untrue. The cardinal beliefs of the Reformed Churches are as old as the Gospel, nay, as the giving of the law from Mount Sinai, nay, as the announcement of salvation made to Eve in Eden. These doctrines,— that the one living and true God is the only legitimate object of divine worship; that Christ is the only Saviour, a perfect sacrifice; that his kingdom is not of this world, but an invisible, spiritual kingdom, composed of the faithful and their infant children; that the condition of union with his spouse, the Church, is regeneration of heart wrought by God's spirit; that the triune God alone can pardon sin; that he and he exclusively is the Lord of the conscience,— are doctrines not only as old as the Reformation, but as old as the inspired Word of God, and as imperishable as the Church itself. But the dogmas of Romanism are a mere novelty in the religious world. Thus the primacy of Peter, a doctrine now considered vital to the system, is of comparatively recent origin. Admitting that Peter was in Rome, we may safely challenge the proof that *he was universal bishop.* And his successors? They were persons so obscure that even Papal infallibility cannot agree upon their names. Though Vicars of Christ, supreme pontiffs, they are never even alluded to by the Apostle John, Peter's survivor for at least forty years. Undutiful son, write so much Scripture, and make no mention of Holy Father! Strange indeed! Notwithstanding Pius IX., in his Invitation "*To all Protestants and other Non-Catholics*," declares, "No one can deny or doubt that Jesus Christ himself . . . . . *built his only Church in this world on Peter; that is to say, the Church, One, Holy, Catholic, and Apostolic,*" we have the heretical hardihood to affirm that the primacy of Peter was entirely unknown in the early ages of the Church. It was devised in the latter part of the sixth century—a means to the accomplishment of an end—to bolster up the assumptions of Rome's proud bishops. So likewise the supremacy of the Pope (never even claimed till A. D. 590) was resisted by Councils, denounced by many of the ablest of the fathers, and condemned by an infallible Pope and canonized saint, GREGORY. (See next Chapter.) The invocation of the dead, now so common with Romanists, did not even begin to manifest itself till the third century. The use of masses, solemnly condemned in the Council of Constantinople, A. D. 700, and again in the seventh Greek Council, 754, was not established till the ninth century. The doctrine of purgatory—the hen that lays the golden egg—was not an essential part of Popery till the Council of Florence, A. D. 1430. The doctrine of celibacy—that mark of the great apostasy, "forbidding to marry," (1 Tim. iv. 3,) is only about 780 years old. For nearly eleven centuries every priest might have a wife, and live a life free from scandal. Now they are "*Fathers*" *without wives.* Transubstantiation—Papal cannibalism—did not originate till about the middle of the fifth century, and was severely denounced by some fifteen or twenty of Rome's most honored fathers. Not till A. D. 1215, in the fourth Lateran Council, was it exalted into a dogma. So also the insufficiency of the Bible as a rule of faith and practice is an assertion frequently and pointedly condemned by at least a dozen of the fathers, Rome's invariable resort. The adoration of relics—that wondrous promoter of traffic in dry bones—originated about the same time as the worship of saints and martyrs. The withholding of the cup from the laity was pronounced by Pope Gelasius (A. D. 492) to be an "*impious sacrilege.*" And to our own times was left the honor—if honor it be to have outstripped the superstition of the dark ages—of promulgating the dogma of the "Immaculate conception of the Virgin," "Mother of God," "Mirror of Justice," "Refuge of Sinners," and "Gate of Heaven." In fact, not till the present year was the system rendered *complete, symmetrical, perfect.* It needed, like Buddhism, its elder sister, the solemn announcement of the infallibility of the supreme pontiff. This, after six months' angry discussion, has been ostentatiously presented to the world as the infallible dogma of five hundred fallible bishops. (How many fallibles may be necessary to make an infallible, possibly Pio Nono can now tell.) Thus we can conclusively show that the distinctive doctrines and rites of Romanism are mere novelties, less ancient than the doctrines and practices of Protestantism.

If by her claim to antiquity, however, is meant that the unhallowed love of forms is as old as the Gospel, we do not deny it. Even in the Apostle's time, depraved man was beginning to corrupt the pure religion of Jesus. "The mystery of iniquity," said Paul, "doth already work, only he who now letteth (hindereth) will let, until he be taken out of the way." As under the tuition of Satan, the deceitful heart developed every system of false religion by which the world had been deluded, so by cunningly employing the truth revealed by Christ, it was commencing to weave a new system of superstition as much like to Paganism, as two garments made from the same material are like to each other. Originating in the preference of the forms of devotion to the spirit—a tendency dating backward to the Fall—this mystery of iniquity, after centuries of gradual development, culminated in Romanism, Satan's last agency for recruiting the armies doing battle with the truth. Though last, its efficiency is by no means least, since the unrenewed naturally turn from the salvation of the Lord to that which, being of their own devising, is more congenial to fallen human nature, easier of attainment, and more flattering to vanity.

In one sense, therefore, we are ready to concede that Popery's claim to antiquity is well founded. Romanism, as ritualism, has always existed, not only in the Pagan world—Paganism is unbaptized Popery—but also in connection with the religion revealed from heaven, and probably will continue to the end of time, and be destroyed only by the brightness of the Saviour's coming. It originated in Eden; at once becoming more pleasing to sensuous man than the worship of God in spirit and in truth. Cain—preferring self-chosen rites to those enjoined by express divine command, and destitute of the spiritual vision of Christ as the sin-atoning Lamb—was a type of Pagan, Jew, Papist, all ritualists. And what was the worship of the wicked antediluvians but one of rites? What was Judaism itself, during almost the entire history of the Jewish nation, but a religion of ceremonies? Its ritual service, though intended and well adapted to keep the vital truths of redemption prominently before the mind, was allowed by many, may we not say by most, to assume such an importance as to *overshadow the tree of righteousness*. Hence, failing to apprehend its true spirit, they crucified him whom the types distinctly prefigured. Coming as "a preacher of righteousness," and not to establish a kingdom in which the forms of devotion should prevail without piety in the heart, he was put to death, and that by those whose mission it was to announce him as the world's spiritual deliverer.

So likewise Phariseeism, loaded with traditions and meaningless moral distinctions, was only Popery under another name. Hostile, then, as ever to the true Church, it was severely denounced by Christ. In his Sermon on the Mount, he laid the axe at the root of the evil, declaring that the righteousness which God accepts is not mere compliance with certain outward requirements of the law and the observance of traditional precepts, but piety in the heart. All, therefore, whether Pharisees or Romanists, who so love the forms of worship and exalt the "traditions of the fathers" as to make "the word of God of none effect," are condemned in terms too explicit to be misunderstood.

Even in the Church of Christ, where the very first requirement is spirituality, this tendency to ritualism manifested itself. As Christianity was the outgrowth of Judaism, some were strongly disposed to place reliance in forms. "Certain men who came down from Judea taught the people, except ye be circumcised after the manner of Moses, ye cannot be saved." Evidently some were trusting to the observance of a profitless rite. The mystery was working. The germ of Popery was developing. For the purpose of crushing this, a council, summoned from the entire Church, consisting of apostles and elders (Peter, it would seem, was not Pope), assembled in Jerusalem. After much discussion, in which Paul and Barnabas and James, as well as Peter, engaged, "the apostles and elders and brethren" (evidently there was as yet no spiritual sovereign) sent letters "unto the brethren of the Gentiles," affirming, "It seemed good to the Holy Ghost and to us to lay upon you no greater burden than *necessary things*." "Believing that through the grace of our Lord Jesus Christ we shall be saved," they condemned dependence on circumcision, on any and every outward form, recommending Christians to the merit of Christ for redemption. Only necessary things, the essentials of religion, were enjoined. Thus the primitive Church, in council assembled, not only furnished evidence of the early working of this "mystery of iniquity," and a refutation of the claim of supremacy for Peter, but in reality most solemnly and emphatically condemned the spirit of Popery, the ever existing and always pernicious tendency to rely upon the outward rites of religion.

Few unbiassed readers will hesitate in conceding that Paul's Epistles, and especially the one to the Galatians, were written with the design of denouncing the tendency to ritualism. He endeavors to refute the errors which were beginning to pervert the Gospel. He directs believers to Christ, and to Christ alone. He condemns dependence on forms—on anything save the blood of Jesus. In holy earnestness he exclaims, "Though we, or an angel from heaven, preach any other Gospel unto you than that we have preached, let him be accursed." Full well did the Apostle discern the tendency of the human heart to become enamored with forms, and in the observance of these, vainly, and perhaps unconsciously, fancy it is working out its own salvation, content without the sense of forgiveness from Christ, or the spirit of godliness in the soul. Therefore, of this "mystery of iniquity" he affirms, "it doth already work."

But although thus sternly reproved, in the lapse of

time, from depraved human nature, it again sprang up, and having established itself, has tyrannized over the souls of men for nearly thirteen centuries. Hence, in one sense, we are ready to admit the claims of the Papists that theirs is the ancient Church. The principles upon which they found their system are as old as the Fall, and as enduring as the human race; but so far from receiving any countenance from Christ and his apostles, they were severely denounced by them; but arising out of corrupt human nature, however frequently refuted, and however severely condemned, they are sure to reappear, and almost certain to find stanch advocates. When these principles, perceptible only in germ in the Apostles' time, had gained the ascendency, Antichrist had arisen; the power and the spirit of godliness were supplanted by dead forms, "*the man of sin*," "*the son of perdition*," "*the mystery of iniquity*," "*that Wicked*," was revealed.

It is scarcely necessary for us to remind the reflecting reader that Romanism, as ritualism, as cold and heartless formalism, not only has ever shown itself the enemy of a pure, spiritual, unfettered Gospel, but the endeared associate of despotism. If not the foe, it certainly has not been the friend of free institutions. Its pomp and glitter, its extravagance and meaningless pageantry, ill comport with the simplicity, economy, and rugged intelligence of Republicanism. Ritualism, Popery, despotism; intelligence, Protestantism, civil liberty, are inseparable friends.

THE CEREMONY OF WASHING FEET. Page 146.

CHAPTER IV.

ROMANISM AN APOSTASY.
(2 Thess. ii. 3–12.)

IN the prophecy of Paul, the organized opposition to the Church is denominated "the man of sin," "the son of perdition," "the mystery of iniquity," "that Wicked." That the passage is a prediction of the rise, progress and overthrow of Popery, an examination, we think, makes clearly manifest. The Apostle affirms that even in that early age the mystery was beginning to work. This we have already found to be true of the Romish Church. His remaining statements await, and in the progress of our work, we trust, shall receive, an examination, proving them not only strikingly applicable to the Papacy, but applicable to no other system of error, religious or political; to no other form of wickedness, personal, social or national. It should exalt itself above all that is called God, or that is worshipped, sitting in the temple of God, claiming to be God. This we shall hereafter find fulfilled in the arrogant assumptions of the proud pontiffs. Its coming should be "with all power and signs and lying wonders." Its relics, its legends, its prodigies and its so-called miracles, "lying wonders," will on examination be seen to be its most efficient agency in spreading and maintaining its soul-debasing superstitions. That God would send its followers strong delusion that they should believe a lie, Paul predicted. Most assuredly observation confirms the testimony of history, that in the Romish Church the willingness and power of the priests to deceive are only equalled by the capability and eagerness of the people to be deceived; deceit producing deceivableness, deceivableness evoking deceit, blinded of God, given over to believe falsehoods. Of this, however, hereafter. So likewise, the prediction that "the man of sin" should continue—not perhaps in organized form as now, but in essential characteristics—during the entire history of the Church on earth, and only be destroyed by the brightness of the Saviour's coming, is precisely the same, as hereafter will appear, with that so emphatically made respecting Romanism. In each, in all of the particulars here enumerated, the prophecy is exclusively applicable to the Church of Rome. This will appear in the course of our work.

The first statement made respecting the "mystery of iniquity" is, that it should arise from apostasy. It was to be a falling away from the faith. We must therefore look for Antichrist among those who once embraced Christianity. In countries Christianized, or at least partially so, and not in those exclusively Pagan, must we expect "*the man of sin.*" And unless in the Papacy, where, in the entire history of the Church, does the prophecy find a fulfilment?

If this be not the apostasy, where is it? Does Protestantism bear the marks? Certainly one or the other is the predicted foe of Christ's kingdom. And if it be Protestantism, then Romanism, with all its abominations, must be all it claims to be, the Church, the only Church, the Holy, Catholic, Apostolic Church.

The inquiry, therefore, which is the predicted "*son of perdition?*" we are entirely willing should await the answer given this question, which form of doctrine and worship has the sanction of the Apostles and primitive Christians? confident that whilst before the beginning of the fourth century there was, as there always has been, and so long as human nature remains unchanged probably always will be, a strong tendency to ritualism, *Popery*—in the form in which it now exists and has cursed the world for nearly thirteen centuries—had no existence.

During the lives of the Apostles, and in times immediately subsequent, the Church was comparatively pure. Believers worshipped God, and God alone, and relied for salvation entirely on the merit of Christ's death. The religion of the humble Nazarene had none of those unmeaning rites, imposing ceremonials, and debasing customs of Romanism. These all came in during the gradual apostasy, and came from Paganism. Prior to this the followers of Jesus were bitterly persecuted, thousands being put to death by every manner of torture which fiendish malignity could invent. They were sawn asunder; they were drowned; they were thrown to wild beasts; they were burned at the stake. Others, covered with the skins of animals, were torn by dogs; others were crucified; others still, besmeared with combustible materials, and suspended by the chin upon sharp stakes, were set on fire, that they might light the gardens of Rome's cruel emperor. And to add interest to the horrid spectacle, and attract the crowd, this heartless exhibition of Satanic malignity was accompanied with horse-racing.

To escape death, the faithful concealed themselves in dens, in caves, in deserts, and in subterranean burial places near the eternal city. During ten successive persecutions, Christianity retained its Apostolic purity. It was persecuted, and partly, no doubt, for this reason was the more spiritual. There was no vast external organization having the Pope at its head, and assuming spiritual power over the entire Church. The worship of images, counting of beads, bowing before altars, adoring the host and worshipping the Virgin, were unknown. Being poor, the Christians had few church edifices; they met for worship in caves and private houses. Magnificent cathedrals, gorgeous vestments, and costly ornaments, which Papists now seem to deem essential to proper worship, were at once impossible and unnecessary to the simple-minded followers of him who had not where to lay his head. Theirs was not the form of godliness, but its power in the heart. Their writings are of the most spiritual type. In these is found incontrovertible proof that the religion then preached was such as we now denominate Protestantism. The Emperor, so far from ruling in ecclesiastical matters, was the bitter enemy of Christianity.

During this period each minister of the Church ruled in his own congregation, and nowhere else. The bishop of the church in Rome was only the equal, in authority, of the humblest shepherd of souls in the most unknown, distant and ignorant part of the empire. Clemens tells us, *"Those who were ordained rulers in the churches, were so ordained with the approbation and concurrence of the whole Church."* Clearly, therefore, Romanism did not prevail. Her system is a despotism, in which the people have no voice in the choice of their spiritual guides.

And the assumptions of Popery, like her mummeries, had no existence during the first three centuries. These the persecutions of Pagan Rome effectually repressed. Therefore, before "the man of sin" could be revealed, this let or hindrance must be removed. "And now," says Paul, "ye know what withholdeth that he might be revealed in his time. For the mystery of iniquity doth already work: only he who now letteth, will let, until he be taken out of the way. And then shall that Wicked be revealed."

In the year, A. D. 306, Constantine succeeded to the throne of his father. This marks an important era in the history of the Church. Having seen, as he claimed, the appearance of a cross in the heavens, exceeding bright, bearing the inscription, "Conquer by this," he embraced Christianity, defeated Maxentius, and in 313, by formal edict, confirmed and extended the privileges of the Christians. Christianity was now established. The Emperor commenced the persecution of Paganism. A profession of the Gospel being no longer accompanied with danger, the churches being richly endowed, the clergy loaded with honors, it was but natural that upon the pure spiritual worship of him who came to abolish all forms, should be engrafted the superstitions of the ignorant heathen. Of a conversion of the heart, there was not even the pretence. With the growth of ignorance and love of ostentation came, not only further importations of unmeaning ceremonies, but also greater assumptions on the part of Rome's bishop, until, in A. D. 606, the Emperor Phocas conferred upon Boniface III. the title of *Universal Bishop*. Thus Romanism, after a desperate struggle of three centuries, established itself. Henceforth none might, with impunity, despise its rites or ridicule its claims.

It must not be supposed, however, that the Roman pontiffs acquired supremacy without long continued efforts, and persistent opposition from those who looked upon the growth of this power as the rise of Antichrist. Protests and refutations were numerous. Irenæus declared that the bishop of Rome was but a presbyter, for Jesus himself was the only bishop of souls. Maurus affirmed that all ministers were bishops, and all bishops were of equal rank. When summoned to Rome to stand trial for such blasphemous heresy, he paid no regard to the summons. When excommunicated he hurled back upon the Pope the sentence pronounced against himself, and continued, in defiance of the Pope's authority, to discharge duty as pastor of his flock. On his death-bed he exhorted his people to continuance in disowning the usurped power of the great Roman Antichrist. The early Councils resisted Papal supremacy. The sixth of Carthage (A. D. 418) resisted three Popes; that of Chalcedon (A. D. 450), Pope Leo. St. Ibar, the Irish divine, wrote, " *We never acknowledge the supremacy of a foreigner.*" Says Theodoret, "*Christ alone is head of all.*" In the early part of the sixth century a fierce contention arose " between Symmachus and Laurentius, who were on the same day elected to the pontificate by different parties." A Council assembled at Rome by Theodoric, king of the Goths, endorsed the election of the former. Ennodius, in an apology written for the Council and for Symmachus, first made the assertion, " The bishop of Rome is subject to no earthly tribunal." He styles him, " judge in place of God, and vicegerent of the Most High." These claims were maintained by the adherents of Symmachus, and detested and refuted by his opponents. Even Gregory, Pope, author and canonized saint—an authority surely with Papists—in his contest with the bishop of Constantinople, denounced the title of *Universal bishop*, as " *vain*," " *diabolical*," "*anti-christian*," "*blasphemous*," "*execrable*," "*infernal*."

He declares, "*Our Lord says unto his disciples, be not ye called Rabbi, for one is your master, and all ye are brethren.*" And again he affirms, "WHOSOEVER ADOPTS OR AFFECTS THE TITLE OF UNIVERSAL BISHOP, HAS THE PRIDE OF ANTICHRIST, AND IS IN SOME MANNER HIS FORERUNNER IN HIS HAUGHTY QUALITY OF ELEVATING HIMSELF ABOVE THE REST OF HIS ORDER. AND INDEED, BOTH THE ONE AND THE OTHER SEEM TO SPLIT UPON THE SAME ROCK; FOR AS PRIDE MAKES ANTICHRIST STRAIN HIS PRETENSIONS UP TO GODHEAD, SO WHOEVER IS AMBITIOUS TO BE CALLED THE ONLY AND UNIVERSAL BISHOP, ARROGATES TO HIMSELF A DISTINGUISHED SUPERIORITY, AND RISES, AS IT WERE, UPON THE RUINS OF THE REST." As the doctrine of Papal supremacy is so strongly condemned by an infallible Pope, surely we ought to be excused for disbelieving it. As the Papacy is declared, by what Romanists deem the highest human authority, to be either Antichrist or his harbinger, further proof that she is the great apostasy is certainly uncalled for. Infallibility has spoken, and for once, we can believe, has certainly spoken the truth.

Two years after the death of Gregory, Boniface III. requested and obtained from the Emperor Phocas—the usurper and murderer—the title of UNIVERSAL BISHOP. This is the date commonly assigned as the origin of Popery. At this time the foundation stone of the entire structure was laid. Grant that the bishop of Rome is the legitimate successor of St. Peter, the primate of the Church, "*the infallible judge in faith and morals*," sole interpreter of Scripture, and the entire system is logically defensible. Even, however, so late as the ninth century, Lewis, son of Charlemagne, owned no supremacy in the Pope, but sustained the power of the bishops and Council against him. To bring men to consent to their arrogant assumptions, the pontiffs now devised a new scheme. They procured, in the year 845, by the aid of their trusty friends, pretended decrees of early Popes, spurious writings of the fathers, and forged acts of synods and Councils, known since as the "*Isidorian Decretals.*" The most important of these documents was the pretended gift from Constantine the Great, in the year 324, of the city of Rome, and all Italy, with the crown, to Sylvester, then bishop of Rome. "We attribute," says the imposture, "to the chair of St. Peter ALL THE IMPERIAL DIGNITY, GLORY AND POWER. Moreover, we give to Sylvester, and to his successors, our palace of Lateran—incontestably one of the finest palaces on earth; we give him OUR CROWN, OUR MITRE, OUR DIADEM, AND ALL OUR PRINCIPAL VESTMENTS; WE RESIGN TO HIM THE IMPERIAL DIGNITY. . . . . WE GIVE AS A FREE GIFT TO THE HOLY PONTIFF THE CITY OF ROME, AND ALL THE WESTERN CITIES OF ITALY, AS WELL AS THE WESTERN CITIES OF THE OTHER COUNTRIES. TO MAKE ROOM FOR HIM, WE ABDICATE OUR SOVEREIGNTY OVER ALL THESE PROVINCES; and we withdraw from Rome, transferring the seat of our empire to Byzantium, SINCE IT IS NOT JUST THAT A TERRESTRIAL EMPEROR SHALL

RETAIN ANY POWER WHERE GOD PLACED THE HEAD OF RELIGION." *

By the aid of these *base forgeries*, approved by the Roman Pontiffs because designed to enrich the primacy of St. Peter, Nicolas I. succeeded, notwithstanding the determined opposition of the reflecting, in instilling into the minds of many the belief that the bishop of Rome was legislator and judge over the whole Church; that other bishops, and even Councils, derived authority solely from him. Nor were the results which flowed from this *huge fabrication* confined to the ninth century. Gradually, but surely, the whole constitution and government of the Church were changed. According to Mosheim, " The wisest and most impartial among the Roman Catholic writers, acknowledge and prove, that from the times of Lewis the Meek, the ancient system of ecclesiastical law in Europe was generally changed, and a new system introduced by the policy of the court of Rome."† The authors of the recent work entitled, "Janus," "*members of a school who yield to none in their loyal devotion to Catholic truth*," affirm : " *The Isidorian Decretals revolutionized the whole constitution of the Church, introducing a new system in the place of the old.*" " *Upon these*," say they,

---

* Of Constantine's pretended donation and the Decretals in general, Dr. Campbell remarks, " They are such bare-faced impostures, and so bunglingly executed, that nothing less than the most profound darkness of those ages could account for their success."

† Mosheim, vol. ii. p. 63.

"*was founded the maxim that the Pope, as supreme judge of the Church, could be judged by no man.*" It was on the strength of these fictions that Nicolas I. affirmed: "*The Roman Church keeps the faith pure, and is free from stain.*" These authors, certainly competent authority, at least with Catholics, affirm: "*Bellarmine acknowledged that without the forgeries of the pseudo-Isidore, . . . it would be impossible to make out even a semblance of traditional evidence,*" for the supremacy. (P. 319.)

As proving that Popery, as it now exists, is an apostasy from the true Church, we present some passages from "Janus," that complete historical refutation of the Papal claim to supremacy and infallibility, which has recently caused the *Catholic World* and other publications of the "infallibles" such immense trouble, and—to say nothing of misrepresentation—such a vast amount of special pleading. They say:

"The Papacy, such as it has become, presents the appearance of a disfiguring, sickly, and choking excrescence on the organization of the Church, hindering and decomposing the action of its vital powers, and bringing manifest diseases in its train."

"The well known fact speaks clearly enough for itself, that throughout the whole ancient canon law . . . there is no mention made of Papal rights."

"When the presidency in the Church became an empire . . . then the unity of the Church, so firmly secured before, was broken up." (P. 21.)

"For a long time nothing was known in Rome of definite rights bequeathed by Peter to his successors."

"The Church of Rome could neither exclude individuals nor Churches from the Church Universal." (Pp. 64–66.)

"There are many national Churches which were never under Rome, and never even had any intercourse with Rome." (P. 68.)

"The Popes took no part in convoking Councils." (P. 63.)

"The force and authority of the decisions of Councils depended upon the consent of the Church, and on the fact of being generally received." (Pp. 63, 64.)

Thus, the sons of "Holy Mother" themselves being witnesses, we confidently affirm that Romanism, in its form of worship, in its system of doctrines, and in its plan of government, is evidently different from the primitive Church. It must, therefore, be "*the mystery of iniquity,*" *the great apostasy,* "*that man of sin,*" "*the son of perdition, who opposeth and exalteth himself above all that is called God, or that is worshipped; so that he, as God, sitteth in the temple of God, showing himself that he is God.*"

The insolent ravings of this foe of the true Church, especially those of the last few months, may well strike us with amazement. Pope Boniface VIII. issued a decree, now embodied in the canon law, which solemnly proclaims:—"We declare, say, define, pronounce it to be of necessity to salvation, for every human creature to be subject to the Roman Pontiff." In the fourth canon of the "Dogmatic Decrees on Catholic Faith," promulgated in the third public session of the Vatican Council, April 24th, 1870, occur these words: "We admonish all that it is their duty to observe likewise the constitutions and decrees of this

Holy See." In the third chapter of the " First Dogmatic Decree on the Church of Christ," passed July 18th, 1870, it is affirmed:—" The decision of the Apostolic See, above which there is no higher authority, cannot be reconsidered by any one, *nor is it lawful to any one to sit in judgment on his judgment*. . . . . We renew the definition of the Œcumenical Council of Florence, according to which all the faithful of Christ must believe that the holy apostolic see and the Roman Pontiff hold the primacy over the whole world, and that the Roman Pontiff is the successor of blessed Peter, the prince of the Apostles, and the true Vicar of Christ, and is the head of the whole Church, and the father and teacher of all Christians." And in the fourth chapter of the same, we find this remarkable assertion, made in this nineteenth century, made after Rome has been again and again proved guilty of entertaining not only doctrines evidently erroneous, but dogmas precisely contradictory—exact opposites:— " KNOWING MOST CERTAINLY THAT THIS SEE OF ST. PETER EVER REMAINS FREE FROM ERROR." Assertion seems their only stock in trade. With this as their formula, " Ubi Petrus, ibi ecclesia," and this as their sole argument, " Thou art Peter, and upon this rock I will build my Church," they pronounce anathemas against all who deny, or even refuse cordially to accept, the doctrines of the supremacy and infallibility of the Pope. In this decree, the first on the Church, the unterrified five hundred thrice pronounce *" anathema sit"* against him who shall presume to call in question the primacy of St. Peter or the legitimate succession of Pius IX., *Holy Father, Vicar of Christ, Vicegerent of God, infallible judge in faith and morals.*

The Romish Church, which now boastingly claims inerrancy, nay even infallibility, has taught errors innumerable, has radically changed her ancient character and constitution, has become thoroughly corrupt in her centre of unity, has changed the forms of worship, has perverted the doctrines of the Gospel; in a word, has, as Paul predicted, *fallen away.*

CHAPTER V.

POPERY, PAGANISM.

ALTHOUGH the claim of the Pope to universal supremacy was not established until A. D. 606 (and is even now vigorously disputed by many loyal sons of Holy Mother), the candid historian is nevertheless ready to admit that the superstition denominated by Paul " an apostasy," was, in all its chief features, distinctly visible prior to the arrogant assumptions of Boniface III. He, in the office of supreme Pontiff, did little more than sanction existing rites and enforce uniformity. The errors in doctrine and practice which have since attained such importance, and produced results so momentous, were most of them engrafted upon Christianity during the three preceding centuries. Whence they came is easily determined. Paganism was their fruitful source.

The motive which prompted to the introduction of these forms, adapting, as was supposed, the new religion to the deep-seated prejudices of the heathen, may have been, nay, we may say, certainly was, praiseworthy. With the fervent desire of becoming all things to all men, that they might by all means save some, the early Christians, with the aid of imposing ceremonies and magnificent rites borrowed from Paganism, thought to win for Christ those who despised the simplicity of Christian worship.*

This policy, laudable in motive, was, however, exceedingly disastrous in its results. To purity of religion consequences the most pernicious ensued. Paganism began to supplant Christianity, leaving little save the name. The change in many doctrines and practices was indeed gradual—Rome boasts of her tardiness, deeming it wise deliberation—but on that account none the less real. Thus, the worship of images, though extensively prevalent in the beginning of the fourth cen-

---

* Gregory, in his instructions given to Augustine, missionary to Britain, says: "Whereas it is a custom among the Saxons to slay abundance of oxen, and sacrifice them to the devil, you must not abolish that custom, but appoint a new festival to be kept either on the day of the consecration of the churches, or the birth-day of the saints whose relics are deposited there, and on those days the Saxons may be allowed to make arbors round the temples changed into churches, to kill their oxen and to feast, as they did while they were Pagans, only they shall offer their thanks and praises, not to the devil, but to God." Says Mosheim: "This addition of external rites was also designed to remove the opprobrious calumnies which the Jewish and Pagan priests cast upon the Christians on account of the simplicity of their worship, esteeming them little better than atheists, because they had no temples, altars, victims, priests, nor anything of that external pomp in which the vulgar are so prone to place the essence of religion. The rulers of the Church adopted, therefore, certain external ceremonies, that thus they might captivate the senses of the vulgar and be able to refute the reproaches of their adversaries, thus obscuring the native lustre of the Gospel in order to extend its influence, and making it lose, in point of real excellence, what it gained in point of popular esteem."

tury, was not established till the ninth. The sacrifice of the mass—Rome's offering of human flesh—though originating about the middle of the fifth century, and almost universally believed in the ninth, being logically and compactly fitted into the system, an essential part thereof, was not erected into a dogma until the time of Pope Innocent III., at the fourth Council of the Lateran, A. D. 1215. (Mosheim, III. chap. iii. part 2.) So likewise the invocation of saints, practised to some extent in the middle of the third century, was without ecclesiastical sanction till the ninth. No less gradual was her adoption of the doctrine of purgatory, that relic of ancient heathenism. So likewise the use of lamps, candles, incense, holy water, and priestly robes, became universal only by silencing opposition continued through centuries. But the gradual importation of these ceremonies, and the slowness with which they grew into favor, in no way affect their heathen origin. That Romanism is Paganism perpetuated, we shall endeavor to prove.

It was during the three centuries that elapsed between the pretended conversion of Constantine and the pontificate of Boniface III. that most of Rome's customs and many of her doctrines were imported from heathenism. The religion of Jesus became a mere form, and not a life. Those who once, as idolaters, worshipped Jupiter and the host of gods, afterward, while worshipping the same images under the names of saints and martyrs, claimed to be Christians. As a necessary result, the same ceremonies, in the main, prevailed in the churches of these so-called followers of Jesus as in the Pagan temples. At the door of the temple stood a vase of holy water, from which the people sprinkled themselves.* How exactly has Rome copied this custom! Go into any Romish chapel or cathedral, and you will find the vessel containing the consecrated water, and modern heathens crossing themselves. The very composition of the water is the same, a mixture of salt with common water.

One of the most ridiculous uses to which this water is applied, the sprinkling of horses, mules and asses, is, like all the other customs, borrowed from ancient Rome. On the Festival of St. Anthony, observed annually in the eternal city, the priest, dressed in sacerdotal robes, after muttering some Latin words, intended as a charm against sickness, death, famine, and danger, sprinkles with a huge brush all the animals brought in from the surrounding country, blasphemously repeating, "In nomine Patris, et Filii, et Sancti Spiritus." St. Anthony, taking literally the command, "Preach the Gospel to every creature," concluded that the "Good Tidings" ought to be proclaimed to the inferior creation, to birds, beasts, and fishes. Hence the Pope has in the Vatican a picture representing even fish as devoutly listening, heads out of water, to a preaching friar! It is on the 17th of January that the festival

---

* "The Amula was a vase of holy water, placed by the heathens at the door of their temples, to sprinkle themselves with."—Montfaucon.

BLESSING ANIMALS. *Page 75.*

of this famous St. Anthony, patron of animals, is celebrated. When this falls on Sabbath, great is the concourse, uproarious is the merriment, profitable indeed is the laughable farce: neighing horses, braying asses, bleating sheep, barking dogs, men, women, and children, each rivalling the other in loquacity, shouting priests, the rattling carriages of cardinals and nobles, and the clink of the fees as they drop into the sacred treasury, produce together a din that Pandemonium might envy, possibly could equal, certainly could not surpass. The entire scene is one that would almost certainly prove fatal to an old Pagan philosopher, should he rise from his grave. A fit of laughter would speedily terminate his second existence. And this benediction in this nineteenth century! The wheel of progress must be moving backwards. The dark age must be the present, the midnight in Rome. And then to see an ass pulled by the tail to the door of the church to receive perforce St. Anthony's blessing, kicking and raising its solemn voice in earnest protest, and going home, tail straight out and head down, sighing, "Life is a failure." Well! human nature, as it exists among Protestants, could endure only one such exhibition.

Even Romanists themselves regard this sprinkling of animals as a Pagan custom, perfected by the touch of infallibility. The old Romans, say they, were accustomed to sprinkle the horses at the Circensian games. It guarded them, it was believed, against evil spirits and accidents in the race. "Once on a time," says a

Catholic legend, "the horses of some Christians outran those of the heathen, because they were sprinkled with holy water." Therefore this custom ought to be perpetuated; it has the sanction of God, the venerableness of antiquity, and was introduced by a saint, *the great Anthony!* The following may be found over the vessels of holy water in the Church of S. Carlo Borromeo, in the Corso, at Rome:

"Holy water possesses much usefulness when Christians sprinkle themselves with it with due reverence and devotion. The Holy Church proposes it as a remedy and assistant in many circumstances both spiritual and corporeal, but especially in these following:

"*Its Spiritual Usefulness.*

"1. It drives away devils from places and from persons.

"2. It affords great assistance against fears and diabolical illusions.

"3. It cancels venial sins.

"4. It imparts strength to resist temptations and occasions to sin.

"5. It drives away wicked thoughts.

"6. It preserves safely from the passing snares of the devil, both internally and externally.

"7. It obtains the favor and presence of the Holy Ghost, by which the soul is consoled, rejoiced, and excited to devotion and disposed to prayer.

"8. It prepares the mind for a better attendance on the divine mysteries, and receiving piously and worthily the most Holy Sacrament.

"*Its Corporeal Usefulness.*

"1. It is a remedy against barrenness in women and beasts.

"2. It is a preservation from sickness.

"3. It heals the infirmities both of the mind and of the body.

"4. It purifies infected air and drives away plague and contagion."

Wonderful water!

Nor is the use of holy water their only conspicuous theft. Clouds of smoke, we are told, arose from the burning incense as the idol worshippers entered the temple.* This custom of using incense for religious purposes was so peculiarly pagan, and felt, both by Christians and their enemies, as so strikingly unbecoming those who worshipped the humble Nazarene, that the method most frequently adopted by the heathen persecutors of testing the fidelity of a Christian to his convictions was to order him to throw incense into the censer. If he refused, he was accounted a Christian; if he threw even the least particle upon the altar, he was acquitted and classed among Pagans. In the churches of the great apostasy no one can fail to notice the use of perfumes. Often their cathedrals remain filled with the fumes of the incense for some considerable time after the services are concluded.

Closer still is Rome's resemblance to Paganism. The heathen worshipper, on entering the temple, knelt before an idol and offered prayers. The devout papist, as he enters the church, often may be found kneeling before an image of the Virgin, praying, "O HOLY MARY! MY SOVEREIGN QUEEN, AND MOST LOVING MOTHER! RECEIVE ME UNDER THY BLESSED PATRONAGE, AND SPECIAL PROTECTION, AND INTO THE BOSOM OF THY MERCY, THIS DAY, AND EVERY DAY, AND AT THE HOUR OF MY DEATH." †

---

* "Thuricremis cum dona imponerit Aris."—Virg. Æn. iv. 453.
† "The Catholic Manual," p. 46.

"O GREAT, EXCELLENT, AND MOST GLORIOUS LADY, PROSTRATE AT THE FOOT OF THY THRONE, WE ADORE THEE FROM THIS VALLEY OF TEARS."* "HAIL! HOLY QUEEN, MOTHER OF MERCY, OUR LIFE, OUR SWEETNESS, AND OUR HOPE! TO THEE WE CRY, POOR BANISHED SONS OF EVE, TO THEE WE SEND OUR SIGHS, MOURNING AND WEEPING IN THIS VALLEY OF TEARS. TURN THEN, MOST GRACIOUS ADVOCATE! THY EYES OF MERCY TOWARDS US." †

"O HOLY MOTHER OF OUR GOD!
TO THEE FOR HELP WE FLY;
DESPISE NOT THIS OUR HUMBLE PRAYER,
BUT ALL OUR WANTS SUPPLY." ‡

Were the most degraded of the heathen ever guilty of idolatry grosser than this?

That they might clearly evidence the heathen origin of their customs, particulars seemingly the most insignificant were not allowed to pass into disuse. Even the arrangement of images in rows around the temple, the most highly prized standing alone in the most conspicuous place, has been slavishly copied, not only in centuries past, but in this late age. Nay, even the priest, dressed in robes apparently after the very pattern of those that decked the priests of ancient Rome, and attended, like his predecessors, by a boy in white, swings his pot of incense precisely as an old heathen in Homer's time may be presumed to have done.

Laboriously endeavoring to exhaust the Pagan ritual,

---

* "The Glories of Mary," Amer. Ed., p. 513, etc.
† "The Catholic Manual," p. 222.   ‡ *Idem*, p. 433.

candles are kept burning before each altar and idol.*
In the churches of Italy they hang up lamps at every
altar, says Mabillon. The Egyptians, says Herodotus,
first introduced the use of lamps in worship. Rollin
says (vol. i., pt. 2, ch. 2), "A festival surnamed the
Feast of Lights, was solemnized at Sais. All persons
throughout all Egypt, who did not go to Sais, were
obliged to illuminate their windows." So strikingly
conspicuous was this part of the heathen worship, that
the early Christians tauntingly said of their foes—
"They light up candles to God as if he lived in the
dark, . . . offering lamps to the Author and Giver of
Light."

Even the fiction of Purgatory, of which Gregory the
Great has generally been represented by Papists as
creator, and which has ever proved a source of immense
wealth to the Pope and the clergy, is evidently an importation from Paganism. Like most of the other customs of the man of sin, it came in soon after Constantine's pretended conversion, when Christianity became
fashionable, and to men ambitious of distinction at the
court, extremely profitable. Unknown to the Christian
Church during the first five centuries, it was, however,
well known in the heathen world even so early as
Homer's time. It is the old fire purification of souls;
and the ceremonies now employed for the relief of those
suffering the tormenting flames are remarkably similar
to those anciently employed by Pagan priests.† In

---

* Virgil, "Æneid," iv. 200. † "Odyssey," xii., and "Æneid," vi.

fact the doctrine was so purely heathen, that not even Popish ingenuity could invent even an argument in its favor. Hence the Jesuit Cottonus, failing to find a passage in Scripture that would infallibly confirm it, implored the devil to assist him. For once even Satan himself was unable to wrest Scripture to his purpose. But, notwithstanding the small, the exceedingly unimportant consideration that no proof, except visions and dreams and assertion, was found, the Popes were able in the end to establish infallibly everything connected with purgatorial fires, and locate them at the earth's centre, 18,300½ miles below the surface. Infallibility don't need to know geography!

Their custom of invoking the dead is of heathen origin. The true Church of God never offered prayers to deceased mortals. The ancient Romans, however, deified their great men, and sought blessings from them. And the Papists, imitating their example, canonize those whom they honor during life, offer incense to them, bow before them and supplicate their assistance. Thus in "The Litany of Saints," found in "The Catholic Manual," their ordinary book of prayer, we find these petitions:

> St. Stephen!
> St. Laurence!
> St. Vincent!
> St. Fabian, and St. Sebastian!
> St. John, and St. Paul!
> St. Cosmas, and St. Damian!

} *Pray for us!*

St. Gervase, and St. Protase!
All ye holy Martyrs!
St. Sylvester!
St. Gregory!
St. Ambrose!
St. Augustin!
St. Jerom!
St. Martin!
St. Nicholas!
All ye holy Bishops and Confessors!
All ye holy Doctors!
St. Anthony!
St. Bennet!
St. Bernard!
St. Dominick!
St. Francis!
All ye holy Priests, and Levites!
All ye holy Monks, and Hermits!
St. Mary Magdalen!
St. Agatha!
St. Lucy!
St. Agnes!
St. Cecily! (etc. for two more pages!) Make intercession for us!

} *Pray for us!*

And from the *Freeman's Journal* (Sept. 24, 1870) we learn that the Archbishop of Cincinnati, in an address delivered at the ceremonies attending the depositing of relics in the convent of the St. Franciscan Sisters (Cincinnati), piously exhorted all devout Catholics to ask the mediation of St. Aureliana. The mortal remains of this saint, after sixteen centuries' quiet rest, were taken (a chance to exercise faith), from the Catacombs of Rome, artistically incased in wax, transported across the Atlantic, and now rest, the object of devout veneration, in the metropolis of the West! This remarkable relic is the fruit of the indomitable perseverance of Mrs. Sarah Peters, the zealous convert whose untiring zeal was rewarded with the rare and blessed privilege of hearing mass said by Pope Pio Nono at the grave of St. Peter, beneath St. Peter's, Rome. The tasteful correspondent of the paper, now so zealously engaged in raising Peter's pence for "the infallible judge in faith and morals, the bishop of the Universal Church," says, "The figure as it lay would have been exquisite, had it not been marred by the ugly gash in the throat, and an appearance of wounds on the hands and feet, caused by pieces of the bones which were encased, being set in the white wax for the better veneration of the faithful." Great indeed must be the faith which prompts persons, of even the least common sense, to venerate as the remains of the "virgin martyr of the proud and royal Aurelian family," a wax figure, with a ghastly gash in the throat, and the bones sticking out! And what must be the superstition which leads to the invocation of this resurrected saint! We live in the year 1871, and boast of the world's progress!

This idolatrous custom no doubt originated in veneration paid to departed worthies. Those, however, who so far conformed to heathen practices, soon offered worship to the creature. So universal became this superstition that even the ancient temple, sacred to

Romulus, where infants were presented by their Pagan mothers to be cured of diseases, was consecrated to a Roman saint, Theodorus, to whom Catholic mothers present their sick children for healing. Nay, even the Pantheon, house of all the gods, the most celebrated heathen temple of antiquity, was rededicated by Pope Boniface IV. "to the blessed Virgin and all the saints." And to this day, with the gods of old Rome bearing the names of Popish saints, the old Pagan worship, in all its essential features, is continued. There the traveller from every Catholic country may find his patron saint, and worship at his altar. And as with the Pantheon so with the other heathen temples; with the same ceremonies they worship the same idols under new names. Diana, Juno, Ceres, and Venus became the Virgin under different titles. Bacchus became St. Joseph. Orpheus and Apollo were regarded as types of Christ. Even the same festivals were perpetuated under new names, and consecrated to the commemoration of Christian anniversaries. The Liberalia were made to yield to the festival of St. Joseph, the ceremonies being slightly changed. The Palilia were retained as a festival in honor of St. John. The feast of St. Peter ad Vincula superseded the festival commemorative of Augustus' victory at Actium. The Floralia, when the streets were strewn with flowers arranged in fantastic forms, were devoted to Our Lady. Even the wild festivities of the Saturnalia were in some measure retained in the excesses which were allowed at Christmas and Epiphany. The Cerealia, in honor of Ceres, the goddess of corn, were transformed into the visitation of the Virgin—the processions of women and virgins, in white robes, vowing chastity and strewing their beds with "agnus castus" being retained. In consequence of the vast increase in the number of saints, the list of heathen festivals was exhausted, so in A. D. 835, Gregory IV. established the feast of ALL SAINTS.

A recent traveller to Rome says:—" You frequently see persons prostrate before images, and in a state of the greatest apparent devotion, even if these images are formed out of materials taken from heathen temples. At Pisa I saw several females prostrate before the statues of Adam and Eve, which are exhibited in a state of almost entire nudity. The celebrated statue of St. Peter, in the Church of St. Peter's at Rome, the toe of which is almost literally kissed away, was originally a statue of Jupiter, taken from the capitol. Many of the altars and ornaments in the churches, are entirely heathen in their origin and appearance. Naked forms in marble abound in all the churches. Many of the vases used for baptismal purposes, and those containing the Holy Water, were anciently used for similar purposes in the days of heathenism."

Such unseemly haste has characterized Rome's propensity to manufacture saints, that some ridiculous mistakes have occured. Thus, they have canonized Julia Evodia, *a heathen*, respecting whom nothing is known except that she erected a tombstone to her heathen mother. They have, by the power of the keys, infallibly converted a mountain into a saint, Mount Soracte, becoming S. Oracte, St. Oreste. They have also a St. Viar, manufactured by a procrustean process from PrefectuS VIARum, overseer of roads; a sainted cloak, and a sainted handkerchief. In honor of the last-mentioned saint, whose surface bears an impression of the Saviour's face, a true image, made as he wiped his face at the execution, Pope John XXII. composed a prayer as follows:—"HAIL HOLY FACE OF OUR REDEEMER, PRINTED UPON A CLOTH AS WHITE AS SNOW; PURGE US FROM ALL SPOT OF VICE, AND JOIN US TO THE COMPANY OF THE BLESSED. BRING US TO OUR COUNTRY, O HAPPY FIGURE, THERE TO SEE THE PURE FACE OF CHRIST." * This sacred relic—preserved in St. Peter's, where is an altar erected by Pope Urban VIII. to the honor of Veronica, "vera icon," the true image—grants, according to Pope Innocent III., ten days' indulgence to all who visit it. Shades of Paganism, did ever superstition equal that! "His Infallibility," Pope Pius IX., certainly deserves commiseration. To be the rock which shall support this mighty fabric of baptized Paganism, must be an oppressive life!

And to make the resemblance to heathenism complete in everything pertaining to saints, "Holy Mother" earnestly recommends every Catholic to select some particular saint as a protecting divinity, a patron,

---

* Bower's "Lives of the Popes."—Life of Innocent III.

Thus, in a "Catechism and Instructions" designed for very small children by M. C. Kavanagh, and having the unqualified commendation of one of Rome's most honored Archbishops, occurs this pious advice, "*You should never be without some object of piety, such as a Crucifix, picture of Our Lady, your good Angel, or Patron Saint, in your bedroom.*" Anciently, every Roman family had its penates, its household gods, a necessary appendage to every dwelling.

Their priestly power is an imitation of Pagan spiritual despotism. In the true Church, "all are kings and priests unto God." Even the most humble, unknown, ignorant, and even sinful creature, "may come boldly unto the throne of grace." But the Papal priests, servile copyists of the heathen, tyrannize over the souls of men, and claim the right to stand between the penitent sinner and his Saviour. All the blessings which he desires, and so much needs, must come through the good-will and efficacious services of priests. And these, forgetting that he who would serve God acceptably in the ministry of the Gospel, must be "least of all" and "servant of all," are too often proud, insolent, tyrannical.

Their processions are of heathen origin. The ancient Romans, on set days, paraded, bearing lighted candles and carrying idols dressed in costly clothing. At these solemnities priests were assisted by the magistrates in ceremonial robes. The youth, gaudily dressed, followed, singing songs in honor of the god whose festival they were celebrating. Most slavishly has this custom been copied in Roman Catholic countries. At the festival of the Holy Virgin, or some other Romish saint, the priests, magistrates, and even ladies and mere boys, with lighted wax candles in their hands, form in solemn procession, bearing images, and chanting hymns. A traveller to Rome thus describes the festival of the Annunciation:—" Processions of penitents are seen silently wending their way along the streets, clothed in long black robes, preceded by a black cross, and bearing in their hands skulls and bones, and contribution-boxes for souls in purgatory. . . . The Pope himself was clothed in robes of white and silver, and as he passed along the crowds of gazing people that lined the streets and filled the windows, he forgot not incessantly to repeat his benediction—a twirl of three fingers, typical of the Father, Son, and Holy Ghost—the little finger representing the latter. Many tiresome ceremonies followed his entry into the church. He was seated on his throne; all the Cardinals successively approached—kissed his hand—retired a step or two—gave three low bows—one to him in front, as personifying God the Father, one to the right, intended for the Son, and one to the left for the Holy Ghost." Most powerfully do such scenes remind us of the pompous ceremonies of ancient Paganism; we seem standing in the midst of some heathen city of the ages past, and witnessing their grotesquely solemn superstitions.

The title of Pontifex Maximus is conspicuously a theft from ancient Rome. All good Papists are stanch advocates of the Pope's supremacy. They consider him the Vicar of Christ, infallible Head of the Church, fountain of all holiness, source of all spiritual blessings, successor to St. Peter. Admitting that Peter was in Rome, and was bishop of the entire Church—which no Papist has ever yet successfully proved—the fact is yet undeniable that the name, the office, the authority, and the functions of the Pope are precisely the same as those of the chiefest pontiff in Pagan Rome. The worldly pomp and splendor that now surround the Papal court, comporting so poorly with what we know of the poverty, self-denial, and simple manners of the ardent, impetuous Apostle, point unmistakably to the Pontifex Maximus of old Rome. He, like his servile imitators, claimed to be the arbiter of all cases, civil and sacred, human and divine. If loyal Romanists, therefore, would say that the present Pope is the legitimate successor of the lordly pontiff who, even when Christ was a babe in Bethlehem, could claim regular succession from pontiffs dating backwards for centuries, they would tell the truth for once, and might add fresh laurels to their boasted claim of antiquity.

The votive offerings so frequently made in Catholic churches are an imitation of a custom practised in Rome long prior to the Christian era. Nothing was more common than votive gifts presented to the gods in consequence of vows taken in times of danger, or for some supposed miraculous deliverance. Of this the authors of Greece and Rome make frequent mention. Even this means of fostering superstition did not escape Romish observation. It was early incorporated into the scheme of Popish worship. Around the shrines of the saints are hung, in almost countless number, these votive offerings, evidences at once of the grossest superstition and of the most servile imitation of Pagan practices. A correspondent of a secular paper, writing recently from Paris, gives an animated description of a scene witnessed in one of the Cathedrals of the French capital on the reception of news by mail from MacMahon's defeated army. Wives, sisters, lovers, were seen presenting their gifts to Our Lady—thanksgiving offerings for the deliverance of their loved ones; others, hanging up their gifts, knelt and tearfully implored the protection of the Mother of God for the exposed, the wounded, the suffering, the dying. Marble tablets, about eight inches by four, graven with sentiments such as these, "In humble thankfulness for the return of my beloved husband from the war," "Honor to Our Lady for her merciful deliverance," "In acknowledgment of the prayer Our Lady answered," covered all the walls and even the pillars overhead, so that the entire church of Our Lady of Victory was literally lined with these records of gratitude. To make the heathen scene complete, there were lighted candles and pictures, officiating priests in gaudy vestments, and a glittering altar loaded with ornaments and votive offerings.

The sacrifice of the mass is a conformity to Paganism

as disgusting as it is slavishly accurate. Christians have always believed that Christ's death is an all-sufficient sacrifice for sin, and has forever done away with the necessity and propriety of any other. "For by one offering he hath perfected forever them that are sanctified." "The blood of Jesus Christ cleanseth from all sin." Popery, however, like Paganism, dishonors this one perfect sacrifice, by substituting others in its stead. It is indeed true that Papists do not offer the blood of bulls and goats; they offer, however, what is far less reasonable and more grossly superstitious, A CONSECRATED WAFER, particles of bread, transubstantiated, by the magic words of the priest, into the "*actual body, blood, soul and divinity of Christ;*" into "*his bones, nerves, muscles;*" and the wine into "*his real blood, which flowed in his veins.*" If priest and people really believe what they so repeatedly affirm they believe, then are they among the most degraded of heathen worshippers—*offering human flesh on their altars, eating human flesh and drinking human blood.* Either, then, human sacrifices are perpetuated, and that, too, in the most shocking, most revolting form, or infallibility errs. Either the priest creates a god, offers him as a sacrifice for sin, and ends in eating him, or all Papists worship FLOUR AND WATER. There is the dilemma! Romanists, choose which horn you please.

But even heathen, in their wildest vagaries, never clung to customs so repugnant to common sense as many that grow out of the doctrine of transubstantiation. For example, the priest, holding a wafer between his thumb and the forefinger of his right hand, says: "Behold the Lamb of God that taketh away the sin of the world," which he thrice repeats, then lays one wafer upon the tongue of each communicant. In winter, the wafers are consecrated twice a month, in summer, once a week. Consecration is oftener in summer than in winter, because the host, by the excessive heat, corrupts, producing worms! A god turned to worms!! It is an injunction of Holy Mother, however, that this corrupted host must be eaten. It is still "the body, blood, soul and divinity of Christ." Again: "If in winter the blood be frozen in the cup, put warm cloths about the cup; if that will not do, let it be put into boiling water near the altar, till it be melted, taking care it does not get into the cup." A god frozen and warmed with bandages or boiling water!! Surely, men have lost their reason! Heathen were never so devoid of common sense. Worse still: "If any of the blood of Christ fall upon the ground by negligence, it must be licked up with the tongue, the place be sufficiently scraped, and the scrapings burned; but the ashes must be buried in holy ground."* "If after consecration a gnat or spider, or any such thing, fall into the chalice, let the priest swallow it with the blood, if he can; but if he fear danger, and have a loathing, let him take it out and wash it with wine,

---

* "Roman Missal," p. 53, etc.—Respecting Defects occurring in the Mass.

and when mass is ended, burn it and cast it and the washing into holy ground."* It was solemnly declared by a reverend father, seconded by several friars, that a dog, which had accidentally caught and eaten the falling wafer, should be henceforth called "the sacrament dog;" that when he died he should be buried in consecrated ground, that he must not be allowed to play with other dogs, and that the woman who owned him must place a silver dog on the tabernacle where the host was deposited, and pay a sum of money to the church. *Surely Popery has out-paganized Paganism itself.*

Nothing is more evident than that asceticism, which is manifestly opposed to the whole spirit of the Bible, is of Pagan origin. It is a vain attempt to work out salvation by severe self-denial, by withdrawing from the abodes of men and the customary pursuits of life, and undergoing penance with the hope that God is well pleased with those who render miserable the life he gave them. The Eremites of the heathen, especially those of Egypt, the Essenes and the Therapeutæ, retiring from the world and all useful occupations, vowing chastity, poverty and obedience, clothing themselves in skins or the coarsest materials, dwelling in caverns, practising tortures, sometimes even scourging themselves with whips, and passing much of their time in silent contemplation, were accustomed to travel from

---

* "Roman Missal," p. 53, etc.—Respecting Defects occurring in the Mass.

house to house, with sacks upon their backs, begging bread, wine, and all kinds of victuals for the support of their lazy fraternities. Precisely the same customs prevail even now in India and Siam, handed down from the same source, Egypt, the fruitful parent of so many gloomy misanthropes. Hordes of mendicant priests, claiming superior sanctity, feed on the people, consuming the fruits of honest industry, and returning no equivalent. After these heathen models, Rome's religious orders of monks and nuns, in their almost endless variety, were unquestionably formed, and that too by the most raving fanatics. These orders have precisely the same vows—chastity, poverty and obedience. They retire into monasteries, nunneries, deserts, or caves, spend their time in filth or useless reverie and idleness; clothe themselves in rags and wretchedness, or in garments powerfully reminding one of their heathen prototypes, and practise severe self-inflicted tortures. So likewise celibacy, so vaunted in the Romish Church, and abstinence from animal food, are among the austerities recommended by Pagans centuries before the Christian era.

That no feature, at least no important feature, of Paganism might be allowed to fall into oblivion, Rome can boast of her sect, the legitimate successors of the Gymnosophists of Egypt, which claims that the perfection of piety consists in an annihilation of every affection implanted in human nature, including e en love of one's parents, which, to any but a heathen, might reasonably be presumed to be innocent. Those voluntarily choosing a hermit life—thus casting slander on the God that made them, and more frequently falling into gross sins than those preferring to remain in society, and there attempt to live worthy of him whose life was spent in labors of love with the multitude—became at one time so numerous in the infallible Church, that in Egypt alone their number was little less than 100,000. In one city, Oxyrinthus, there were 20,000 virgins and 10,000 monks. To find from 7000 to 10,000 lazy monks under the superintendence of one abbot was by no means unusual.

And even the self-whipping, copied from the priests of Isis, Papists have retained. True, the sect of the Flagellantes no longer exists, but then in the eternal city, during the season of Lent, fleshly discipline is still practised. Only a short time since, in one of the churches of Rome, after a brief season of prayer, the candles being extinguished, a company of the faithful, for the space of an hour, sacredly devoted themselves to the use of the consecrated whip—either upon their backs or upon the benches. Seneca, referring to this same custom in Pagan Rome, says: "If there be any gods that desire to be worshipped after this manner, they do not deserve to be worshipped at all; since the very worst of tyrants, though they have sometimes torn and tormented people, yet have never commanded men to torture themselves." And the Emperor Commodus, shrewd old Pagan as he was, being opposed to people wearing unearned laurels, ordered these self-whippers "to lash themselves in good earnest, and not feign it merely and impose upon the people."

Even so trifling a circumstance as kissing the Pope's toe is borrowed from the heathen Emperor and tyrant, Caligula. When first the pontifical toe of the old pagan was introduced to the public, it aroused a violent storm of indignation, being taken as the greatest possible insult to freedom. Now, however, in Christian Rome, it scarcely ruffles the serenity of even the proudest and most honored Papist. It is the condition of access into the awe-inspiring presence of *"Our Lord God the Pope, infallible judge in faith and morals."* And as he is the legitimate successor of the lordly pontiff who was conducted to the castle of Toici, in France, by two kings, one walking on either side of his horse, and holding the bridle rein; and of Gregory VII., who compelled the Emperor Henry IV. to remain three full days at his palace gate, barefoot and fasting, humbly suing for admittance, it would be too cruel to deny the Holy Father of all christendom the small honor of having the faithful kiss his jewelled slipper.

Instead of tracing the remaining characteristic features of Romanism back to their heathen origin, we must content ourselves with bringing forward a few authorities substantiating the position that Popery is perpetuated Paganism. The first shall be Dean Waddington. "The copious transfusion of heathen ceremonies into Christian worship, which had taken place before the end of the fourth century, had, to a certain extent, Paganized (if we may so express it) the outward form and aspect of religion, and these ceremonies became more general and more numerous, and, so far as the calamities of the times would permit, more splendid in the age which followed. To console the convert for the loss of his favorite festival, others of a different name, but similar description, were introduced; and the simple and serious occupation of spiritual devotion was beginning to degenerate into a worship of parade and demonstration, or a mere scene of riotous festivity."

Aringhus, a Roman Catholic witer, acknowledging the conformity between Pagan and Popish rites, explains and defends it as follows:—"The Popes found it necessary, in the conversion of the Gentiles, to dissemble and wink at many things and yield to the times, and not to use force against customs which the people are so obstinately fond of, nor to think of extirpating at once everything that had the appearance of profane."

Dr. Middleton, in his letters from Rome, to which we acknowledge ourselves indebted for many of the above-mentioned facts, affirms:—"All their ceremonies appear plainly to have been copied from the rituals of primitive Paganism; as if handed down by an uninterrupted succession from the priests of old, to the priests of new Rome." After carrying out the comparison to an extent which would be wearisome were it not so deeply interesting, he employs this language:—"I could easily carry on this parallel, through many more instances of the Pagan and Popish ceremonies, to show from what spring all that superstition flows, which we so justly charge them with, and how vain an attempt it must be to justify by the principles of Christianity a worship formed upon the plan and after the very pattern of pure heathenism."

Considering the evidence we are able to present of the strikingly accurate conformity of modern Popery to ancient Paganism, who is not ready to believe that if Cicero should rise from his grave in the Campus Martius, and wandering through Rome should enter St. Peter's, he would certainly imagine that the successors of the old priests, in scarcely a circumstance changed, were, with the same fopperies, which in the times of the Cæsars excited the ridicule of the learned, worshipping Diana, or Venus, or Apollo?

If, as we believe has been successfully proved, modern Romanism is only the Paganism of Antechristian times perpetuated, then we may expect to find it bearing a close affinity to Buddhism, the oldest known religion of the Indo-European race. For unless Dwight and Max Muller, and in fact all philologists are incorrect in their oft-repeated declaration that India and Greece and Rome were peopled by kindred tribes, speaking cognate languages and having essentially the same religion, then is modern Popery the same as Buddhism of the present day, barring only the slight changes that have occurred since the separation. And as each prides itself in veneration of the past, in inerrancy and immutability, these may be presumed to be few.

That Romanism is indeed the twin sister of the Buddhist religion none surely can deny. A comparison of the two will force conviction upon even the most incredulous. Antedating Christianity by several centuries, and spreading over all the countries inhabited by what are now known as the Indo-European races, Buddhism has ever had, and now has, precisely those features which mark the Papal Church, consisting partly of maxims of morality and partly of dogmas of faith on subjects transcending the reach of reason, it rests conjointly on the authority of certain sacred books and the decisions of early councils—called, like Rome's, œcumenical, and blindly venerated. The worshippers of Buddha in Burmah, Siam, and the Chinese Empire—numbering more than the adherents of any other religious system known in either ancient or modern times—have their relics and their images, the objects of supreme veneration; their temples costing fabulous sums of money; their saints canonized by ecclesiastical authority; their priests with shaven heads, vowing chastity, poverty and obedience; their wax candles burning night and day; their penances and self-inflicted tortures; their endless traditions, and hair-splitting moral distinctions; *and even their confessional.* They have also their Lent, when for four or five weeks all the people are supposed to live on vegetables and fruits; their acts of merit, repetition of prayers, fasting, offerings to the images, celibacy, voluntary poverty, enforced devotions, and munificent gifts to temples, monasteries and idols. Even the rosary, a string of beads used in saying prayers, and supposed by Papists to be a device specially revealed to St. Dominic, is part of the sacred machinery of the devout Buddhist. And their monasteries, into which priests retire from the world, and engage in the instruction of the young, especially in the mysteries of their sacred books, almost startle one by their close resemblance to those of Popery. And to see the worshippers of Buddha, each with a rosary in his hand, prostrate themselves before an image and repeat their prayers, whilst priests in gaudy vestments, bowing before lighted candles, mutter their incantations in a language which has long since ceased to be spoken, forces upon even the least reflecting the conviction that though Rome has ever claimed the power of working miracles, she has shown little inventive genius. Not even are shrines and sacred places a monopoly with Rome. There are plenty of them, and pilgrims too, in India. And why not, since they have their preaching friars, spending their time alternatively in sacred oratory and in begging. Nay, even modern miracles, though by no means so numerous, and certainly not so astounding, are performed by Rome's elder sister. And to complete the picture, they have their infallible pontiff. At Lhassa, as well as at Rome, dwells one whom the faithful *make believe* cannot err when speaking *ex cathedra*. With two infallibles, one in

Asia and one in Europe, the world certainly ought not to err in faith and morals. And then, like the Romanist and the ancient Egyptian, the learned Buddhist indignantly repels the charge of idolatry, affirming that he only employs idols as a visible image of the invisible Buddha, an aid in spiritual worship. Alike in most things, and antedated only in one, infallibility, Rome is, as yet, ahead in the mad chase after superstition. Buddhism has no indulgences, no purgatory, no living Eucharist, that is, human sacrifices:—Paganism has been outstripped.

PART II.

Popery essentially hostile to Christianity.

CHAPTER I.

ARROGANCE.
(2 Thess. ii. 4.)

HAVING proved—we trust to the satisfaction of unprejudiced minds—that Romanism is the predicted foe of Christ's kingdom, the mystery of iniquity that even in the Apostles' time was beginning to work, the great apostasy, *baptized Paganism,* it remains for us to show that she is, in spirit, doctrine and practice, hostile to the true Church of Christ; that in her leading characteristics she is necessarily antagonistic to Christianity, nor less so in this enlightened nineteenth century, than in the world's midnight, Rome's golden age; that her changes have most of them been for the worse, towards grosser superstition, greater pride, and more absurd dogmas.

In Paul's glowing description of the rise of Antichrist, occur these remarkable words: " *Who opposeth and exalteth himself above all that is called God, or that is worshipped; so that he, as God, sitteth in the temple of God, showing himself that he is God.*" No arrogance that the world has ever witnessed can compare with that of the Papal Church. It claims not only immutability but also inerrancy, not merely the right to bind the conscience and destroy the body, but even to damn the soul. It boastingly proclaims itself able to work miracles, to forgive sins, and to create the world's Creator. Its proud pontiff calls himself God's vicegerent on earth, Vicar of Christ. By his subjects he is denominated, "HIS HOLINESS," "OUR LORD GOD THE POPE." The celebrated canonist, Prospero Fagnani, the oracle of the court of Rome, in his commentaries on the Decretals, thus defines the Pope:

"He may make laws and institutions for all the world. He has power over all men, even infidels. *The Pope judges all men, and can be only judged of God.* He cannot be judged of councils; nay, *were the whole world to pronounce in any particular against the Pope, it would be right to submit to his judgment against the world.* Everything he does is done by divine authority. The Pope may, by himself alone, determine the symbols of faith, since it belongs to him only to decide in matters of faith. The Pope is not subject to the decisions of his predecessors—*not even to that of the Apostles;* for there is no power that can limit the power of the keys. *He may dispense with the observance of the divine laws and the Gospel precepts.* The Pope may grant every species of dispensation, with the exception of one, to marry one's father, or one's mother. He may depose magistrates and princes, and free their subjects from their obligations to loyalty. He is king of kings and ruler of rulers; he is the prince of bishops, *the judge of all men. He can create a law where before there was none."* If this is not dethroning the King of heaven, what shall we call it?

Innocent III., in his coronation sermon, said :—" Now you may see who is the servant who is placed over the family of the Lord; truly is he the Vicar of Jesus Christ, the successor of Peter, *the Christ of the Lord, the God of Pharaoh; placed in the middle between God and man, on this side of God, but beyond man; less than God, but greater than man; who judges all, but is judged by none."* *

Bellarmine wrote :—" *If the Pope should err by enjoining vices or prohibiting virtues, the Church, unless she would sin against conscience, would be bound to believe vices to be good and virtues evil.*" What can we say to men who profess such doctrines?

Another writer, in defining the limits between Papal and secular power, affirms :—" The Pope is bound by no forms of law; his pleasure is law. The Pope makes right of that which is wrong, and can change the nature of things. He can change square things into round."

Nor must it be imagined that these doctrines are only the legacy of the dark ages. They are the beliefs of the living present, held more firmly now than ever.

---

* A contemporary poet addressed Innocent :—
"Non Deus es, nec homo ; sed neuter et inter utrumque,
Quem Deus elegit socium ; soci aliter egit
Tecum partitus mundum, sibi noluit unus
Omnia, sed voluit tibi terras et sibi cœlum."

The *Freeman's Journal and Catholic Register* of New York, under date of Oct. 1, 1870, holds this language:— "It is as obligatory to hear the voice of Pius IX., when he speaks, avowedly to the universal Church, as it is to listen to the voice of Jesus Christ."

The Papal Church has the effrontery and the blasphemy to claim, even in this age, that she is, always has been and ever will be, immutable. *Le Universe*, an Ultramontane journal of France, lately contained the following:—

"The Catholic Church is in the commencement of all things. It has always existed and will always exist. It was before time, it is in time, it will be after time, without spots, or wrinkles, *or any change.* It does not change; it is developed. It is from God, it is through God, it will be God, for God has constituted it to fill the human race with divinity, that it may become an increase of God."

This, in face of Rome's numberless changes, her countless contradictions and variations (see "Edgar's Variations"), is a faith that may well be denominated sublime. The present Pope is a firm believer in transubstantiation, but Pope Gelasius I. wrote:— "The substance of the bread and wine ceases not to exist." The doctrine of purgatory is, with all true Catholics of the present day, an essential part of that perfect, unchanged and unchangeable system. But this doctrine, little more than four hundred years old, is condemned by more than twenty of the fathers, including

St. Augustine, Justin Martyr, Cyprian, Tertullian, Ambrose, the two Cyrils, Chrysostom, Athenasius, and Jerome. Not always was Rome so unreflecting as publicly to proclaim her damnable avarice, her heartlessness and inhumanity in allowing the souls of her "beloved children" to lie "broiling in the fiercest flames" till a few coppers, wrenched from her poverty-stricken victims, drop into her accursed coffers. Pio Nono, and all intelligent Papists, it is fair to presume, agree with the teachers of science, as to the diameter of the earth. But Pope Gregory, and Bellarmine, and Dr. Rosaccio placed purgatory at the earth's centre, more than 18,000 miles below the surface. They must be correct, for infallibility, it seems, has measured it. The Inquisition of Rome, in 1633, guided by the Vicar of God, infallible Pope Urban, in condemning Galileo, affirmed:— "The proposition that the earth moves is absurd, philosophically false, and theologically considered, at least, erroneous in faith." As infallibility cannot correct itself, in what a dilemma the Papal world finds itself! They are living on a flat, immovable planet, the centre of the universe. Similar countless contradictions and variations of Popery in no way stagger the faith of true Romanists, however. The children of Holy Mother, evidently believing some things because they are absurd, give us touches of arrogance that are truly sublime. Le Père Lacordaire, the noted Dominican preacher, in a sermon delivered not long since in Notre Dame, exclaims:—

"Assuredly the desire has not been wanting to lay hold of us, or put us to fault against immutability; for what a weighty privilege to all those who do not possess it: a doctrine immutable when everything upon earth changes! a doctrine which men hold in their hands, which poor old men in a place called the Vatican guard under the key of this cabinet, and which without any other defence resists the course of time, the dreams of sages, the designs of kings, the fall of empires—always one, constant, identical with itself! What a prodigy to deny! What an accusation to silence!"

A little farther on he represents the Pope, after refusing the demand of the present age for change, and scorning a million of men under arms, as indignantly exclaiming, when offered half of Cæsar's sceptre on condition he will change just a little:

"Keep thy purple, O Cæsar! to-morrow they will bury thee in it; and we will chant over thee the Alleluia and the De Profundis, which never change."

Since this eloquent bombast was penned, Pio Nono has yielded his temporal crown to a few shouting Liberals. Yet such is the grandeur of Papal arrogance that, ignoring changes, the Pope's loyal sons shout: "'Man's extremity is God's opportunity.' We stand by now; and wait to see how the Lord will bring safety for our Church out of what, humanly considered, is a desperate case. But let the enemy take note of our confidence! We acknowledge we know not how, but we are sure of a deliverance. We do not know what the Holy Father will do. Perhaps the Holy Father does not know what he will do a month hence." *

So the boasted immutability has been shivered to pieces by the waywardness of the Pope's "*poor misguided sheep.*" And since infallibility is unfortunately not foreknowledge, even "Our Lord God the Pope" does not know what will come of his having so peremptorily refused the half of Cæsar's crown, offered him by the vivid imagination of "*the great Dominican.*"

The Church of Rome claims the exclusive right to interpret Scriptures. According to Popery, individual believers have no right whatever to form for themselves opinions as to the meaning of the Bible. In religious matters they have no right to think. It is their duty to believe and to obey. It is the exclusive right of the sovereign Pontiff to think and to command.† God has indeed given all men reason and conscience, but they may not use them except according to Papal rule. The Pope gives to the Word of God all the authority it can possess! Without his sanction it has no binding force. He can abrogate the laws of the Creator. He can declare the commands of Christ of no effect. If God should speak in an audible voice from heaven, we would not be required to obey unless the Pope endorsed the

---

* *Freeman's Journal*, Oct. 8, 1870.

† In the bull of Gregory XVI., dated May 8, 1844, occur these words: "Watch attentively over those appointed to expound the Holy Scriptures, that they dare not, under any pretext whatever, interpret or explain the holy pages contrary to the traditions of the Holy Fathers, or to the service of the Catholic Church."

command. Nay, the case is even worse. For the spiritual despot in the eternal city has actually forbidden his subjects to read, or even possess, the will of heaven revealed for our salvation. The bull of May 8th, 1844, contains this remarkable prohibition:

"MOREOVER, WE CONFIRM AND RENEW THE DECREES RECITED ABOVE, DELIVERED IN FORMER TIMES BY APOSTOLIC AUTHORITY, AGAINST THE PUBLICATION, DISTRIBUTION, READING AND POSSESSION OF BOOKS OF THE HOLY SCRIPTURES TRANSLATED INTO THE VULGAR TONGUE."

Thus an erring creature presumes to tell the King of heaven that he may not make known his will to his own creatures. Has not Romanism "exalted itself above all that is called God?"

In entire consistency this mystery of iniquity has denounced the American Bible Society as "a most crafty device, shaking the foundations of religion," "a pestilence," "a defilement of the faith most eminently dangerous to souls." Again: "It is greatly feared that Bible societies will, by a perverse interpretation, turn Christ's Gospel into a human Gospel, or, what is worse still, into a Gospel of the devil." In a letter dated June 26th, 1816, and addressed to the Primate of Poland, Pius VII. said: "*It is evident, from experience, that the Holy Scriptures, when circulated in the vulgar tongue, have, through the temerity of men, produced more harm than benefit. Warn the people intrusted to your care, that they fall not into the snares prepared for their everlasting ruin.*" In the nineteenth century language

BURNING BIBLES IN CHAMPLAIN, N.Y.

such as this falls from lips claiming superior sanctity and even supernatural guardianship! If our versions are so shockingly dangerous, and that, too, when simple translations without note or comment, one would suppose they would industriously circulate a translation of their own. Instead of doing so, however, this proposition, "It is useful and necessary to study the Scriptures," one of the Popes branded as "*false, shocking, scandalous, seditious, impious, blasphemous.*" It would seem that in the judgment of Rome the Bible is the most dangerous book in existence. And yet, strange to say, this immutable, infallible Church has, by solemn decree, granted her priests the privilege of selling licences to read God's Word. Among the ten rules enacted by the Council of Trent respecting prohibited books, we find this:

"It is referred to the judgment of the bishops, or inquisitors, who may, by the advice of the priest or confessor, PERMIT THE READING OF THE BIBLE TRANSLATED INTO THE VULGAR TONGUE BY CATHOLIC AUTHORS, TO THOSE PERSONS WHOSE FAITH AND PIETY, THEY APPREHEND, WILL BE AUGMENTED, AND NOT INJURED BY IT; AND THIS PERMISSION THEY MUST HAVE IN WRITING."

Thus God's Vicegerent tells him: "We will grant our subjects permission to read your message of life if they will pay us for the privilege." Standing between the Creator and the creature, the Pope says to the former: "You may not speak to my subjects;" to the latter: "You may not receive the message of your Maker, unless you have the means of purchasing my permission." And even this presumption is sustained by Roman logic. "The Pope has the chief power of disposing of the temporal affairs of Christians, in order to their spiritual good." Wealth corrupts men. By every conceivable means, therefore, it should be taken from them. Verily we are prepared to read this claim: "The Pope has power above all powers in heaven and in earth." "He, as God, sitteth in the temple of God, showing himself that he is God."

It is a maxim with Popery that ignorance is the mother of devotion. If this be true—and infallibility has affirmed it—the devotion of the mass of Papists must be the deepest, the purest, the noblest, and the most spiritual the erring creatures of God have ever rendered him. And hence arises a reason, all powerful with Romanists, why popular education should be opposed. And accordingly they are, and always have been, opposed to the freedom of the press, to the general diffusion of knowledge, to the progress of the arts and sciences. Pope Gregory, in his bull of 1832, denounces liberty of opinion, of conscience, and of the press, as "absurd and erroneous doctrines; pregnant with the most deplorable evils; and pests of all others most to be dreaded in a state." And those who proclaim censures such as these irreconcilable with the rights of men, are charged with "falsity, rashness, and infamous effrontery." Catholicism is, in interest, in principle, and in policy, the uncompromising foe to modern ideas of education. What Protestants denominate the dark ages Romanism calls the golden age. It disdains the civilization, intelligence, and sterling activity of the present, and were the power hers, no doubt the wheels of progress would be turned backwards four or five centuries.

The Church of Rome claims ability to forgive sins. Confession being made and the money demanded handed over, absolution is unconditionally granted. This is their claim. And in accordance therewith is their practice. We are indeed aware of the affirmation of many, that the priests, in granting absolution, merely declare, that to the penitent, sin is remitted by God. We affirm, however, that the Church claims the inherent power of forgiving sin. One of the anathemas of the Council of Trent, certainly no mean authority, is: "If any one shall say that the sacramental absolution of the priest *is not a judicial act, but a naked ministry of pronouncing and declaring that sins are remitted to the person confessing, provided only they be believers* .... *let him be accursed.*" Here forgiveness of sin is claimed as a judicial act of the priest. He sits in Christ's seat, granting pardon. And against each and every apologist, whether Papal or Protestant, who, smoothing down the asperities of Popery, would reconcile it with reason, Rome's last argument is fulminated, "*anathema sit.*"

And their theological works contain arguments to prove that to the Pope has been given the right of granting this pardoning power to every priest. Did not Christ say to Peter, "Whatsoever thou loosest on earth shall be loosed in heaven?" Every priest, therefore, holding his commission from Peter's successor, has ability to pardon the sinner. And why not? Is there not a storehouse of good works? Has not the Pope the key? May he not disinterestedly sell the merit accumulated from the obedience of the faithful above all that God required? Absolutions are, therefore, only the transfers of merit, of the supererogatory works of Rome's renowned saints. And surely he who can make virtue vice, and vice virtue, can set some of this treasure to the account of the sinner who proves the genuineness of his desire for it by paying the stipulated price. Nay, "the Mother of Harlots" can do more than forgive sins. She has the right to sell indulgences. And every sin has its price. Did space permit, it would furnish a pitiable exhibition of the innate depravity of man to run over the list prepared by this trafficker in human souls. There is the price of an indulgence to "murder one's father, mother, brother, sister, wife, or other relative, one dollar and seventy-five cents;" "for theft, sacrilege, rapine, perjury, two dollars;" "for incest with a sister, a mother, or any near relative, two dollars and a quarter." At the end of one of the chapters in this, the "Pope's Chancery Book," it is said: "Note well: Graces and dispensations of this kind are not conceded to the poor, because they have no means, therefore they cannot be comforted." Poor creatures! Their poverty is their only sin! That the traffic in these indulgences is now dull, is not because Rome has willingly abandoned the lucrative business, but because the light of the Reformation has ruined the trade. Even yet, however, they are purchasable by prayers, and especially by the repetition of Mary's rosary. "The Catholic Manual," a collection of devotional exercises, promises a plenary indulgence on each of the solemn feasts of Christ and of the blessed Virgin Mary, to those who, with these beads, pray devoutly at least once a week. Whoever repeats a Hail Mary in the morning, is promised "an indulgence of a hundred days, each day of the week, and seven years and seven times forty days on each Sunday." By carefully following the sixteen instructions on indulgences in "The Catholic Manual," a devout Papist, by laboring with the machinery of devotion about four hours each day for five years, could, we think, very easily purchase a thousand years' unbridled licence in sin. About one hundred monks, working diligently, could, we believe, lay up merit adequate to pardon the entire world of sinners. They might thus open a new spiritual bank and rival the Pope in making merchandise of souls. Why, therefore, should the subjects of Pio Nono tremble with apprehensions of the torments of perdition? The infallible Church has granted, and therefore, of course, can again grant, permission to commit any sin, engaging to extinguish the flames of hell. None, to whom he grants a claim to the joys of the redeemed, can be finally lost. None can enter paradise without his passport. Did not Jesus say to Peter, "I will give unto thee the keys of the kingdom of heaven?" These keys have been handed down from Peter to the present Pope! Therefore, "He openeth, and no man shutteth; and shutteth, and no man openeth." On what condition will he open heaven to the soul? When the dues to the Church are paid. Did ever assumption equal this?

Claiming sovereignty over his people not only in this world but also in the world to come, the Pope controls even purgatorial fires. How long souls are kept in the purifying flames would seem to depend entirely on the willingness of living friends to pay money for the celebration of masses. Archbishop Hughes, when on earth, was lauded as one of the holiest of men. It required, however, a long time to pray his soul out of purgatory. "How hardly shall they that have riches enter into the kingdom of heaven."

Nor does Papal presumption stop even here. In the doctrine of the real presence, according to which in every crumb of bread and in every drop of wine Christ's entire nature, human and divine, is comprehended, we have arrogance the most blasphemous which it is possible to conceive. Christ, in his undivided humanity, is present in heaven and on the countless Popish altars of all countries and all ages, entire, perfect, complete in every particle of the consecrated elements. And yet, lest human weakness should be horrified with eating flesh and drinking blood, the form, appearance, qualities, and taste of bread and wine remain unchanged. And this self-contradictory miracle, the most stupendous ever imposed upon human credulity, it is affirmed, is daily wrought by priestly power. A learned Cardinal says: "*He that created me gave me*, if it be lawful to tell, *to create himself.*" And Pope Urban affirmed: "The hands of the pontiff are raised to an eminence granted to none of the angels, OF CREATING GOD THE CREATOR OF ALL THINGS, and of offering him up for the salvation of the whole world." One shudders as he reads such blasphemy. And to find in the *Freeman's Journal* of Sept. 3, 1870, such language as this, "How many prayers have they (the French priests praying for unhappy Napoleon III.) offered *even with the Most Holy in their hands*," too plainly proves that Popery is the same unchanged monster of iniquity.

Add to the above list of assumptions, the last and greatest of all, infallibility, so recently exalted into a dogma, and you have all that it would seem possible for man to claim; all that the proudest and most cruel tyrant could desire. The arrogance is complete; the despotism is perfect. The Pope has the right to enslave the body; nay, even to take life, to bind the conscience, and to damn the soul. And in the exercise of these divine prerogatives, *to err is impossible.* These assumptions the faithful are not only expected to believe with the whole heart, but to yield unresisting obedience to the tyranny thence resulting.

> "I'd rather be a dog, and bay the moon,
> Than such a Roman."

CHAPTER II.

INFALLIBILITY.
(2 Thes. ii. 4, and 1 Tim. iv. 2.)

THE year 1870 will be forever memorable in the history of the Papacy. It has witnessed the grotesquely solemn ascription of one of the attributes of deity to the pretended successor of Peter. "Speaking lies in hypocrisy," and raving in a delirium of passion, the sovereign pontiff shouts:—

"I am the Pope: the Vicar of Jesus Christ; the chief of the Catholic Church, and I have called this Council, which shall do His work, ... I say,—I, who can not but speak the truth, —that if we would establish liberty, we must never fear to speak the truth, and to denounce error. I too would be free as well as the truth itself." *

"And there are those now who are in fear of the world! They fear revolution! . . . . They will sacrifice all the rights of the Holy See, and their love for the Vicar of Jesus Christ. Miserable men, what must they do? They seek the applause of men. We, my children, we seek the approbation of God. You must sustain the claims of truth and righteousness. It is the duty of the bishops fearlessly to fight in the defence of truth alongside of the Vicar of Jesus Christ. My children, do not forsake me." †

---

* Allocution, Jan. 9th, 1870.

† From the Pope's speech to the Vicars Apostolic, March 23d, 1870.

THE INFALLIBLE POPE.

In answer to this pathetic appeal the unterrified made the Vatican ring with cries, "*No, No, No, Vive l'Infallible! Vive l'Infallible!! Vive l'Infallible!!!*" At the public reception, May 14, 1870, one continuous deafening shout was heard, "*Long live the Infallible.*" Was Paul picturing this scene when he wrote, "Who opposes himself, and exalts himself against all that is called God, and against all worship: even to seat himself in the temple of God, and take on himself openly the signs of Godhead?" (Conybeare and Howson's Version.)

Preparations for this solemn farce were made even so early as the year 1864. Then was issued the Encyclical and Syllabus, since so famous, which commend most of the arrogant assumptions of previous Pontiffs, and denounce, in no measured terms, the civilization, progress, religion and education of the present. With characteristic impudence they claim for the Pope the right of abrogating civil law, of enforcing obedience to Catholic dogmas, of employing corporal punishment, and even of compelling princes to execute civil penalties for ecclesiastical offences. They insist, in language not to be mistaken, that to Holy Mother belongs the exclusive right to educate the young, that priests are not subject to civil governments, that the Pope rules, *jure divino*, in temporal things, that the right to solemnize marriage is the exclusive possession of the priesthood, that Catholicism is the only system of faith entitled to man's suffrage, and, accordingly, that Protestant worship ought not to be tolerated, and where it can be suppressed, as in New Granada and in Rome, *must be*. Not content with endorsing Gregory's condemnation of liberty of conscience as an insanity, His Infallibility denominates it the liberty of perdition. The privilege of embracing that religion which, led by the light of reason, a man conscientiously believes to be right, is repeatedly and emphatically denied. Even the will of an entire nation, though calmly, kindly and intelligently expressed, can by no possibility constitute law; cannot lawfully demand the respect of Christ's Vicar. Having thus condemned all liberty, personal and national, civil and religious, he commits himself unqualifiedly to despotism, by anathematizing those who demand that the Roman Pontiff should harmonize himself with progress and modern civilization, and by denying to the down-trodden even the God-given right of rebellion. Fitly is this proud tyranny crowned with the unblushing assertion, that the judgments, decisions, dogmas and practices of the Church are infallible.

Conceived in iniquity, this now famous dogma was brought forth by the suppression of free discussion. Protests against its adoption, though respectfully worded and courteously presented, were sent back without comment or communication, and in some instances even unread. Arguments in every way deserving of serious attention obtained no answer.* The German prelates,

---

* "I protest," said Father Hyacinthe, "against the pretended dogma of the Pope's infallibility, as it is contained in the decree of the

in a carefully prepared protest, said, "Unless these (the great difficulties arising from the words and acts of the Fathers of the Church, as contained in authentic documents of Catholic history) can be resolved, it will be impossible to impose this doctrine upon Christian people as being a revelation from heaven." And yet far from succeeding, scarcely an effort was made in removing the difficulties. "All religion," said Cardinal Schwarzenberg, "is at an end in Bohemia if this definition is affirmed." "No words," said another prelate, "can express the evils which will accrue to the cause of religion throughout Hungary, if infallibility is affirmed." These, like all the bishops who dared to anticipate social and political evils from the adoption of this new dogma, were treated as disturbers of the peace, as disloyal to Christ's Vicar, as grossly impertinent and

---

Council of Rome. It is because I am a Catholic, and wish to remain such, that I refuse to admit as binding upon the faith of the faithful a doctrine unknown to all ecclesiastical history, which is disputed even now by numerous and eminent theologians, and which implies not a regular development, but a gradual change in the constitution of the Church, and in the immutable rule of its faith. It is because I am a Christian and wish to remain such, that I protest with all my soul against these almost divine attributes to a man who is presented to our faith—I was about to say to our worship—as uniting in his person both the domination which is opposed to the spirit of that Gospel of which he is a minister, and to the infallibility which is repugnant to the clay from which, like ourselves, he is formed. One of the most illustrious predecessors of Pius IX., St. Gregory the Great, rejected as a sign of Antichrist the title of Universal Bishop which was offered to him. What would he have said to the title of Infallible Pontiff?"

presumptuous. A correspondent of the *Liberté* gives an account of a strange scene between the Pope and the Syrian Patriarch of Babylon. The Patriarch, who, before leaving for Rome had taken solemn oath to defend the liberties of the Oriental Churches, said in Council: "We Orientals reserve our rights, which moreover have been recognized by the Council of Florence." The Pope, irritated, sent for him. The venerable Prelate immediately repaired to the Vatican. The Pontiff, pale and greatly agitated, presented a paper by which the Patriarch renounced all his rights and privileges. "Sign that," said Pius IX. "I cannot," replied the Prelate. The Pope, seized with one of his violent fits of anger, striking his hand on the table, exclaimed: "You cannot leave without signing it." The Patriarch reminded him of his oath. "Your oath is a nullity, sign." After an hour's useless struggle the Prelate submitted, appending his signature.

Those who, with irresistible logic demanded unanimity as the condition of promulgating a new dogma, especially one so important and far-reaching in its consequences, were insulted, threatened with deposition, and in the end forced either to absent themselves or to vote infallibility.* The Pope, as in the preparations for the Council, so in its proceedings, assumed to

---

* The votes were as follows:—

	July 13th.	July 18th.
Placet,	451	533
Placet juxta modum,	62	
Non-placet,	88	2

decide the gravest questions. He ostentatiously proclaimed himself as by divine appointment the infallible head of the Church. By lauding and honoring the friends of infallibility, and insulting and denouncing their opponents, denominating them "bad Catholics," he showed himself the worthy head of the order of Jesuits. Freedom of opinion became a mere name; discussion only a pretence. The result was predetermined; known when the Council was called. The French bishops, in a manifesto portraying with just indignation the successive steps taken in suppressing all freedom, affirm: "Debate in general convocation has been a mere illusion: discussion has been muzzled, and free speech gagged. Passion is dominating more and more: old traditions and usages are abandoned, just claims forgotten, and the most elementary rules set at nought. . . . . A good cause does not need to be supported by violence."

By such agencies as these an assembly of bishops, who according to ancient Roman law had no right to originate dogma, but simply to express in formula doctrines which had ever been held as objects of universal belief, promulgated a dogma as dishonoring to God as it is insulting to man.

And the arguments by which this monstrous claim was supported, are, like those by which St. Liguori proves Mary a proper object of worship, so excessively weak as to excite contempt. We do not affirm that those who employ them are men of feeble intellect.

This, in many instances, is certainly not the case. But men of powerful minds, when thoroughly committed to an absurdity, are, of course, forced to bring forward arguments which strike every unbiassed listener as simply ridiculous. And to hear mitred bishops and self-inflated cardinals, and a host of priests repeatedly and solemnly declaring that the doctrine of infallibility is as old as the Christian Church, would certainly excite universal laughter, were not the consequences of the claim so appalling. And the argument from silence, so much employed, how conclusive! For ten centuries you find no protest against it. The fathers never mention it. They present no labored arguments in its favor. The councils uttered no anathemas against those refusing adhesion to it. The Popes, those sacred custodians of truth, have held no allocutions respecting it, have issued no bulls against those who questioned it. Therefore, of course, it must have been the universal faith from the time of the Apostles. Now, however, for the first time, some damnable heretics have presumed to call it in question. It is on this account that we deem it necessary to proclaim what has ever been the faith of those constituting the Church. Why this argument would not prove that two and two make five it would be difficult for a Protestant to conceive. But Papists, apparently, deem it entirely conclusive. The Rev. James Kent Stone, a recent convert to Catholicism, expands it to great length, and seemingly considers it unanswerable. Surely arguments must be scarce.

Dr. Henry Newman, another champion of Romanism, in his "Essay in Aid of a Grammar of Assent," appeals to common sense in proof of infallibility! He undertakes to show that the principles of assent applied to the ordinary affairs of life, logically lead to an enforced belief in the last dogma of Rome. We have the same reasons for believing that the Pope is infallible that we have for believing that Napoleon III. is a prisoner, viz., a great many people say so. We Protestants, upstarts of three centuries, ought to have the modesty to confess ourselves unable to see the force in metaphysical disquisitions so abstruse.

Then there is the Scriptural argument so laboriously drawn out in the *London Vatican* of July 29th, 1870: "Did not Christ say: 'Thou art Peter, and upon this rock I will build my church?' (We fancy we have heard that quoted before by Papists.) Even this, however, was not enough for the Most High to say to the first primate. Hence he adds, 'And the gates of hell shall never prevail against it.' Not enough yet. The sovereign Pope must reign in both worlds at once. 'I will give unto thee the keys of the kingdom of heaven.' Not sufficient still. 'And whatsoever thou shalt bind on earth shall be bound in heaven, and whatsoever thou shalt loose on earth shall be loosed in heaven.' Then, moreover, Jesus said to Peter, not to John (the records must needs be amended, so the facts of Peter's fall, denial and profanity are cautiously and very considerately suppressed): 'I have prayed for thee that thy faith fail not.' God's Vicar could not err, because his fall would have been the ruin of the Church." (The sacred record, you see, must be incorrect. Peter must have remained firm, for the Church has been infallible ever since. This passage must be like that other, which speaks of Peter's wife's mother, whereas Peter could by no possibility have been guilty of having a wife, since all his successors, following his illustrious example, vow celibacy.) Then follows the admonition addressed to the first pontiff, and through him to the long succession of Holy Fathers, "Confirm thy brethren." So you see, or don't you see?—the Pope is infallible. Can't you say with "the greatest theologian of the age," "There is hardly a doctrine of Christianity which is so conspicuously vouched in Holy Scripture, or which its divine author thought proper to reveal by such an astonishing iteration of words and acts, as that of the primacy and inerrancy of his Vicar?" This famous passage which does battle everywhere, which proves that priests can forgive sins, that the Pope can send a man to hell, to heaven, or to purgatory, that Peter was primate, that the Catholic Church is as unchangeable as a rock, that no man can be saved unless within its sinless pale, that Popery, in the exact form in which it now exists, shall continue till the Church militant becomes the Church triumphant, that corporal punishment for spiritual offences is heaven-ordained, and that Peter never fell, also, according to Papal logic, incontestably, unmistakably, irresistibly proves that Pio Nono, in this nineteenth century, is infallible.

Lastly, we have the argument of the bishop of Poitiers, which elicited such applause in the Vatican Council:—
"St. Paul was beheaded; consequently his head, which represents the ordinary episcopate, was not indissolubly united to the body. St. Peter, on the contrary, was crucified with his head downwards, to show that his head, which was the image of the Papacy, sustained the whole body." So you perceive the present Pope must be infallible. HE SAYS SO. And how otherwise could he sustain the entire Church?—how be a Rock?

Proved, to the satisfaction of Papists by arguments such as these, infallibility was, July 18th, 1870, exalted into a dogma. The entire Catholic world must henceforth believe, on pain of eternal damnation, "that when the Roman pontiff speaks *ex cathedrâ* . . . . he possesses . . . . . infallibility.* In interpretation of this the New York *Freeman's Journal and Catholic Register*, of September 3d, 1870, says: "In his personal character as Pope, without awaiting the agreement of the Catholic Episcopate, the Pope is infallible *personally*. The expression *personal infallibility of the Pope* is therefore correct."

So the famous and long-continued discussion, where resides the infallibility of the Church—in the Pope, in a General Council, or in the concurrent voice of both?—

---

* Dogmatic Decree on the Church of Christ, chap. iv.

is at last ended. No second Dean Swift need tauntingly say, "Really, Holy Mother might as well be without an infallible head, as not to know where to find him in necessity." Five hundred and thirty-three robed bishops have solemnly proclaimed that he lives in Rome, or did, and is the legitimate successor of the fallible Peter. He eats bread, drinks wine, rides out daily in his coach, twirls his finger in an ecstasy of delight as he pronounces benedictions on those who shout, "Vive l'Infallible," and scowls with rage as he utters anathemas against the Protestant failure.

As this last and most insolent dogma of Popery has been established without argument, or rather in spite of argument, it certainly were folly for Protestants to dignify it by attempting a formal refutation. To argue a shouting crowd into silence is impossible. And a cloud, dense, dark, impalpable, portending storm, is not dissolved by man's howling out a few syllogisms. Many an error has been argued into respectability by its opponents. For some absurdities no argument is more powerful than ridicule; for some pretensions no treatment so galling as silent contempt. And Protestants can certainly well afford to let bishops, priests, and people tell each other that they believe, or make believe, Pio Nono is infallible. If, however, any desire to examine a complete demolition of Rome's last arrogant claim, we commend to their careful perusal, "The Pope and the Council," by Janus. This work, originating in the bosom of the Papal Church, written by persons claiming to be genuine Catholics, and proving with inexorable logic that the doctrine of infallibility is a mere novelty in the religious world, has caused much uneasiness even in the seared conscience of the Papal Church, and called forth a vast amount of fruitless effort at refutation. We have seldom seen such pitiable exhibitions of the inherent weakness of a cause as may be seen in the absurdly feeble attempts to answer Janus. The *Catholic World* of New York (June, July, and August numbers, 1870), contains articles which, for feebleness and clumsy special pleading, are, we firmly believe, entitled to the first place in the literature of the last half century. Every unprejudiced reader must certainly rise from their perusal thoroughly convinced that the reception of the infallibility dogma *is purely an act of faith*. If that is Rome's best showing, her proud claim evidently rests exclusively on bold and oft-repeated assertion and specious falsehood.

Since at last we have an infallible man, we ought to know how his decrees are to be transmitted to us fallibles. He is accessible only to a limited few. How can he make every child of Holy Mother infallibly certain what the truth is? Are all archbishops and bishops and priests to be next declared infallible? Are we to have a set of infallible telegraph operators, and infallible printers, who shall inform prelates and bishops, who in turn shall peddle out infallibility's last announcement to every loyal Papist? And unless this is done, of what use is an infallible head?* Must the faithful take an infallible system on the testimony of fallibles? Are they required to believe by proxy? The Pope says, "All must believe what I believe, because I believe what all believe." Then every Romanist, it is to be presumed, believes everything contained in "the whole Word of God, written and unwritten." This requires belief in at least one hundred and fifty folio volumes, a cart-load of contradictory doctrines and clashing traditions. If employing private judgment, the layman conscientiously endeavors to eliminate truth from this mass of useless rubbish, he is guilty of a damnable heresy. And how is he to know with infallible certainty what is the interpretation of Pius IX.? Must he go to Rome? Must he await the next Œcumenical Council which shall decree Papal transmission infallible? Or must he content himself with this circular argument? I believe what the Pope believes. The Pope believes what I believe. We both believe exactly the same. He and I are therefore infallible. And if *he is,* surely *I must be.* An unerring head and an erring body and members, were a kind of nondescript, a monster known neither in heaven, on earth, nor in hell.

This marvellous prerogative, it is now claimed, has always belonged to the successor of Peter. Has it ever decided a single controversy?—ever healed a single

---

* The absence of a comma in one of the recent Decrees came near making the entire Catholic world believe a falsehood.

dissension?—ever settled a single quarrel either in private, in social or in national life? In this intensely practical age men therefore ask, what good is to result from this dogma? The fiercely bitter strifes between the Calvinistic Jansenists and the Arminian Jesuits, between the Franciscans and the Dominicans touching the kind of homage due the transubstantiated wafer, between the advocates and the opponents of the Immaculate Conception of the Virgin Mary, were they, even in the slightest degree, alleviated or repressed by Christ's infallible Vicar? And of what value was the inerrancy of Pope Liberius who embraced the Arian heresy? An infallible primate endorsing a doctrine which had already been repeatedly and emphatically anathematized, and by the present "Infallible Judge in faith and morals" is deemed no less heinous than infidelity itself, is surely a strange proof of indefectibility. And of what value was this boasted prerogative to Pope Honorius, that old transgressor, whose doctrinal errors cost the last Œcumenical Council such an immense amount of arguing and falsifying? Being unanimously condemned by the sixth General Council for holding doctrines then, since, and now considered heretical, the advocates of Papal infallibility are placed in the awkward dilemma of being forced to believe that exact contraries are precisely the same. Benediction and anathema, assertion and denial, truth and error, are one and the same thing to those who can legislate vice into virtue and virtue into vice. Of what practical worth is that infallibility which in the seventeenth century, "desirous of providing against increased detriment to the holy faith," solemnly affirmed: "The proposition that the earth moves is absurd, philosophically false, and theologically considered at least, erroneous in faith;" and in this nineteenth century, not merely believes the Copernican system, but with brazen-faced effrontery endeavors to deny that Galileo suffered persecution for opinion's sake? And then, too, unless His Infallibility can reconcile the two thousand variations between the authorized Vulgate Bible of Pope Sextus, the infallible, and that of Pope Clement, the infallible, the unbelieving world will continue to smile at the deliverance of the invincible five hundred.*

Let Rome's arguments and anathemas therefore be never so powerful, an infallibility which suspends civil law, spreads rebellion and celebrates a Te Deum for the massacre of heretics; which corrupts the doctrines of the Bible, opposes popular education, and hangs on the skirts of progress shouting halt; which inveighs against the civilization of the present, stops commerce, fetters science, enslaves the mind, impoverishes the nations, and mingles even with her prayers curses against civil and religious liberty, is a dogma which this age at least can contemplate only with mingled horror and derision. Were it less ridiculous we might

---

* Says Dr. John, an eminent Romanist, "The more learned Catholics have never denied the existence of errors in the Vulgate; on the contrary, Isidore Clarius collected 80,000."

almost weep tears of blood over the spiritual thraldom of one hundred and eighty millions of human beings henceforth forced, on pain of excommunication, refusal of the sacraments and everlasting damnation, to believe an erring mortal "infallible judge in faith and morals," Christ's inerrant Vicar. Were it less fatal to the freedom, the morals, and the eternal hopes of enslaved Papists we might give way to uproarious laughter, and shame the absurdity off the world's stage. We can view it however only as a declaration of war against civilization; only as a death knell to the hopes of those who are subject to the Roman priesthood. Henceforth Popery is to be narrower, more bigoted, more impenetrable to truth than ever. While the Protestant world is advancing in liberty, intelligence, morality and material prosperity, the Papal seems destined to stagnation, if not, alas, to even grosser superstition, deeper ignorance and more abject spiritual servitude.

What results may flow from this last arrogant assumption of Rome's proud Pontiff, it is yet too soon to predict. The struggle of the last three centuries—a struggle between intelligence and superstition, between progress and reaction, between light and darkness, between all that makes this age hopeful and made the middle ages the world's midnight—has ended, ended in the triumph of bigotry. In this we may, perhaps, discover the beginning of the end. Certainly Catholic aggression in civilized countries is henceforth impossible. The absurdity is too apparent to impose upon even common intelligence.

134   *INFALLIBILITY.*

Infallible but powerless! French troops withdrawn, Napoleon dethroned, Catholic France beaten and helpless, the Pope's temporal power gone, his erring sheep following the guidance of liberal ideas, himself, though claiming to be Supreme Judge over all kings, virtually a prisoner, bishops in scores denouncing the infallibility blunder,* the entire Catholic world in momentary apprehension of yet more terrible calamities, surely we are powerfully reminded of that ancient and honorable declaration, "In one hour is she made desolate." What wonders has God wrought! How suddenly have her woes come upon her! † "This is the Lord's doing, and it is marvellous in our eyes."

And now from all parts of the Catholic world may be heard one long drawn sigh over Popery's helpless condition, one deep wail of terror, harmonized from the

---

* Bishop Héfélé, of Rottenberg, with his entire chapter and the theological faculty of Tubingen, have determined to persevere in the opposition to the Vatican Council, come what may. Lord Acton says: "The Vatican Council has pronounced its own condemnation. Some of the most distinguished of the prelates characterized it as a 'conspiracy against Divine truth and right,' 'a disgrace for all Catholics.'"

† 1870. July 14. Infallibility proclaimed, Protestantism condemned.
　　　July 15. War declared by Napoleon III. against Protestant Prussia.
　　　Sept. 1. The oldest son of Holy Mother captured by a heretic.
　　　Sept. 20. The Pope and Rome captured by an excommunicated king.
　　　Oct. 2. The Roman people's love for the Pope expressed by 40,805 negatives against 46 affirmatives.

cry of the impotent infallible, the half frantic whinings of bishops and priests, and the evil forebodings of pamphlets, magazines, periodicals, and papers. Plainly, whatever results were fondly anticipated from the consummation of the work for which the Council was summoned, Holy Mother deems herself in dreadful agonies. Says the *Tablet*, a Roman organ, "There is, alas, no room for doubt that a heavy calamity has befallen the Holy Church of Rome and the Apostolic See. The infidels have converted and educated the bad Catholics up to the reception of certain opinions and principles of their own." So even Romanists will think for themselves, notwithstanding there is an infallible Pope to think for them. And even now, after all their efforts, Italy is tainted to the very core with love of liberty; private judgment is even now untrammelled. The vengeance sworn against Republicanism, were it not so impotent, might strike terror. It is evidently, however, only the wail of despair.

A cloud, portentous, though small, may be seen on the horizon. An ominous increase in the number of Jesuits, those unprincipled political tricksters, has taken place. In Germany, France, England, and even in the United States, the Catholic papers are sounding "*a call for a new Crusade.*" With this as their watchword, "*Rome belongs to the Catholic Church,*" they are seeking to fire the hearts of the young. Already we learn on Papal authority, that "The Catholic youth of Europe are stirring, and preparing for the conflict. In our own land thousands of hearts, of young Catholic men, are burning with desire to add their part to the Grand Crusade." In New Orleans an immense mass meeting has been held, and that too on Sunday, in utter disregard of the rights of Protestants and the laws of the country, to express sympathy with and secure material aid for the "Infallible Judge in faith and morals." All this may, most likely will, end in smoke. Possibly, however, they may be so infatuated as to continue their repinings over the terrible fate of Christ's Vicar, perhaps may inaugurate agencies for his restoration, possibly may "take up arms against a sea of troubles," and thereby hasten the end. The old Romans, whose Pagan religion these modern heathen have inherited, had an adage containing a mine of good sense, "Whom the gods design to destroy they first make mad." Are we witnessing the infatuation which precedes destruction? *

---

* "We call for a Crusade of the whole of Christendom, to put him (the Pope) on his throne. . . . . Neither the 'King of the monkeys' (Victor Emmanuel), or any other being, should hold as a subject the Pope that is head of our Church." "At this moment St. Peter is in chains, in the person of his successor."—*Freeman's Journal and Catholic Register*, Nov. 19, 1870.

CHAPTER III.

DESPOTISM.
(2 Thess. ii. 9.)

NO political tyrant, no despotic Nero, even in his most frenzied mood, ever arrogated claims over man so cruelly tyrannical as those of Popery. Despots have indeed tortured the body till death granted release; but to tyrannize over the mind, to traffic in the eternal destinies of the soul, to trample at will upon man's dearest hopes, those that stretch beyond this troubled life, are abominations known only to Romanism. The only usurpations worthy of comparison with hers are the monstrous assumptions of Brahminism. And even these, though having the same parentage, and manifesting similar dispositions, sink into insignificance when compared with those of that mystery of iniquity whose coming, it was predicted, should be *"with all power."*

To render the spiritual control complete, the Papal Church has made her seven sacraments so many instruments of despotism. These, in connection with her doctrine of INTENTION, form a power of oppression truly appalling. In the decree of the Council of Trent we read: " If any one shall affirm, that when the minister performs and confers a sacrament, it is not necessary that they should, at least, have the *intention* to do what the Church does, let him be accursed." Could anything, we ask, place the Romanist more completely under the power of the priest? Through him must come all spiritual blessings. Here centre all hopes. In administering the ordinances of the church, however, the officiating priest may, through negligence, or to gratify personal resentment, or with the diabolical purpose of leaving the suppliant unblessed, withhold the intention, giving the form without the substance. Thus the poor penitent is entirely at the mercy of his spiritual despot.

The faithful are taught that marvellous grace comes through eating the bread transubstantiated by the prayer of the priest into the very body of Christ. Suppose, however, that when the words are pronounced, "This is my body," the celebrant has in reality no intention of changing the wafer to flesh. Then the worshipper, ignorant of the secret purpose of the minister's heart, but required by a Church claiming infallibility to believe that the visible wafer "is the body and blood, soul and divinity, of Christ," is not merely guilty of believing a falsehood, but of the grossest idolatry—the worship of flour and water. On pain of eternal damnation, he is ordered to believe an absurdity, and to bow in adoration before what he cannot know to be a God; nay, what reason and the senses testify is bread. If, trusting these, he refuses homage, he is threatened by a Church, claiming to possess the keys of heaven and hell, with the endless torments of perdition. If he adores the host, then, on the concession of Rome herself, he may be guilty of worshipping the creature, a sin for which, according to the Papal Church, there is no forgiveness. If he follows common sense, Rome thunders her anathemas against him. If he obeys the Church, he may be rendering his damnation doubly more certain. Did ever despotism equal this? Eternal happiness is suspended on the mere whim of a priest, and he, perhaps a revengeful, licentious, drunken wretch.

Take the sacrament of baptism. In the "Abridgment of Christian Doctrine," it is asked, " Whither go the souls of infants that die without baptism? *Answer*. To that part of hell where they suffer the pains of loss, but not the punishment of sense; and shall never see the face of God." Tearfully, almost in hopeless despair, may the loyal Papist ask, as he kisses the pallid lips of the coffined babe, Do any reach the joys of the redeemed? The sweet whisperings of a hope natural to the parental heart are silenced by the stern voice of Holy Mother, " *Unbaptized, unsaved*." How many chances against the innocents! The parents neglect their duty: the babe is lost. It is brought to the priest and its brow sprinkled with water. Through carelessness or fiendish malignity, however, the *intention* is wanting. The helpless infant is eternally exiled from God. Perhaps the priest himself was never baptized;

or if baptized, perhaps never ordained. Though these ordinances may have been administered, the *intention* may have been wanting. In either case the child is doomed to endless woe. Nor is this a mere fancied difficulty. No genuine Romanist can by possibility possess satisfactory evidence that either he himself or his child is validly baptized. And yet he is taught to believe that without this baptismal regeneration salvation is impossible. The legitimate result of such teaching is to produce a race of the most abject slaves, crouching, spiritless.

The dying Papist, as he receives penance and extreme unction, feels in his inmost soul that all his hopes for time and eternity are suspended on the *intention* of the priest, who, " sitting in the tribunal of penance, represents the character and discharges the functions of Jesus Christ."* To heaven, to hell, or to purgatory, as best suits his fancy, he can send the departing spirit. However deep may have been its guilt, however black its crimes, however polluted its thoughts, the priest "*can confer dying grace*," and "*open the gates of paradise:*" he can send the most devout Romanist to endless despair, eternally beyond the reach of hope. Was ever another system devised, even in the hotbed of Pagan superstition, so perfectly fitted to crush its victims? What could produce slavery more abject, of reason, will, soul and body? All the efforts of the poor vassal must be directed to-

---

* " Trent Catechism," p. 260.

wards propitiating the priest, who henceforth stands to him in the place of a god.

Two youthful hearts, innocent and pure, present themselves in the first fervor of new-born love, to be united in the bonds of holy matrimony. Hope paints a radiant future. They are pronounced husband and wife. If intelligent Catholics, however, and earnestly desirous of true union, they may well ask, as they turn from the priest, Are we really married? Perhaps there was no intention on the part of him professing to confer the sacrament; perhaps the bride, perhaps the groom lacked the intention. In either case, Holy Mother infallible affirms, the marriage contract is null.* By the negligence or wickedness of him who should have conferred the matrimonial sacrament, two persons, though innocent, pure-minded and conscientious, live in mortal sin, and should death overtake them in that state—and how can they ever possess assurance that they are truly married?—they must sink down to endless perdition. Worse still; one of the parties may, when the health, wealth or beauty of the other is lost, declare under oath that the marriage ceremony, by the lack of intention on his or her part, was a nullity. The code of Rome declares the union dissolved. And what shall hinder an adventurous wretch from designing this beforehand, and thus sending to eternal woe one whose greatest, almost only sin, was a lavish bestowment of the entire wealth of her affections upon an object so unworthy?

---

* "Abridgment of Doctrine," p. 76.

To the other sacraments of Romanism, we need not refer. The despotism is of the same character as that apparent in all parts of her organized system of traffic in the souls of men.

As an engine of spiritual despotism, none, perhaps, is so powerful as *the confessional*. It crushes the poor deluded Papist to the very dust. Even for the forgiveness of sins committed against God, he looks to the priest. "Absolution is not a bare declaration that sin is pardoned by God to the penitent, but *really a judicial act.*" The subjection is complete. Are such down-trodden slaves ever likely to "become kings and priests unto God?" Could we expect them to seek the closet, and before the High-priest of our profession seek and obtain pardon in the blood that cleanses from all sin? And as for becoming guardians of civil liberty, the very idea is preposterous. They who, at the nod of Rome's mitred bishops, lick the very dust and swear eternal loyalty to a distant spiritual despot; who openly proclaim that their first allegiance is due to Rome's Sovereign Pontiff; who are educated under a system bitterly hostile to all existing forms of government, and especially to those founded on equal rights; who anxiously, prayerfully, imploringly await the return of the nations to the despotic forms of government now so exceedingly obnoxious; who denounce the Reformation as the fruitful source of all the worst evils that have ever afflicted human society; who oppose our common school system, ridicule the right of private judgment, repress the sterling activity which has enriched the nations, transforming continents as if by magic, and determinedly resist the onward march of liberty, personal and national, civil and religious,—can such victims of Papal superstition ever become good citizens in a free enlightened republic?

Even the claim of ability to forgive sin, presumptuous as it is, and their yet more arrogant claim of power to send the soul to purgatory, or to release it from the purifying fires, are surpassed by that masterpiece of heartless malignity, the solemn assertion of a God-given right "*to damn the souls of rebellious and refractory men.*" The bull against Henry VIII., as also that against Queen Elizabeth, the memorable patroness of literature, is the "excommunication and damnation of the Sovereign." And more than once have the Popes pronounced anathemas against the entire Protestant world. Surely Paul was predicting Popery when he wrote: "Whose coming is after the working of Satan with *all power.*" Over those believing her doctrines Rome's power is absolute. Nero himself could desire no more.

To render the bondage still more abject, if that were possible, one Pope, Stephen, laid the talent of Peter under contribution. When Aistulphus, king of the Lombards, burning with rage against the Pope, laid siege to Rome, Stephen, driven by stern necessity, dispatched a messenger to Pepin, king of France, with a letter purporting to come from St. Peter, servant and

Apostle of Jesus Christ. The epistle, direct from heaven—written on mundane paper—earnestly entreated and peremptorily ordered "*the first son of the Church*" to earn an eternal reward "*by hastening to the relief of the city, the Church, and the people of Rome.*" Then, apparently fearing that his own requests and orders should be despised by king Pepin, Peter considerately adds: "Our Lady, the Virgin Mary, mother of God, joins in earnestly entreating, nay, commands you to hasten, to run, to fly, to the relief of my favorite people, reduced almost to the last gasp." Pepin obeyed. The letter from heaven was effectual. "The monarch of the first, the best and the most deserving of all nations," marched immediately with a large army into Italy. Aistulphus was forced to surrender a part of his dominions to the Pope, "to be forever held and possessed by St. Peter and his lawful successors in the See of Rome." Thus the Pope became a temporal sovereign. How mildly Stephen's successor, Pius IX., has ruled, let the vote of his subjects so lately taken testify. If ever a ruler was emphatically pronounced a despot, the present Pope has been.*

And to judge from his denunciations of liberty, so repeatedly and emphatically made, especially in the documents preparatory to the Vatican Council, the Italian people are certainly not wide of the mark. His pious soul seems inflamed with holy indignation

---

* The vote stood: for Dethronement of Pope, 40,805; against, 46.

against the present forms of government. "Anarchic doctrines," he affirms, "have taken possession of men's minds so universally, that it is not possible now to discover a single State in Europe that is not governed upon principles hostile to the faith." And this proud potentate assumes the right to lord it over princes as well as people: "It is not he (the Pope) who has given up the State; it is the State that has revolted from him; the old days of the Passion have returned; the nations will not have this man to rule over them, so they give themselves to Cæsar."* Nor is this embodiment of despotic power, who claims spiritual and even temporal dominion over all secular princes, any more ready to acknowledge the authority of a General Council. Such a Council can convene only at his bidding. "And if, under some circumstances, all the bishops did meet, and formed themselves into a Council, their acts would be null, unless the Pope consented to them."† Even to the decisions of a Council properly convoked, the Pope, it is affirmed, is not required to submit. "As the Pope is higher than all bishops, none of them could have jurisdiction over him. . . . Not even of his own choice could he yield obedience. . . . He could not submit to their jurisdiction voluntarily, because his power is a divine gift."‡ Did ever another's power reach so lofty an altitude as to render voluntary obedience an absolute

---

* "The Year of Preparation for the Vatican Council," p. 18.
† *Idem*, p. 12. ‡ *Idem*, p. 22.

impossibility? Even when seated in the Council, surrounded by those who are nothing more than counsellors of the supreme judge, his Holiness IS STILL THE POPE. "He is there as the Pope." "The whole authority resides really in himself, for though he communicates of his powers to the assembled Prelates, yet he does not divest himself of his own. . . . Thus the supreme jurisdiction of the Church never passes away from the Supreme Pontiff, and does not even vest in a General Council. . . . The reason assigned for this lies in the fact that the gift of infallibility is not communicated to the Council, but abides in the Pope." * No wonder the Pope so tenderly commends that "teaching which makes the Church our Mother, and all the faithful little children listening to the voice of St. Peter."

As an appropriate and suggestive conclusion to this chapter, we beg the privilege of introducing the reader to this lordly potentate, this king of kings, and bishop of bishops, this Infallible Judge in faith and morals, in the act of proving himself a servant of servants. Graphically is the scene described in the *Catholic World* of July, 1870. An eye-witness, evidently and certainly a loyal subject of Pius IX., touches the picture with an artist's hand. During Holy Week in Rome, the bishops of the Vatican Council being present, the Sovereign Pontiff gave proof, to Papists entirely satisfactory, that he was of all men the humblest.

---

* "The Year of Preparation for the Vatican Council," pp. 27, 28.

On a raised platform, in the full view of several thousand of his adoring subjects, His Humility prepares himself for the ceremony of washing and kissing the feet of thirteen pilgrim priests to Rome, one a Senegambian negro. As the voices of the choir, in soul-subduing melody, intone, "A new command I give you," the humble servant—his head adorned with a mitre, typical, we suppose, of the poverty and humble station of St. Peter, his predecessor—girds on an apron. Before him are the thirteen travellers, dressed in long white robes, cut in the style of a thousand years ago, and wearing white rimless stove-pipe hats, surmounted by tufts. Shoes and stockings spotlessly white complete the costume of these weary pilgrims from distant climes. An attendant, full robed and exceedingly dignified, with studied precision, unlaces the brand new, stainlessly white shoe, and lets down the immaculate stocking on the right foot of the nearest pilgrim. Breathless silence reigns. All eyes are intensely fixed. A vessel of water, and span clean towels are handed the Pontiff. He washes the instep, wipes it, kisses it, and gives the happy possessor a nosegay—minus the gold coin of former and better days, when the traffic in indulgences was brisk. A murmur of applause, like the ripple of many waters, runs through the vast cathedral. Another and another instep is washed and kissed. "The jet black negro," as a new anthem rings through the vast arches of St. Peter's, and the assembled spectators, in an ecstasy of humbled devotion, whisper in half-broken accents, "*Vive l'Infallible,*" finds his instep pressed by the infallible lips of His Holiness, the Supreme Judge of all men. The ceremony is ended. During its continuance an hundred human beings have gone down to death. Infallibility can find no fitter employment than such exhibitions of mock humility! Washing the clean feet, and crushing the blackened souls!! Feigning the humility of the poor, despised, lowly Nazarene, and blasphemously claiming the attributes of Deity!!!

PROCESSION WITH RELICS IN CINCINNATI.

CHAPTER IV.

FRAUD :—RELICS.

THE coming of the mystery of iniquity, Paul predicted, should be not merely with "*all power,*" but with "*signs and lying wonders.*" Could language more accurately describe the countless relics which Rome's votaries venerate ?—*Lying wonders.* Without attempting to furnish a complete list—the bare catalogue would make a large octavo volume—we present a few, enough to determine the character of all.

The early Christians, it would seem, must have been particularly careful to preserve the bones of their dead. In the Cathedral of St. Peter, at Rome, they have an arm of St. Lazarus; a finger and arm of St. Ann, the Holy Virgin's Mother; and the head of St. Dennis, which he caught up and carried the distance of two miles after it had been cut off. In France they have four heads of John the Baptist. In Spain, France, and Flanders they have *eight* arms of St. Matthew! and *three* of St. Luke! In the Lateran Church, in Rome, they have the *entire* heads of St. Peter and St. Paul; and in the convent of the St. Augustines, at Bilboa, the holy monks have a *large* part of Peter's head, and the Franciscans a large part of Paul's. At Burgos they have the tail of Balaam's ass, a part of the body of St. Mark, and an arm and finger of St. Ann. At Aix-la-Chapelle they have two teeth of St. Thomas; part of an arm of St. Simeon; a tooth of St. Catharine; a rib of St. Stephen; a shoulder blade and leg bone of St. Mary Magdalene; oil from the bones of St. Elizabeth; bones of Sts. Andrew, James, Matthias, Luke, Mark, Timotheus and John the Baptist. Perhaps it is for the purpose of carrying all these sacred relics that Rome has *five* legs of the ass upon which our Saviour rode into Jerusalem.

Nor are bones their only precious mementoes. In almost every chapel in Europe may be found pieces of the cross on which our Lord was crucified. If these were all collected, no doubt they would furnish an amount of material equal to that contained in one of the largest dwellings in America. In Rome they have also the cross of the good thief; also the entire table on which our Lord celebrated the Paschal Supper. And a recent publication, "The Living Eucharist manifested by Miracles," assures us, "this is the true table of the Lord, that on which the world's Redeemer and God, Jesus, offered the first eucharistic sacrifice." And on the same authority we learn that at the cathedral of Valencia, in Spain, they have "the cup in which His blood was first laid, the chalice elevated from the table by his divine hands." "At St. Mark's, in Venice," says the same author, "the knife used by our Lord in *touching, not cutting,* the bread, is exposed each year, on Holy Thursday for the veneration of the faithful." Even the old room, that very upper chamber in Jerusalem, in which our Lord wrought that miracle of miracles, transubstantiating the bread into his actual flesh and blood, is even now "retained in a tolerable state." Fearing that no Protestant can possibly believe men so credulous, and that my honesty in reporting these "*lying wonders*" may be called in question, I refer the reader to the little tract published in London, A. D. 1869, written by George Keating, "The Living Eucharist manifested by Miracles." Here he will find what is enough to make one shudder with horror as he contemplates the abyss of superstition into which Papists have fallen.

And they have yet more wonderful mementoes than bones and wood. In more than one cathedral they have specimens of the manna of the wilderness, and a few blossoms of Aaron's rod. In Rome they have the very ark that Moses made, and the rod by which he wrought his miracles. At Gastonbury they have the identical stones which the devil tempted our Lord to turn into bread. In another of their chapels they have the dice employed by the soldiers in casting lots for the Saviour's garments.

They have St. Joseph's axe and saw; St. Anthony's millstone, on which he crossed the sea; St. Patrick's staff, by which he drove out the toads and snakes from Ireland; St. Francis' cowl; St. Ann's comb; St. Joseph's breeches; St. Mark's boots; "a piece of the Virgin's green petticoat;" St. Anthony's toe-nails, and "the parings of St. Edmund's toes."

Then, also, there are in their convents, all carefully suspended from the walls, most precious relics preserved in hermetically sealed bottles. There is a vial of St. Joseph's breath, caught as he was exercising himself with the very axe and saw now in their possession. There are several vials of the Holy Virgin's milk; and—will you doubt it, poor deluded Protestants?—a small roll of butter and a little piece of cheese made from her milk. They have also hair from the heads of most of their saints, and twelve combs, one from each of the Apostles, with which to dress it. And what is a little marvellous, these combs are declared to be "nearly as good as new."

To end our enumeration of her sacred relics; they have a small piece of the rope with which Judas hanged himself; "a bit of the finger of the Holy Ghost;" the nose of an angel; "a rib of the Word made flesh;" "a quantity of the identical rays of the star which led the wise men to our infant Saviour;" Christ's seamless coat; two original impressions of his face on two pocket-handkerchiefs; a wing of the archangel Gabriel, obtained by the prayers of Pope Gregory VII.; the beard of Noah; a piece of the very same porphyry pillar, on which the cock perched when he crowed after Peter's denial, and even the comb of the cock; and then the pearl of the entire collection, "one of the steps of the ladder on which Jacob, in his dream, saw the heavenly

ST. FRANCIS RESISTING THE DEVIL.　　*Page* 156.

host ascending and descending." A recent traveller to Rome not merely saw these wonders, but was considerately and affectionately told that inasmuch as he was a "*devout man*," he could obtain a small portion of these precious relics at a moderate price. He was offered a feather from Gabriel's wing for twenty-five cents.*

If we add to the above idolatries, their adoration of statues and images and the consecrated wafer, we have a system of superstition, such as no Pagan in his wildest vagaries ever dreamed of. And that they do worship these relics is, alas, too evident. We speak not merely of the ignorant masses, perhaps for their debasing idolatries the Church is not entirely responsible (although this may be fairly questioned, since her whole system is, in its very nature, adapted to produce the grossest superstition), but we charge this idol worship upon the most highly educated of their clergy.

---

* A noted Catholic historian tells us that when St. Ambrose needed relics with which to consecrate a church at Milan, "immediately his heart burned within him, in presage as he felt of what was to happen." By a dream he was directed to the spot where he would find the bones of St. Gervasius and St. Prostasius. "Having discovered their skeletons, all their bones entire, a quantity of blood about, and their heads separated from their bodies, ... they arranged them, covered them with cloths and laid them on litters. In this manner they were carried towards evening to the Basilica of St. Fausta, where vigils were celebrated all night, and several that were possessed received imposition of hands. That day and the next there was a great concourse of people, and then the old men recollected that they had formerly heard the names of these martyrs." "Profane and old wives' fables."

Thomas Aquinas says, "If we speak of the very cross on which Christ was crucified, it is to be worshipped with divine worship." And the prayers which are to be said in the adoration of these sacred bits of wood are given in the "Roman Missal."

> "Oh, judgment! thou hast fled to brutish beasts,
> And men have lost their reason."

CHAPTER V.

FRAUD :—MIRACLES.

ROME ever has claimed, and does still claim, the power of working miracles. One of her most eminent historians says : " The Catholic Church being always the chaste spouse of Christ, continuing to bring forth children of heroical sanctity,—God fails not in this, any more than in past ages, to illustrate her and them by unquestionable miracles." The Rev. James Kent Stone, a recent convert to Romanism, in his "Invitation Heeded" repeatedly and emphatically claims for the Church of his adoption the unquestioned ability to work miracles. He even undertakes a defence of those she has published to the world, affirming that they are as credible, nay, in some instances more so, than those recorded in the Bible. Here is a specimen :—" In 1814, a man who had his back-bone broken was made whole by making a pilgrimage to Garswood, and there getting the sign of the cross made on his back by some unknown priest called Arrowsmith, who was killed in the wars of Charles I." The bull of the Pope assigning a reason why the Virgin Magdalene should be canonized, reads thus: " Not without good reason with that incorruption and good odor of her body, which continues to this day." A "*delicious odor*" was emitted from her grave. St. Patrick sailed to Ireland on a millstone, and drove out all the snakes and toads with his staff.

St. Francis, founder of the Franciscan order of monks, who "had no teacher but Christ, and learned all by an immediate revelation," and of whom St. Bridget had a marvellous vision testifying that "the Franciscan rule was not composed by the wisdom of men, but by God himself," was, on one occasion, sorely tempted by a devil in the form of a beautiful, facinating lady. On a certain evening, however, when again tempted, "he spit in the devil's face." His biographer solemnly adds, "Confounded and disgusted the devil fled." A miracle! This same holy St. Francis predicted the day of his death, and even after his decease wrought miracles by his intercessory prayers. He had a vision of a seraph, the effect of which was that "His soul was utterly inflamed with seraphic ardor, and his body ever after retained the similar wounds of Christ." In consequence of these wounds, and the miracles he performd, so great became his honor, that in Roman books it is written, "Those only were saved by the blood of Christ who lived before St. Francis; but all that followed were redeemed by the blood of St. Francis."

Miracles were wrought in favor of the Immaculate Conception, and miracles were wrought against it. And what to Protestants seems strange, Rome confirmed both classes, and canonized those who achieved miracles in favor of, and those who achieved miracles against, this precious doctrine.

Take another of Rome's unquestionable miracles. St. Wenefride being a nun, of course could not marry. Her suitor, young Prince Caradoc, in anger at this, cut off her head. This gave rise to three miracles: 1. St. Beuno caused the earth to open, and young Caradoc was swallowed up; 2. A well opened on the spot where the nun's blood was shed, and the holy waters of this healing fountain work miracles unto this day; 3. St. Beuno placed the nun's head on the bleeding body, prayed to the "Mother of Christ," and behold St. Wenefride was immediately restored to life. Who will dare to say that these miracles are not far more wonderful than any recorded in Scripture? Protestants, in their ignorance, may be inclined to call them "*lying wonders*," but Roman infallibility has pronounced them "*unquestionable miracles*."

St. Dominic, on one occasion, during a dreadful tempest, exhorted the inhabitants of Toulouse to appease the wrath of heaven by reciting their prayers. The arm of the wooden image of the Virgin in the church was raised in a threatening attitude. "Hear me," shouted St. Dominic, "that arm will not be withdrawn till you have obeyed my commands." The terrified worshippers instantly set to work, counting their beads. Dominic, satisfied with their spiritual devotions, gave the order, and the arm of wrath immediately fell. The storm abated. The thunder and lightning ceased.

The blood of St. Januarius, preserved in a small bottle at Naples, is wont to liquefy, and sometimes boil, when exposed to the adoration of the faithful. This miracle, Protestants might be excused from believing, especially as on one occasion, when it refused to dissolve because the French soldiers occupied the kingdom, it afterwards concluded to do so, inasmuch as the Vicar of the bishops received this order from the French Commander: "If in ten minutes St. Januarius should not perform his usual miracle, the whole city shall be reduced to ashes." The obstinate saint came to terms! The blood boiled furiously!

But perhaps some one may be inclined to question whether miracles so preposterously absurd are now offered to the faith of Papists. Possibly some, by reading "The Aspirations of Nature," a work written to make converts to Catholicism, may imagine that Romanists are less credulous, less superstitious, less blindly bigoted now than in the middle ages. For the benefit of such we refer to miracles whose long drawn accounts are to be found in books now issuing, in this very country, under the official and authoritative endorsement of Rome. In the "Living Eucharist manifested by Miracles," the infallible, authoritative, apostolic Church, the unerring teacher of divine truth, in this nineteenth century actually records some twenty or more miracles wrought in proof of the real presence.

Bishops, priests and nuns, we are solemnly told, certainly saw the wafer, after the benediction of the priest, changed into an infant. The bread became real flesh and blood, a perfect infant, Jesus himself. In one case a priest was seen laying a beautiful babe, Jesus, on the tongue of each communicant. Wafers carried several days in the pocket of a bishop, on being blessed became little infants. Did ever blasphemy and irreverence equal this? Dogmatically affirming that the testimony of the senses is not to be taken in matters of faith, Papists endeavor to establish a doctrine which is in itself so repugnant to reason that one would suppose none but an idiot could believe it. And this publication has the sanction of Papal infallibility. Now, therefore, heretics, doubt no longer. Believe that the priest creates a god, worships him, and then eats him. Presume not to smile at this precious doctrine of transubstantiation, this sublime mystery, which the Rev. James Kent Stone (who in a short fifteen months passed from a public defender of Episcopacy to a most ardent advocate of the Papacy) affirms is a doctrine so spiritual that purblind Protestants cannot be expected to comprehend it.

Another tract, published in London, " The Miracle of Liège, by the use of the water from the fountain of Our Lady of Lourdes," deserves attention. This also can be purchased in almost any Catholic bookstore. " Mr. Hanquet's Narrative."—He was taken, he affirms, extremely ill in 1862. Continuing to grow worse, in July 1864 sitting up even for a few momemts was an impossibility. In 1867, ulcers, erysipelas, "a back bent like a bow," "a chest like a fiery oven," and "bloodless withered legs," rendered life a burden. The physician affirmed: "I find symptons of almost all diseases." In 1869 all hope of recovery faded away. His brother, however, on Oct. 13th, found in a bookstore the account of Our Lady of Lourdes. Already the dying man was praying most importunately to the Mother of God, Blessed Lady, Mary Immaculate. A bottle of water was sent for. A glass of it was poured down the throat of the dying man. Mary's aid was invoked. For an instant the death rattle was heard; then one bound, and the man, well and strong, seized his hat and went out doors wholly restored. A miracle indeed !!! And this, my dear Protestant friend, has the sanction of Papal infallibility. Who will not henceforth pray with devout Hanquet: "Holy Virgin, deign to ask for me from your divine Son that grace which is best for me, to die, to suffer or to be cured," *especially the last, to be cured?* This wonderful account of a very remarkable miracle—unless you are sacrilegious enough to call it one of Rome's lying wonders—this incontestable proof of the efficacy of prayer to the Blessed Virgin, you can make your own for twelve cents. This in the year 1870, and in New York.

M. C. Kavanagh, in her catechism and instructions for confession designed for very young children, having heartily commended the patience of St. Joseph, who, when a little lad, though bathed in tears, offered no reproach to those destroying his highly prized little garden (tradition, *i. e.* fiction pure and simple), our authoress gives, by way of enforcing the duty of penance, "a story of Our Blessed Lady." Little Mary when three or four years old, informed the priest that she had imposed upon herself penances, to eat no fruit except one kind, to drink no wine or vinegar of which she was very fond, to eat no meat or fish, and to rise three times in the night to pray. Heartily do we join in the ejaculation of the narrator, "This at the age of three years!" We certainly think that the dogma of infallibility is really needed. How otherwise could such a dose as this be forced down even a Papist's throat. The second instruction closes with this pious admonition: "Do not fail to pray to Our Lady and St. Jeseph to help you." Fed upon such food, is it any wonder that the children of our Catholic fellow-citizens grow up in the grossest ignorance, in superstition that would disgrace a heathen in Central Africa?

But the third instruction contains the gem, "*a true miracle.*" Only five years ago, in a village of France (how unfortunate, these miracles always occur in some distant land), there resided a certain curé. Among those who came to him was a gentleman who had great temptations against faith in the Blessed Eucharist. (Not so unreasonable when he was asked to believe, contrary to the testimony of his senses, that bread was flesh.) One day, as this doubter came to communion, the sacred host left the hands of the curé and placed itself on the tongue of the gentleman. Our authoress, in holy fervor exclaims, "What a miracle of love!" And we are impious enough to respond, *What a transparent falsehood!*

Obedience is a Christian duty which certainly ought to be commended to children. Here is Rome's way of enjoining it. St. Frances whilst saying the office of Our Lady, which she did daily (how adroitly Mary's worship is commended), was called by her servant. Leaving her prayers she attended to the request. Returning, scarcely had she begun the psalm when she was called a second time. Without loss of patience again she left her book to obey the command. Just after she had resumed her prayers for the third time her husband called. Leaving all, she ran to him. Returning, what was her surprise to find the words, written in letters of gold: "Now, therefore, dear children, always obey the calls of duty."

Lengthy as our list has become, we cannot pass the two hundred or more remarkable miracles contained in the ever-memorable book, so celebrated in Catholic communities, "The Glories of Mary," by St. Alphonsus Liguori.* This book was never intended for Protestant eyes. The original having been carefully examined, and every line, even every word found in perfect harmony with the doctrines of Holy Mother, and the translation in like manner *"expurgated,"* *approved and*

---

* A life of this saint, in four vols , by Cardinal Villecourt, has been recently published.

earnestly commended to the faithful, the work was introduced "with the hope that it might be found to retain the spirit of the learned and saintly author, and be welcomed by the devout in this country with the same delight which it has universally called forth in Catholic Europe." Whatever miracles are herein found may therefore be taken as duly attested and approved by Papal infallibility. Here is one. A gentleman devoted to Blessed Mary was accustomed often in the night to repair to the oratory of his palace to bow in prayer to an image of the Virgin. His wife, jealous and angered, asked him, "Have you ever loved any other woman but me?" He replied, "I love the most amiable lady in the world; to her I have given my whole heart," meaning Mary (?) The wife still more suspicious asked, "When you arise and leave the room, is it to meet this lady?" "Yes." "Deceived and blinded by passion," this wife, one night during her husband's long absence, "*cut her throat and very soon died.*" The heart-broken husband on learning this, implored help of Mary's image. No sooner was this done than the living wife, throwing herself at his feet, bathed in tears, exclaimed, "Oh, my husband, the Mother of God, through thy prayers, *has delivered me from hell.*"

"The next day the husband made a feast, and the wife told her relatives the facts, and showed the marks of the wound." Now, heretics, doubt if you dare.

Let us have one in the exact language of "the

learned and saintly author." "There lived in the city of Aragona a girl named Alexandra, who, being noble and very beautiful, was greatly loved by two young men. Through jealousy, they one day fought and killed each other. Their enraged relatives, in return, killed the poor young girl, as the cause of so much trouble, cut off her head, and threw her into a well. A few days after, St. Dominic was passing through that place, and, inspired by the Lord, approached the well, and said: 'Alexandra, come forth,' and immediately the head of the deceased came forth, placed itself on the edge of the well, and prayed St. Dominic to hear its confession. The Saint heard its confession, and also gave it communion, in presence of a great concourse of persons who had assembled to witness the miracle. Then St. Dominic ordered her to speak, and tell why she had received that grace. Alexandra answered, that when she was beheaded, she was in a state of mortal sin, but that the most Holy Mary, on account of the rosary, which she was in the habit of reciting, had preserved her in life. Two days the head retained its life upon the edge of the well, in the presence of all, and then the soul went to purgatory. But fifteen days after, the soul of Alexandra appeared to St. Dominic, beautiful and radiant as a star, and told him that one of the principal sources of relief to the souls in purgatory is the rosary which is recited for them; and that, as soon as they arrive in paradise, they pray for those who apply to them these powerful

ALEXANDRA'S HEAD CONFESSING.

prayers. Having said this, St. Dominic saw that happy soul ascending in triumph to the kingdom of the blessed."—" Glories of Mary," American Ed., p. 274.

Of others we have merely time to give the briefest outline. Mary's image furnishes written prayers to a penitent (p. 76); rescues a condemned murderer from the gallows (p. 78); bows to a murderer (p. 213); becomes and continues a nun fifteen years, in order to shield a devotee who wilfully deserted the paths of virtue (p. 224); leaves a church during the trial, condemnation and beheading of an infamous bishop (p. 391); speaks to a young man about to commit sin (p. 559), etc., etc., almost *ad infinitum.*

Blessed Mary herself cools the cheek of a dying devotee with a fan (p. 110); with a cloth wipes the death damp from the brow of "a good woman" dying in a home of poverty (p. 112); secures from the devil a paper given by an abandoned sinner containing a written renunciation of God (p. 198); furnishes a letter to one of her ardent admirers (the same lady had entertained her admirers all night in "rooms richly furnished and perfumed as with an odor of paradise!") (p. 454); burns an inn in which her children were sinning (five of the rescued affirm, on oath, that Mary, the Blessed Virgin, lighted the flames) (p. 659); by a second revelation of herself restores sight to one eye of a man who had regularly bargained with her for total blindness, if he might be permitted twice to behold her (p. 512).

By the assistance of Our Lady, an ape becomes and declares himself a devil, and at the command of a priest goes through a hole in the wall, which hole no mechanical genius could fill up (p. 251); a man in spirit form comes to his friend and says, My dead body is in the street, my soul in purgatory, *and I am here* (p. 265); at the repetition of the magic rosary devils have been known to leave wretched men (p. 683). There, that is a dose sufficient for any Protestant stomach! If any, however, desire more, there are plenty in the "Glories of Mary." Don't the immutable Church need the dogma of infallibility? Barring the sense of shame for our race produced by such exhibitions of moral depravity and mental weakness, these "examples" are more interesting and certainly far more startling than the most exciting modern novel. And they are published as truth, approved by Papal inerrancy, earnestly commended to the devout, believed by Papists! They are sold in New York, Philadelphia, Baltimore, and all large towns—sold in this nineteenth century, and in educated, enlightened, civilized, Christianized America! Can a republic long rest secure on a foundation of superstition? Judged by such literature, the present must indeed be the world's midnight of ignorance! Did the dark ages produce anything more grossly absurd? And Rome anathematizes the times because there are some men so heretical, so unprecedentedly blasphemous as to make jest of such absurdities.

May we not apply to Popery the words of Pollok?

> "The hypocrite in mask! He was a man
> Who stole the livery of the court of heaven
> To serve the devil in."

If any desire to see the account of a recent miracle, with all the embellishments, drawn out "*ad nauseam,*" we refer them to "Our Lady of Lourdes, by Henri Lasserre," found in the *Catholic World* (September, October, November, December, 1870, and January, February, March, and April, 1871).

At a grotto near Lourdes, in France, a poor, simple-minded, invalid, fourteen-year-old shepherdess, who could neither read nor write, knowing almost nothing except the superstitious use of Mary's rosary, had, we are gravely informed, daily visions, for more than two weeks, of the Blessed Virgin, and gave accurate, full, elegant descriptions of her dress, features and beauty. The honored recipient of Mary's favors, Bernadette, so named for her patron, St. Bernard, saw the heavenly vision, though no single observer of a vast crowd was able to see anything save the barren rock and the climbing eglantine; and heard words from lips seemingly lisping prayers for poor sinners as her fingers counted the beads of her glittering rosary. After days of ecstatic beholding, this wonderful message was sent from the "Queen of Heaven and Earth," by the vision-beholding Bernadette, to the priests—those prudent men who received the current rumors of the wildly excited populace with dignified silence, looks of disapprobation, and words of suspicion—"*Go tell the priests that I want a chapel built on this spot.*" When these words were spoken in ordinary tone, in the midst of several thousand breathless spectators of Bernadette's transfiguration, no ear caught the sound save that of the little, ignorant, simple-minded, pale-faced, nervous peasant girl.

At a subsequent vision this command was received: " Go drink and wash at the fountain, and eat of the herbs growing at its side." Fountain?—there was none. Bernadette, however, essaying obedience, walked on her knees over the rocks, and into the furthest corner of the grotto. As she dug up the earth with her hands a fountain sprung up. This, which has since flowed unceasingly for thirteen years and wrought miracles innumerable, possessed, from its first outgushing, miraculous healing properties. A quarryman, rubbing his blinded eye with the first water that filled the cavity, and kneeling in prayer to the Blessed Virgin, " immediately uttered a loud cry and began to tremble in violent excitement." " Cured." " Impossible," said the physician. " It is the Holy Virgin," said the devout Catholic. Many arose from beds to which they had been confined for years. Paralyzed limbs were instantaneously restored. Sores were cured. Deaf ears were unstopped. A dying child—the shroud already made—plunged by its mother into "the icy cold fountain,"* and held there for more than fifteen

---

* It was February, 1858.

minutes, was completely restored to health, and the next day, in the absence of the parents, "left the cradle and walked around the room," its first effort at walking! Remarkable baby! Wonderful water! One morning, says the author, twenty thousand, many of whom had spent the previous night at the grotto, witnessed, in rapt silence, the ecstasy of the little saint. Even if the waters had wrought no miracles, superstitious faith might have manufactured at least one or two tolerably decent counterfeits. So we think. So evidently thought the Editor of the *Ere Imperiale*, a local paper.

"Do not be surprised," said the organ of the Prefecture (Catholic), "if there are still some people who persist in maintaining that the child is a saint, and gifted with supernatural powers. These people believe the following stories :—

"1st. That a dove hovered the day before yesterday over the head of the child during the whole time of the ecstasy.*

"2d. That she breathed upon the eyes of a little blind girl, and restored her sight.

"3d. That she cured another child whose arm was paralyzed.

"4th. That a peasant of the Valley of Campan, having declared that he could not be duped by such scenes of hallucination, his sins had, in answer to her prayers, been turned into snakes, which had devoured him, not leaving a trace of his impious body.

---

* March 4th, A. D. 1858.

"This, then, is what we have come to, but what we would not have come to if the parents of this girl had followed the advice of the physicians, who recommended that she should be sent to the lunatic asylum"

CHAPTER VI.

IDOLATRY.

IT was against the worship of idols that the early Christians most solemnly and most determinedly protested. "We Christians," says Origen, "have nothing to do with images, on account of the second commandment; the first thing we teach those who come to us is to despise idols and images; it being the peculiar characteristic of the Christian religion to raise our minds above images, agreeably to the law which God himself has given to mankind." * And Gibbon affirms, "The primitive Christians were possessed with an unconquerable repugnance to the use and abuse of images." † Again: "The public worship of the Christians was uniformly simple and spiritual."

Most cunningly was this spirituality undermined and idolatry substituted. In the early part of the fourth century, after the subversion of Paganism, some bishops began to encourage the use of pictures and images as aids to the devotion and instruction of the ignorant. Even till the time of Gregory it was the prevalent opinion that, if used at all, images must be used merely

---

* "Origen against Celsus," lib. v. 7.
† "Decline and Fall," chap. xlix.

as books for the unlearned. The Pontiff, however, so far encouraged their erection that almost every church in the west could boast of at least one. Before these the multitude soon learned to bow; to these they offered prayers.

So disgusting became this growing superstition that in 700 the Council of Constantinople solemnly condemned the use of images, and ordered their expulsion from the churches. But in 713 Pope Constantine pronounced an anathema against those who "deny that veneration to the holy images which the Church has appointed." A few years later began that famous controversy between the Emperor Leo and Gregory II. which continued to distract the Church for more than fifty years. The Emperor and his successors, Constantine V., and Leo IV., strenuously endeavored to restore Christianity to its primitive purity. Gregory II., and the Popes succeeding him, with a zeal bordering on fanaticism, undertook a defence of image-worship. The Emperors were charged with ignorance, rudeness, pride, contempt of the authority of the sovereign Pontiff, and opposition to the teachings of the Church. Defying the wrath of the Pope, however, and encouraged by the unanimous decision of the Seventh Greek Council (A. D. 754), which condemned idolatry, Constantine V. burned the images and demolished the walls of the churches bearing painted representations of Christ, of the Virgin, and of the saints. The efforts of his son, Leo IV., were directed to the same end. But the Emperor dying suddenly—as is generally supposed from the effects of poison administered by his wife, Irene—the contest ended in a victory for the image-worshippers. Irene, prompted by a desire to occupy the throne, ordered her own son, Constantine VI., to be seized and his eyes put out. The order was faithfully executed, and with such cruelty that the unhappy son almost immediately expired. To this wretched and terribly brutal woman Papists are deeply indebted. Assisted by Pope Adrian, she extended idolatry throughout the entire empire, and in 787 summoned a Council at Nice, which decreed "That holy images of the cross should be consecrated, and put on the sacred vessels and vestments, and upon walls and boards, in private houses and in public ways. And especially that there should be erected images of the Lord God, our Saviour Jesus Christ, of our blessed Lady, the Mother of God, of the venerable angels, and of all the saints. And that whosoever should presume to think or teach otherwise, or to throw away any painted books, or the figure of the cross, or any image, or picture, or any genuine relics of the martyrs, they should, if bishops or clergymen, be deposed, or if monks or laymen, be excommunicated." *

Owing a debt of gratitude to Irene, Papists have endeavored to defend her monstrous wickedness. Unable to deny the cruelties practised upon her son, they attempt to justify them, nay, even to commend them, applauding her for so far overcoming the feelings of

---

* Plotina's "Lives of the Popes."

humanity, through love for the true Church and its honored doctrines, that she could sacrifice her own son, who stood in the way of her aiding in the establishment of image-worship.*

From that day to the present idolatry has been one of Rome's chief characteristics. It is now so intimately interwoven with her forms of worship as to defy all opposition. Most probably it will hold its place until the prophecy of John finds fulfilment, *"Babylon, the great, is fallen, is fallen."*

Nor are their images confined to churches and chapels. They are also set up by the road-side. In Popish countries, and especially in Italy, these images, fit successors of the old Roman gods that presided over the highways, are frequently to be met with. As the traveller passes, he uncovers his head, and reverently bows, or, time permitting, turns aside to kneel before the idol and implore a blessing. Did ever heathenism more unblushingly offer insult to common sense?

As our space will not permit an extended reference to the monstrous falsehoods, intrigues, and deceptions by which the priesthood succeeded in securing for these images the devout homage of the multitude, and the treasury of the Church the rich gifts so much coveted,

---

* "An execrable crime," says Baronius, "had she not been prompted to it by zeal for justice. On that consideration she even deserved to be commended for what she did. In more ancient times, the hands of parents were armed, by God's command, against their children worshipping strange gods, and they who killed them were commended by Moses."

we must content ourselves with calling attention to one or two specimens. In the "Master Key to Popery," by Anthony Gavin, we have an historical account of the "Virgin of Pillar," an image religiously worshipped in Saragossa, Spain. The Apostle St. James, the account informs us, with seven new converts, came to preach the Gospel in Saragossa. While sleeping upon the brink of a river, an army of angels came down from heaven with an image on a pillar, which they placed on the ground, saying, "This image of Our Queen shall be the defence of this city. By her help it shall be reduced to your Master's sway. As she is to protect you, you must build a decent chapel for her." The order was obeyed. A chapel was built, which became the richest in Spain.*

The crucifix of St. Salvador, when there is great need of rain and the barometer indicates a speedy change, is sometimes carried through the streets, while

---

* For "Our Lady of Pillar" a chaplain was provided, whose business it was to dress the image every morning. Through him, the Virgin Lady once addressed a solemn admonition to the people of Saragossa, accusing them of illiberality, want of devotion, and the basest ingratitude, and expressing her determination to resign her government to Lucifer, unless the people should come for the space of fifteen days, every day with gifts, tears, and penitence, to appease her wrath and secure a return of her favor. They were exhorted to come with prodigal hands and true hearts, lest the Prince of Darkness should be appointed to reign over them. They were also assured that from this sentence there was no appeal, not even to the tribunal of the Most High. This device, enriching the Church, nearly beggared the inhabitants of the threatened city.

the accompanying priests sing the litany and repeat prayers, imploring rain. This well-timed ceremony is almost invariably followed, within a few days, by rain. All exclaim, "A miracle wrought by our Holy Crucifix."

Not to multiply instances, we have the authority of Pope Gregory for affirming that wonders and miracles wrought by images are by no means rare. In an epistle addressed to the Empress Constantina, who had requested from him the head of St. Paul, for the purpose of enshrining it in the church which she was erecting in his honor, the successor of St. Peter says: "Great sadness has possessed me, because you have enjoined upon me those things which I neither can, nor dare do; for the bodies of the holy Apostles, Peter and Paul, are so resplendent with miracles and terrific prodigies in their own churches, that no one can approach them without awe, even for the purpose of adoring them. . . . . The superior of the place having found some bones that were not at all connected with that tomb; and having presumed to disturb them and remove them to some other place, he was visited by certain frightful apparitions and died suddenly. . . . Be it known to you that it is the custom of the Romans, when they give any relics, not to venture to touch any portion of the body; only they put into a box a piece of linen, which is placed near the holy body; then it is withdrawn and shut up with due veneration in the church which is to be dedicated, and as many prodigies are wrought by it as if the bodies themselves had been carried thither. . . . . But that your religious desire may not be wholly frustrated, I will hasten to send you some parts of those chains which St. Paul wore on his neck and hands, if indeed I shall succeed in getting off any filings from them." *

So, dear Empress Constantina, be it known to you, that Rome will not part with the hen that lays the golden egg, nor even allow you, much less the infidel world, to examine the nest. These holy bodies are surrounded by a more sacred divinity than doth hedge a king. Death is the penalty of approaching them unbidden by the infallible Pope. He will sell you relics —linen rags and iron filings—which will work as great wonders as the head you so much covet. No doubt of it ! ! !

Notwithstanding the distinction made by Romanists between absolute and relative, proper and improper worship, between latria, dulia, and hyperdulia, there can be no doubt they offer to these images an idolatrous homage. Devised evidently for the sole purpose of warding off the charge so frequently brought against them, of offering to pictures, images and relics that adoration due to Deity alone, this hair-splitting distinction has no influence in modifying the worship of the vast mass of Rome's devotees. The images are the real objects worshipped.

One of the ablest expounders of Papal doctrines

---

* " Gregory's Epistles," lib. iv. epist. 30. A large part of the original may be found in " Greseler," vol. i. p. 350.

says:—" From God, as its source, the worship with which we honor relics, originates, and to God, as its end, it ultimately and terminatively reverts." Assuredly the worship which originates with God, and returns ultimately to God, must be that true and proper homage due to him alone.

In proof that Papists offer adoration to images, we refer to the custom of serenading, on Christmas morning, all the statues of the Holy Virgin in the streets of Rome. The reason assigned for this grand musical entertainment is that the Virgin is a great lover and an excellent judge of good music.

A recent visitor to the church erected about the house where it is said Blessed Mary was born, saw miserable women, very personifications of gross superstition, dragging themselves on their knees around the venerated building, counting beads, kissing the marble foundations, repeating prayers before the idol, and ordering masses to be said for the benefit of themselves and friends. Disgusting beggars, trafficking in superstition, clamorously promise to supplicate the idol on behalf of those who favor them with alms. Dealers in the implements of devotion hawk their sacred wares, rosaries, pictures, medals, and casts of the Madonna.

Certainly no one except an idolater will deny that real homage is offered when the worshipper, bowing before an image, hymns its praises, and to it offers his prayers. Papists indeed say, " We do not worship the image, but the personage represented, not the statue, but the

WOMEN CREEPING INTO CHURCH.

Virgin, not the cross, but the Saviour suspended thereon." Gregory III., in writing to the Emperor Leo, says:—" You say we adore stones, walls, and boards. It is not so, my Lord; but these symbols make us recollect the persons whose names they bear, and exalt our grovelling minds." Intelligent Pagans have ever rendered precisely the same excuse.* They who knelt before the shrine of Jupiter, claimed that they were worshipping the invisible and spiritual by means of the visible and material. Those in India who now worship the images of Gaudama, do the same. Are we then to believe that there are not, never have been, and never can be, persons so degraded as to be properly denominated idolaters? Have all who employed images been capable of fully appreciating this sentimental distinction? Has not even superstitious ignorance worshipped the seen and forgotten the

---

* Plutarch, in explaining the worship of Egypt's two most famous deities, Osiris and Isis, holds the following language:—"Philosophers honor the image of God wherever they find it, even in inanimate beings, and consequently more in those which have life. We are therefore to approve, not the worshippers of these animals, but those who, by their means, ascend to the Deity; they are to be considered as so many mirrors, which nature holds forth, and in which the Supreme Being displays himself in a wonderful manner; or as so many instruments, which he makes use of to manifest outwardly his incomprehensible wisdom. Should men, therefore, for the embellishing of statues, amass together all the gold and precious stones in the world, the worship must not be referred to the statues, for the Deity does not exist in colors artfully disposed, nor in frail matter destitute of sense and motion."

unseen? Admitting that in the Papal Church only the less gross idolatry exists, is this justifiable? Is it not condemned in Scripture? The prohibition reads:— "Thou shalt not make unto thee *any* graven image, or any likeness of *any thing*." There has been given us, in the person of Jesus Christ, a visible image of the invisible God. Bowing before him, and crying, "My Lord and my God," we worship the seen, God in human form, "*the likeness of the Father*," "*the express image of his person*," and yet are not idolaters. Having so far accomodated himself to the constitution of our nature, he allows no other object to come between himself and the penitent heart.

Among Rome's numerous idolatries, none certainly is more conspicuous, none more ardently advocated, none less inexcusable than the adoration offered to the Virgin. Her mere titles, as found in that ever-famous book, "The Glories of Mary,"* and in her litany, a solemn supplicatory prayer, would fill more than a page of our present volume. She is denominated Queen of heaven, of earth, of mercy, of angels, of patriarchs, of prophets, of apostles, of martyrs, of confessors, of virgins, and of all saints; Mother of God, of penitents, and especially of obdurate and abandoned sinners; Ravisher of heart, finder of grace, hope of salvation, defence of the faithful, helper of sinners; our

---

* Translated from the Italian of St. Alphonsus Liguori. New York: Cath. Pub. House; approved of +John, Archbishop, January 21, 1852.

only advocate, our refuge, our protection, our health, our life, our hope, our soul, our heart, our mistress, our lady, our loving mother; secure salvation, Redeemer of the world, Virgin of virgins, Mother undefiled, unviolated, most pure, most chaste, most amiable, most admirable, most prudent, most venerable, most powerful, most merciful, most faithful; mirror of justice, seat of wisdom, cause of joy, spiritual vessel, vessel of honor, mystical rose, tower of David, house of gold, ark of the covenant, gate of heaven, morning star, comfort of the afflicted, etc., etc.

Liguori, since enrolled as a saint, mainly as the reward of his untiring efforts to supplant love of the Creator by love of the creature, boldly and unqualifiedly asserts that Mary co-operated in the original work of redemption :—

"When God saw the great desire of Mary to devote herself to the salvation of men, he ordained that by the sacrifice and offering of the life of this same Jesus, she might co-operate with him in the work of our salvation, and thus become mother of our souls." (P. 43, American Ed.)

"God could indeed, as St. Anselm asserts, create the world from nothing; but when it was lost by sin, he could not redeem it without the co-operation of Mary." (P. 186.)

He also asserts that Mary is the only fountain of life and salvation. "God has ordained that all graces should come to us through the hands of Mary." (P. 13.) And how is this proved? In true Catholic style, by authority. St. Augustine mentions Mary's name and affirms, "All the tongues of men would not be sufficient to praise her as she deserves." St. Bonaventure declares, "those who are devoted to publishing 'The Glories of Mary' are secure of paradise." Did these fathers ever make these assertions? And if they did, is assertion proof? These two questions remorselessly pressed would leave all Liguori's fine-spun arguments floating together distractedly in an ocean of balderdash. And here is a second kind of proof, Rome's clinching argument, a miracle—each section of the book has one, besides the eighty-nine additional. In the revelation of St. Bridget, we are told that Bishop Emingo, being accustomed to begin his sermons with the praises of Mary, the Virgin one day appeared to St. Bridget, and said: "Tell that bishop I will be his mother, and he shall die a good death." He died like a saint. Now, therefore, all you Catholics bow the knee and repeat one of St. Liguori's prayers to the Virgin. You have a fine selection from which to choose, well nigh a hundred. But the chief proof here, as elsewhere, is assertion. Here are a few specimens:—

"The kingdom of God consisting of justice and mercy, the Lord has divided it: he has reserved the kingdom of justice for himself, and *he has granted the kingdom of mercy to Mary*, ordaining that *all the mercies* which are dispensed to men should pass through *the hands of Mary*, and should be bestowed according to *her* good pleasure." (Pp. 27, 28.)

"St. Bernard asks: 'Why does the Church name Mary Queen of Mercy?' And answers: 'Because we believe that *she* opens the depths of the mercy of God, *to whom she will, when she will, and as she will;* so that not even *the vilest* sinner is lost if Mary *protects him.*' " (P. 31.)

" In Mary we shall find every hope. . . . In a word, we shall find in Mary *life and eternal salvation.*" (Pp. 173, 174.)

" For this reason, too, she is called *the gate of heaven* by the Holy Church. . . . St. Bonaventure, moreover, says that Mary is called the gate of heaven, because *no one* can enter heaven if he does not pass through *Mary, who is the door of it.*" (P. 177.)

" Richard, of St. Laurence, says : ' Our salvation is in the hands of Mary.' . . . Cassian absolutely affirms that the *salvation of the whole world* depends upon the *favor and protection* of Mary." (P. 190.)

" O how many, exclaims the Abbot of Celles, who merit to be condemned by the Divine justice, are saved by the mercy of Mary! for she is the treasure of God, and the treasurer of *all graces;* therefore it is, that our *salvation* is in her hands." (P. 300.)

" Thou hast a merit that has *no limits*, and an entire power over all creatures. Thou art the mother of God, the mistress of the world, the Queen of heaven. Thou art the *dispenser of all graces*, the glory of the Holy Church." (P. 673.) [The italics are ours.]

He assures his readers that Mary is omnipotent :—

" Do not say that thou canst not aid me, for I know that thou art *omnipotent*, and dost obtain *whatsoever* thou desirest from God." (P. 78.)

" Says St. Peter Damian, 'The Virgin has *all power in heaven and on earth.*'" (P. 201.)

" Yes, Mary is *omnipotent*, adds Richard, of St. Laurence, since the Queen, by every law, must enjoy the same privileges as the King. . . . And St. Antoninus says: 'God has placed the whole Church, not only under the patronage, but also under the *dominion* of Mary.'" (P. 203.)

Infallibility has also approved these assertions of her canonized saint :—

"Not only Most Holy Mary is Queen of heaven and of the saints, but also of hell and of the devils; for she has bravely triumphed over them by her virtues. From the beginning of the world God predicted to the infernal serpent the victory and the empire which our Queen would obtain over him, when he announced to him that a woman would come into the world who should conquer him." (P. 155.) "Mary, then, is this great and strong woman who has conquered the devil, and crushed his head by subduing his pride, as the Lord added, 'She shall crush thy head.' . . . The Blessed Virgin, by conquering the devil, brought us *life* and *light*." (P. 156.)

"'Very glorious, O Mary, and wonderful,' exclaims St. Bonaventure, 'is thy great name. Those who are mindful to utter it at the hour of death have *nothing to fear from hell*, for the devils at once abandon the soul when they *hear the name of Mary*.'" (P. 163.)

Greater blasphemy still! Liguori affirms that God the Father is under obligation to Mary, and cheerfully obeys her commands:—

"St. Bernardine, of Sienna, does not hesitate to say that *all obey* the commands of Mary, *even God himself*." (P. 202.)

"Rejoice, O Mary, that a son has fallen to thy lot as thy *debtor*, who gives to all and receives from none." (P. 210.)

"She knows so well how to appease Divine justice with her tender and wise entreaties, that God himself blesses her for it, and, as it were, *thanks her*, that thus she restrains him from abandoning and punishing them as they deserve." (P. 220.)

"Rejoice, O mother and handmaid of God! rejoice! rejoice! thou hast for a *debtor* him to whom all creatures owe their being. We are all debtors to God, but *God is debtor to thee*." (P. 327.)

We have scarcely heart to quote from the petitions offered to the Virgin. In "The Glories of Mary," one prayer, intended as the beautiful blossom or perfected fruit of the finished argument, very appropriately closes each section. Besides these, there is an interesting collection from Rome's most honored saints—in all over three score. In their books of devotion,—the number and names of which are exceedingly perplexing to a poor heretic,—no prayers are more frequent, none more ardent than those offered to the Blessed Virgin, Mother of God :—

"O Mother of my God, and my Lady Mary, as a poor wounded and loathsome wretch presents himself to a great queen, I present myself to thee, who art the Queen of heaven and earth. From the lofty throne on which thou are seated, do not disdain, I pray thee, to cast thine eyes upon me, a poor sinner," etc. ("Glories of Mary," p. 37.)

"I *venerate*, O most pure Virgin Mary, thy most sacred heart. I, an unhappy sinner, come to thee with a heart filled with all uncleanness and wounds. O mother of mercy, do not, on this account, despise me, but let it excite thee to a greater compassion, and *come to my help*." (P. 140.)

"O Mother of God! O Queen of angels! O hope of men, listen to him who *invokes* thee, and has recourse to thee. Behold me to-day *prostrate* at thy feet; I, a miserable slave of hell, *consecrate* myself to thee as thy servant *forever*, offering myself to serve and honor thee to the utmost of my power all the days of my life." (P. 153.)

"O Lady, I know that thou dost glory in being merciful as thou art great. I know that thou dost rejoice in being so rich, that thou mayest share thy riches with us sinners. I know that the more wretched are those who seek thee, the greater is thy desire to *help and save them*." (P. 252.)

"O Mary! O my most dear mother, in what an abyss of evil I should find myself, if thou, with thy kind hand, hadst not so often *preserved* me! Yes, how many years should I already have been in hell, if thou, with thy powerful prayers, hadst not *rescued* me! My grievous sins were hurrying me there; divine justice had already condemned me; the raging demons were waiting to execute the sentence, but thou didst appear, O mother, not invoked nor asked by me, and *hast saved me*." (P. 266.)

"Hearken, O most holy Virgin, to our prayers, and remember us. *Dispense* to us the gifts of thy riches, and the abundant graces with which thou art filled. All nations call thee blessed; the whole hierarchy of heaven blesses thee, and we, who are of the terrestrial hierarchy, also say to thee: Hail, full of grace." (P. 329.)

"Holy Virgin, Mother of God, *succor* those who implore thy assistance. . . . To thee *nothing* is impossible, for thou canst raise even the *despairing* to the *hope of salvation*. . . . Thou dost love us with a love that no other love can *surpass*. . . . *All* the treasures of the mercy of God are in *thy* hands." (P. 331.)

For want of space we pause. Scores of other passages, equally or even more revolting, lie open before us. If any one desires to see Romanism as it is, let him purchase a "Catholic Manual," and "The Glories of Mary." Thenceforth, semi-political papers, like *The Freeman's Journal and Catholic Register*, and Jesuitical pamphlets, like the *Catholic World*, will charm in vain, charm they never so sweetly.

Did space permit, quotations innumerable, as blasphemous as those already adduced, could be given from "The Manual," "The Key of Paradise," "True Piety," "The Christian's Vade Mecum," and the several other Catholic collections of prayers. One, from Dr. John Power's "Catholic Manual," must suffice:—"Confiding in thy goodness and mercy, I cast myself at thy sacred feet, and do most humbly supplicate thee, O Mother of the Eternal Word, to adopt me as thy child."

Bonaventure, a Roman saint (worshipped annually, July 14: see Catholic Almanac), has actually gone over most of the Psalms of David, striking out the words Lord, God, etc., and inserting, Blessed Virgin, Our Lady, Holy Mother, etc. Psalm cx.:—" The Lord said unto Our Lady, sit thou on my right hand." Psalm xxv.:—" Unto thee, O Blessed Virgin, do I lift up my soul." Psalm xxxi.:—" In thee, O Lady, do I put my trust."

Pope Pius IX., who considers the dogma of the Immaculate Conception the glory of his reign, in his Encyclical of November 1, 1870, condemning the usurpers of the States of the Church, addresses to all devout Catholics this earnest exhortation: " Going altogether to the foot of the throne of grace and mercy, let us engage the intercession of the Immaculate Virgin Mary, mother of God."

If we may not apply the word idolatry to these abominations of Popery, then, certainly, we have no need of the word. The future Noah Webster may as well omit it from his dictionary. Comment, however, is certainly uncalled for. "And a mighty angel took up a stone like a great millstone, and cast it into the sea, saying, Thus with violence shall that great city Babylon be thrown down, and shall be found no more at all." " Idolaters shall have their part in the lake which burneth with fire and brimstone, which is the second death."*

---

* " These wise logicians (heretics) of the world
　　Can prove with reasoning clear
　How he, in heaven, will welcome those
　　Who scorn his Mother here ! . . .
　And this is reason ! this is light !—
　　A light that blinds the eyes,
　And leads to the fire of endless night,
　　And the worm that never dies."
　　　　　The Catholic World, Jan. No., 1871, p. 532.

CHAPTER VII.

WILL—WORSHIP.

WILL-WORSHIP, self-imposed restriction, producing excessive spiritual pride, but leaving the heart impure and the life unchanged, is evidently a noteworthy characteristic of Popery. In Paul's portraiture of the fatal apostasy these words occur: "Commanding to abstain from meats." This passage, restricted in its application to an organization once truly Christian, must of necessity refer to the Romish Church; no other has made abstinence from animal food a religious duty. Popery, however, has enacted, that "meats eaten during Lent, or on Friday, pollute the body and bring down *eternal damnation on the soul.*" And must we, then, believe, on the authority of a Church which evinces its much-vaunted infallibility by abrogating its own immutable laws, that something from without, beef-steak, defiles the man?* The proud occupant of Peter's chair, by a single word, may reverse the teachings of the humble Nazarene!

---

* Formerly it was enacted: "No meat shall be eaten during Lent, on Fridays, or on Saturdays." One of the Popes, however, by a new unalterable law suspending all previous immutable enactments, granted universal and perpetual indulgence on Saturdays. A Pope's word makes the eating of animal food healthful or a damning sin!

Must the conscientious Protestant, his life an epistle of love, eternally bear the frown of an incensed God because, alike on all the days of the week, he temperately enjoyed the gifts of God's bounty? Shall the Catholic, his heart unrenewed, his life a slander on the religion of the spotless Jesus, find, in the hour of death and the day of judgment, heaven's favor richly bestowed simply because, by an act of will, he refused animal food on one day in seven?

Even mortal sins, it seems, can be committed with impunity if the Pope grants permission. The bull of Clement XI., in favor of those who should assist Philip V. in the holy war against the heretics, "grants to all who should take this bull, that during the year . . . . they may eat flesh in Lent and several other days in which it is prohibited. . . . . that they may eat eggs and things with milk." His Infallibility makes known when and for what services his subjects may eat eggs without incurring eternal damnation. Important business! In the world's midnight, Popery's palmiest days, even heretics could purchase indulgence to commit the heinous sin of dining on roast chicken.*

Paul, discerning the natural tendency of the human heart to place reliance in self-imposed outward requirements, and disregard inward piety, affirmed: "Bodily exercise profiteth little, but godliness is profitable unto all things." The entire system of penance is here condemned. Popery, however, losing sight of the very

---

* Price $2.75.

kernel of the Gospel, that the blood of Christ cleanses from all sin, has ever taught that self-chosen torture, will-worship, is an efficient aid to piety—is in fact itself piety. Merit wrought by self-effort is by Rome considered as acceptable to God as it is pleasing to the carnal heart. Suffering sent of heaven may indeed if rightly received strengthen and deepen devotion, but self-imposed penances, engendering spiritual pride, produce a type of piety—if indeed it be piety—far more resembling heathen fanaticism than the self-denial of him who, in obedience to the will of the Father, offered himself to death that man might live. Between the sufferings of Christ and those of an anchorite, who does not see a world-wide difference? In what respect a senseless, useless, hermit life, like that of the sainted Simeon,* is a copy of our Lord's, most certainly infallibility alone can perceive. Are we, then, to believe that useless reverie and Pagan asceticism, with all their disgusting filth, ignorance, beggary, and superstition, are services more acceptable to God than feeding the hungry, clothing the naked, instructing the ignorant, reforming the vicious, and living, in the sphere in which God has placed us, a life of active obedience to the precepts of his Word?

Another predicted characteristic of the fatal apostasy

---

* This monk, who lived for thirty-six years on a solitary pillar in the mountains of Syria, exposed to summer's heat and winter's cold, refusing to speak even with his mother, has ever been considered, by the Papal Church, a paragon of piety.

was this: "Forbidding to marry." Among those bearing the Christian name, none, except the Papists, have ever denied to a certain class the inalienable right of matrimony. They alone have pronounced that unholy which God's Word declares *"honorable in all."* "A bishop," says Paul, "must be blameless, the husband of one wife." This—even supposing it does not recommend marriage to the clergy—certainly at least accords them the privilege. Since the days of Gregory VII., however, whose profligate life would have disgraced even Pagan Rome, the marriage of a priest has been looked upon as a sin incomparably greater than adultery, or fornication, or even incest. A priest may associate with prostitutes and escape Church censure, but to marry a virtuous woman is, in the casuistry of Rome, one of the greatest of sins.*

This enforced celibacy, there can be no doubt, has been exceedingly disastrous to the cause of morality. With no desire of dwelling upon facts the bare recital of which produce shuddering disgust, we refer our readers to the confession of a priest in Gavin's "Master-Key

---

* *The Catholic World*, July, 1870, p. 440, says: "It is against these (licentiousness and low views of marriage) that the Church opposes her laws of marriage, and the absolute supernatural chastity of her priests and religious." Thereby she "provides herself with angels and ministers of grace to do her will, accomplish her work, perform her innumerable acts of spiritual and corporeal mercy, and be literally the god-fathers and god-mothers to the orphaned human race, while they obtain for themselves and others countless riches of merit." Chastity supernatural! Riches of merit countless!

to Popery," p. 35; to those of a nun, p. 43; and to the "Confessions of a Catholic Priest," translated by Samuel F. B. Morse. From revelations frequently made, as in the "Memoirs of Sipio De Ricci," and of "Lorette," it would seem that in some instances at least monasteries and nunneries are dens of infamy in comparison with which the temples of ancient Babylon were pure.* Even the halls of the Holy Inquisition were not unfrequently converted into harems. ("Master-Key to Popery," pp. 169-188.) In South America and Spain priests are among the most regular frequenters of the "house of her whose feet take hold on hell." Lest, however, we may be charged with slander, we close by quoting the language of St. Liguori, certainly good authority with Papists: "Among the priests who live in the world, IT IS RARE, VERY RARE, TO FIND ANY THAT ARE GOOD."

As human nature is much the same everywhere, is it not fair to charge this wickedness—the extent of which is scarcely conceivable by those who have given the subject no examination †—upon the scarlet-colored

---

* A few months since a motion was made, and carried by a small majority in the British Parliament, to appoint a committee to "Inquire into Conventual and Monastic Institutions." It was found there were 69 monasteries and 233 nunneries in which Rome claimed the prerogative to detain men and women against their will, and even transport them to convents upon the continent. Rome is above law.

† A few extracts—the least objectionable—from the confessions of a priest ("Master-Key to Popery") we append: "I have served my parish sixteen years. I have in money 15,000 pistoles, and I have

Beast whose forehead bears this inscription, "*Mystery, Babylon the great, the Mother of harlots and Abominations of the earth?*"

---

given away more than 6000. My money is unlawfully gotten. My thoughts have been impure ever since I began to hear confessions. My actions have been the most criminal of mankind. I have been the cause of many innocent deaths. I have procured, by remedies, sixty abortions. We, six priests, did consult and contrive all the ways to satisfy our passions. Everybody had a list of the handsomest women in the parish. I have sixty nepotes alive. But my principal care ought to be of those I had by the two young women I keep at home. Both are sisters, and I had, by the oldest, two boys; and by the youngest one, and *one which I had by my own sister is dead.*"

CHAPTER VIII.

CREDULITY.

(2 Thess. ii. 11; and 1 Tim. iv. 2.)

IN examining the leading characteristics of Popery one instinctively asks, how can rational men even pretend to believe such monstrous absurdities, such palpable errors? Paul gives apparently the only possible explanation. Referring to the adherents of the "man of sin," "the great apostasy," he affirms:—"God shall send them strong delusion, that they should believe a lie." Surely, in perfect fairness we may ask, has there ever been, or is there now, among those who have fallen from the faith, a more conspicuous fulfilment of this prophecy than is furnished by the victims of Popish superstition?

If, as the best authority affirms, it was because "God gave them over to a reprobate mind," that the heathen became guilty of such revolting immoralities and "worshipped and served the creature more than the Creator," how else shall we account for the deeper degradation and the grosser idolatry of Papists? Paganism never sanctioned such enormities as have found strenuous advocates in the bosom of "Holy Mother." True, in some ages they deified every vile passion that rankles in the heart of man. Those gods, however, were never placed on loftier thrones than Jupiter. Venus and Bacchus were not allowed to purchase Jove's pardon of unbridled indulgence. Over all other gods there was ever one whose anger could be appeased, and whose favor could be secured only by earnest effort after a life of virtue. It was left for "the trader in human souls" to promulgate the doctrine that by gold and silver given to the priest forgiveness of all sins, even the most heinous, could be purchased from the High and Holy one who inhabits eternity, the King of kings and Lord of lords. He who in his Word so repeatedly proffers a free salvation, is thus represented as conferring upon an arrogant and corrupt priesthood the right of selling pardons to the highest bidders; nay, worse, of granting indulgences, permission to sin to the wealthiest knaves, and the most unprincipled miscreants. The heathen worshipped gods which their own hands had made, it is true. They never so far degraded themselves, however, as to bow in adoration before a morsel of consecrated flour. Such disgusting idolatry is found only among the advocates of transubstantiation.

Except that God had given them up to believe a lie, how could Papists found a hope of heaven on the absolution granted by a priest? Turning from the throne of free grace, they hasten to a confessor for pardon. A frail, sinning man, forgives sins committed against God! A criminal pardons his fellow-criminal! A creature forgives the violation of the Creator's laws! Rome's most honored Council has pronounced an anathema against all who deny that the act of the priest in granting absolution is properly a judicial act. "He sits on the judgment seat representing Christ, and doing what Christ does." In the catechism sanctioned by the Council of Trent, it is said:—" In the minister of God, who sits in the tribunal of penance, as his legitimate judge, the penitent venerates the power and person of our Lord Jesus Christ; for, in the administration of this, as in that of the other sacraments, the priest represents the character and discharges the functions of Jesus Christ." When a large number of the ignorant are so credulous as to believe that this claim is founded in truth, is it any wonder that we witness from even the most atrocious murderers such disgusting exhibitions of hopes belonging alone to the devoutly penitent? And certainly it need scarcely strike us with surprise, if in almost every community not a few were found who, goaded by conscience to seek remission of sin, bow at the feet of the priest confidently expecting to purchase forgiveness with a part of the wages of iniquity. This done, why should they not return with even intensified delight to their former mode of life? An earnest, long-continued endeavor to imitate the pure life of Christ could not be expected from those who are taught to believe that the favor of God can be purchased with dollars and cents. Even if left to the promptings of nature, untutored by an infallible church, man would be far more likely to become enamored of virtue. Consciously burdened with a sense of guilt, he might be driven to him who alone "has power on earth to forgive sin."

That Paul's prophecy finds a fulfilment in the history of Romanism is apparent in the doctrine of the real presence. In this the faithful, on pain of eternal damnation, are expected to believe that bread and wine, by the enunciation of the magic words, "*Hoc est corpus meum*," are changed into Christ's "*body, blood, soul, and divinity.*" It is *flesh*, though it tastes like bread. It is *blood*, though it tastes like wine. Did ever delusion equal this? Men claiming common sense deliberately profess disbelief in the testimony of their own senses. On the mere declaration of a priest, they contemn one of God's immutable laws, that to which they are indebted for all the knowledge they have of an external world. In being faithful to Rome, they become the worst of infidels, without faith in themselves and without faith in the God that made them.

Instead of denominating this a delusion, perhaps, so far as intelligent Papists are concerned, it were more charitable to characterize it as a "*lie spoken in hypocrisy.*" Evidently it is "a commandment of men," defended as an essential part of a perfected system of extortion. Without it there would be a manifest absurdity in claiming ability to forgive sins. Represented, however, as a "bloodless sacrifice," offered by the priest to the Father of all mercies, the appearance of consistency is retained. Merit purchasable is also marketable. Transubstantiation, like the doctrine of supererogation, is food for the hen that lays the golden egg.

And what shall we denominate the doctrine of purgatory,—a profitable delusion, or a lie spoken in hypocrisy? What could be better calculated to make market for masses? "Saints," says the Council of Florence, "go to heaven; sinners to hell; and the middling class to purgatory." Among the middlings, the priests now cunningly manage, for an obvious reason, to include nearly all. Saints in heaven, and sinners in hell, are beyond the reach of further extortion. From the fires of purgatory, however, unbloody sacrifices, if well paid for, can secure release. Whilst belief in this intermediate state is either a delusion borrowed from Paganism, or a hypocritical falsehood intended to fill Rome's coffers, the pretence that the offering of a consecrated wafer can open to the soul the gates of paradise, is a delusion or hypocrisy still more inexplicable; and most unaccountable of all is the claim that the Church can determine when the soul is released from the purifying flames. To those whom God has given up to believe a lie, is any delusion too great for credence?—any profitable falsehood too hypocritical for advocacy?

This monstrous doctrine of purgatory the deluded victims of Popish superstition believe, notwithstanding it is written, "The blood of Christ cleanseth from all sin;" notwithstanding the Saviour's promise to the thief on the cross, "This day shalt thou be with *me* in paradise;" notwithstanding the parable of the rich man and Lazarus, in which the former is represented as lifting up his eyes in hell, being in torments, the latter as safely folded in Abraham's bosom. They credit this absurdity whilst professing to accept as of inspired authority the declarations of Paul, "I have a desire to depart and to be with Christ, which is far better;" "For me to live is Christ, and to die is gain;" "To be absent from the body is to be present with the Lord." Blinded of God, the intelligent strenuously advocate, and the ignorant superstitiously believe, a doctrine which effectually "makes merchandise of the souls of men."

And her doctrine of supererogation is a delusion no less absurd. It is gravely said, "Men can do more than God's holy law demands." Many have done so. These works have merit. This merit, collected from the deeds of thousands of worthies, has been gathered into a treasury of which the Pope has the key. Hence he can deal out these good works in the form of indulgences and absolutions. What a mine of wealth! And every man, however wicked, may thence derive merit that will atone for any sin he may commit, even theft, adultery, or murder, on the simple condition that the price of the requisite amount of treasured goodness is paid for in current coin. Is this a delusion?—or is it rascality? With the ignorant masses it is no doubt the former. But the educated—do they really believe that the Pope collects the merits of those who are more virtuous than God requires into a fund for insuring souls against the torments of perdition, and sells life policies to the highest bidder? If so, alas for frail humanity! Superstition, it would seem, can silence common sense!

That the Popes are legitimate successors of St. Peter, bishops over all Christendom, is another of Rome's delusions. Though unable to determine whether the rock upon which Christ founded his Church was Peter, the Apostles, Peter's faith, Peter's confession, or the Saviour's own meritorious offering, infallibility yet confidently affirms that upon the Pope in Rome is founded the true, holy, Catholic, Apostolic Church, out of which none can even hope for salvation. Supposing the Apostolic office still continues—a purely gratuitous assumption, since none can show the requisite qualifications, personal knowledge of our Saviour's resurrection, a call direct from his lips, infallibility in teaching truth, the gift of tongues, the power of working miracles, and a commission to teach truth to the entire human family in all countries and all ages—the claim of an unbroken succession from Peter has never been established. No Papist, even with the aid of inerrancy, has been able to trace the line. On the concession of Rome's most honored historians, Bellarmine, Alexander, Du Pin and others, at least 240 years remain from the beginning of the Christian era in which no vestiges of Papal authority can be discovered. The most ancient of the fathers, Irenæus, Justin, and Clemens of Alexandria, make no mention of it, direct or indirect. And it is undeniably true that in the tenth century abandoned women ruled in Rome, by whom false pontiffs, their paramours, were intruded into the Papal chair. Will any Romanist have the hardihood to affirm that grossly immoral men, thus illegally thrust into office, were successors of the holy Apostles? Moreover, there have been times in the history of the Church when the line of succession cannot be traced even through such monsters of iniquity, no one even claiming universal spiritual sovereignty. For fifty years there were two infallible pontiffs, one at Avignon, another at Rome, each claiming to be the only legitimate successor of St. Peter. Both of these were deposed by the Council of Pisa, and Alexander elected. This resulted in giving Holy Mother three infallible heads. These being deposed by the Council of Constance, each took solemn oath to yield obedience. Each immediately resumed the claim: thus there were three, *all perjured*. In the face of such facts, admitted by all candid historians, Papal as well as Protestant, it evidently requires no small amount of credulity to believe not merely that the Popes are true successors of St. Peter, but that the Church founded on them is the only Church of Christ on earth.

The Church of Rome assumes to be in possession of the keys of heaven, although it has forsaken the fundamental doctrines of the Gospel. It denies that regeneration of heart and purity of purpose are necessary to salvation. Christ's meritorious offering, the only sufficient atonement, is practically rejected. That justification is solely by faith in the Lord's righteousness, and that sanctification is the work of God's spirit, are repeatedly and emphatically denied. It condemns the declaration of Paul, that "there is no righteousness in us," claiming merit from nature and justifying righteousness from the deeds of the law. Contradicting the teaching of the Apostle, it affirms, "Man can be just before God, *yea, holier than his law requires.*" The assertion of Scripture, "By the deeds of the law there shall no flesh be justified," is met with the declaration, "We are set free from sin on account of our works." That "God desires or wills that all men should repent," and that "repentance is the gift of God," are condemned in severe terms. These propositions: "Believers are about to enter into their rest," "The Bible is the only infallible rule of faith and practice," are pronounced "*damnable heresies.*" And although the New Testament has given this, "forbidding to marry," as one of the marks of the man of sin, yet they prohibit marriage in the clergy while permitting concubinage. Could delusion surpass this, that men should believe themselves the true Church of Christ whilst they have apostatized from almost every essential doctrine of the Gospel?

Unless we accept one or other of Paul's explanations —either believing them strongly deluded or hypocritically false—how shall we account for their use of incense; their solemn consecration of bells and burial places; their burning of wax candles; and their sprinkling of horses, asses, and cattle? Formerly pious solicitude was taken in the proper solution, by an infallible Church, of the vitally important question, "Shall the hair of the monks be shaved in the form of a semicircle or circle?" Do not such things evidence the presence of seducing spirits cunningly turning the thoughts from the state of the heart to unmeaning forms?

And by what terms shall we characterize those endless frauds by which superstitious people were made to believe pretended miracles; or those silly dreams by which the most unprincipled impostors that ever disgraced humanity pretended to be directed to the tombs of saints and martyrs? And the bones thus obtained, how powerful! "By them," so says an infallible Church, "Satan's cunningest machinations were successfully defeated: diseases both of body and mind, otherwise incurable, were instantaneously healed." In one thing at least they were exceedingly potent. They filled Rome's empty treasury. That, in the Romish code of morals, is all that need be demanded. "It is an act of virtue to deceive, and lie, when, by that means, the interests of the Church can be promoted." Falsehood, sometimes adroitly conceived, always persistently adhered to, has ever been one of Rome's most efficient agencies in establishing and perpetuating her power.*

---

* As specimens of the agencies employed by Rome to keep her children from straying from the fold, take these drafts upon the credulity of the ignorant: "The Holy Scriptures are far more extensively read among Catholics than they are by Protestants."—Plain Talk about

"God," says Paul, "shall send them strong delusion, that they should believe a lie." "The spirit speaketh expressly, that in the latter times some shall depart from the faith, giving heed to seducing spirits, and doctrines of devils; speaking lies in hypocrisy, having

---

the Protestantism of To-Day, p. 121. "Tradition has in itself as much authority as the Gospel."—*Idem*, p. 127. "Heresy is in itself a more grievous sin, an evil far greater and more baneful, than immorality and the inordinations of sensuality."—*Idem*, p. 27. "Christianity and Catholicity are one and the same thing."—*Idem*, p. 56. "To be a Christian is to be a Catholic: outside of Catholicity you may be a Lutheran, a Calvinist, a Mahommedan, a Mormon, a Free Thinker, a Buddhist, but you are not, you cannot be a Christian."—p. 58. " 'Tis not very hard to be a good Protestant. Believe whatever you please in matters of religion. Believe nothing at all, if it suits you better. Be honest, as the world understands it. Read the Bible or not, as it pleases you; go to church, or do not go; forget not to subscribe to one, or two, or three Bible and evangelical societies; but, above all, hold the Catholic Church in abomination—and you shall be a good Protestant."—p. 20. "One is poor, and wishes to emerge from his poverty; another is swayed by passions, which he does not wish to control; a third has too much pride, and is loath to subdue it; a fourth is ignorant, and allows himself to be led away. For such reasons people become Protestant."—p. 37. "As for him who becomes a Protestant. . . . . Poor apostate! for him, no more the beautiful ceremonies of the Church. The images of our Lord, of the Blessed Virgin, and of the saints, become emblems of idolatry!—no more crucifix, no more the sign of the cross: it is idolatry!—no more prayers: no more respect or love for the Mother of God: idolatry!—no more trusting the intercession of saints, patrons in heaven, advocates, protectors near God: idolatry!"

"And when the hour of death is drawing near—when the unfortunate *man is left to himself*, about standing before God, covered with the sins of his whole life—no priest to administer the last sacraments of the Church, no priest to tell him, with all the power of divine au-

their conscience seared with a hot iron; forbidding to marry," etc.—1 Tim. iv. 1–3.

Among the delusions of Romanism, none, perhaps, is more transparently absurd than their much-vaunted immutability. Bossuet, the celebrated Bishop of Meaux, detailed, with seemingly intense delight, the alleged variations of Protestantism, assuming, indeed asserting, that "Catholicity ever has been, is, and ever will be, as unchangeable as its Author." In face of all the facts, for a Protestant to listen to this claim without a smile,

---

thority, 'Poor sinner, take courage; thou canst die in peace, because *Jesus has given me the power to forgive thee thy sins.*' "—*Idem*, p. 233.

"The death-bed of the founders of Protestantism—all apostates, and, for the most, apostate priests—bears us out in our assertions, and with terribly overwhelming evidence."

"Luther despaired of the salvation of his soul. Shortly before his death, his concubine pointed to the brilliancy of the stars in the firmament.

"'See, Martin, how beautiful that heaven is!'

"'It does not shine in our behalf,' replied the master, moodily.

"'Is it because we have broken our vows?' resumed Kate, in dismay.

"'May be,' said Luther.

"'If so, let us go back.'

"'Too late! the hearse is stuck in the mire.' And he would hear no more.

"At Eisleben, on the day previous to that on which he was stricken with apoplexy, he remarked to his friends: 'I have almost lost sight of the Christ, tossed as I am by these waves of despair which overwhelm me.' And after a while, 'I, who have imparted salvation to so many, cannot save myself.'

"He died forlorn of God—blaspheming to the very end. His last words were an attestation of his impenitence. His eldest son, who had doubts about the Reformation and the Reform, asked him for a

certainly requires no ordinary measure of gravity. And for Papists to yield it cordial belief, imperatively demands either extreme ignorance, obstinate credulity, or gross bigotry. No doubt the Church which once condemned the revolution of the earth upon its axis, must now be, as it ever has been, *immutable.* Unchangeable as Deity, and lasting as time, Popery's great argument is a pathetic appeal to antiquity. By this the doubting faithful are confirmed, and heretics silenced. It is an end of all controversy. This question, "Where was

---

last time whether he persevered in the doctrine he preached. 'Yes,' replied a gurgling sound from the old sinner's throat—and Luther was before his God. The last descendant of Luther died not long ago a fervent Catholic."

"Schusselburg, a Protestant, writes: 'Calvin died of scarlet fever, devoured of vermin, and eaten up by ulcerous abscess, the stench whereof drove away every person.' In great misery he gave up his rascally ghost, despairing of salvation, evoking the devils from the abyss, and uttering oaths most horrible and blasphemies most frightful.

"Spalatin, Justus, Jonas, Isinder, and a host of other friends of Luther, died either in despair or crazy. Henry VIII. died bewailing that he had lost heaven; and his worthy daughter Elizabeth breathed her last in deep desolation, stretched on the floor—not daring to lie in bed, because, at the first attack of her illness, she thought she saw her body all torn to pieces and palpitating in a cauldron of fire.

"Let, then, in the presence of such frightful deaths and of the thought of eternity, those of our unfortunate brethren who may be tempted to abandon their Church, remember that a day will come when they will also be summoned to appear before God! Let them think, in their sober senses, of death, and of judgment, and of hell, and I pledge my word they will not think of becoming Protestants."— Plain Talk about the Protestantism of To-Day, p. 236. Boston: Patrick Donahoe, 1870. *Imprimatur, Joannes Josephus, Episcopus Boston.*

your Protestant Church before the Reformation?" is the rallying cry of the advancing hosts of Papacy, and is expected to be the requiem sung over the lifeless corpse of soulless, godless Protestantism, "that spawn of hell," destined, as infallibility assures us, speedily to go to his own place. Where was Protestantism three hundred years ago? Where were the Augean stables before they were cleansed by Hercules?—where the decaying palace before its crumbling towers, and ivy-bound walls, and tottering foundations were repaired, strengthened, and beautified? The doctrines of Protestantism are as old as the promulgation of the Gospel. Romanism is the intruder. Its characteristic doctrines are mere novelties in the religious world.

By what terms shall we characterize that blindness which, disregarding the foul stains upon her history, denominates the Papal Antichrist "Holy Mother," the one true, Catholic, Apostolic Church, out of which is no salvation? Pope John XII. was guilty of blasphemy, perjury, profanation, impiety, simony, sacrilege, adultery, incest, and murder. "He was," says Bellarmine, "nearly the wickedest of the Popes." * John XXIII., however, exceeded him. His Holiness, Infallible Judge in faith and morals, was, by the Council of Constance, convicted of denying the accountability of man, the

---

* When summoned to attend a Council and answer the charges brought against him, he refused, and excommunicated the Council in the name of God. Though deposed, he regained the Papal throne. Caught in adultery, he was killed, probably by the injured husband.

See Edgar's "Variations of Popery," p. 110.

immortality of the soul, the resurrection of the body, and all the institutions of revealed religion. But his errors in faith were venial and few compared with his immoralities. He was found guilty of almost every crime of which it is possible to conceive. The list enumerated no less than seventy; among these, simony, piracy, exaction, barbarity, robbery, murder, massacre, lying, perjury, fornication, adultery, incest, and sodomy. Of Alexander VI., another infallible Pope, a trustworthy historian says: "His debauchery, perfidy, ambition, malice, inhumanity, and irreligion, made him the execration of all Europe." He died from drinking one of the poisoned cups prepared by him for the rich cardinals whose possessions he intended to seize. Humanity disowns the monster. His successor, Julius II., inherited, along with the tiara, all the immoralities of the Papacy. Having secured the triple crown by bribing the cardinals, no crime was too great to appal his unterrified conscience. Assassination, adultery, sodomy, and bestial drunkenness, are scarcely a moiety of his enormities. "He was a scandal to the whole Church. He filled Italy with rapine, war, and blood." Pope Leo X. denied the immortality of the soul, and in fact every doctrine of Christianity, denominating it a "lucrative fiction." "Paul III., and Julius III., were such licentious characters that no modest man can write or read their lives without blushing." The former, the convener of the Council of Trent, made large sums of money by selling indulgences and licenses to houses of ill-fame. At least four pontiffs, Liberius, Zosimus, Honorius, and Vigilius, were convicted of heresy; seventeen of perjury, and twenty-five of schism. According to Genebrard, "For nearly 150 years about fifty Popes deserted wholly the virtue of their predecessors, being apostate rather than apostolic." Baronius, himself a Papist, as if unable to repress the intensity of his disgust for the abominations of the Papal See, exclaims: "The case is such, that scarcely any one can believe, or even will believe it, unless he sees it with his eyes, and handles it with his hands, viz., what unworthy, vile, unsightly, yea, execrable and hateful things the sacred Apostolic See, on whose hinges the universal Apostolical Church turns, has been compelled to see. . . . . To our shame and grief, be it spoken, how many monsters, horrible to behold, were intruded by them (the secular princes) into that seat which is reverenced by angels!" "The Holy See is bespattered with filth," "infected by stench," "defiled by impurities," and "blackened by perpetual infamy!" Guiciardini, another defender of Holy Mother, speaking of the Popes of the sixteenth century, says: "He was esteemed a good Pope, in those days, who did not exceed in wickedness the worst of men."

Of the Councils which have given us the dogmas of Romanism, some have been immortalized not less by villainy than by heresy. That of Constantinople is described by Nazianzen as "A cabal of wretches fit for the house of correction." That of Nice, in approving a disgusting story, sanctioned perjury and fornication. Of the Council of Lyons, Cardinal Hugo, in his farewell address to the retiring president, Pope Innocent, presents this picture: "Friends, we have effected a work of great utility and charity in this city. When we came to Lyons, we found three or four brothels in it, and we have left at our departure only one. But this extends, without interruption, from the eastern to the western gate of the city." The Council of Constance, composed of 1000 holy fathers, which solemnly decreed that "no faith shall be kept with heretics," and consigned John Huss to the flames, although he had given himself into their hands only on the express pledge of protection given by the Emperor, was attended by 1500 public prostitutes. This same Council ordered the bones of Wyckliffe to be "dug up and thrown upon a dung-hill." Well does Baronius exclaim: "What is, then, the face of the holy Roman Church! How exceedingly foul it is!" To believe that an organization, characterized, according to the assertions of its own historians, by such unheard-of abominations, is the only true Church, demands a credulity fitly termed, "delusion sent of God."

On pain of unending woe, every genuine Romanist must now believe that Pius IX. is infallible. Here is a specimen of his inerrancy. Arguing for his temporal power (since needing stronger support than infallible reasoning), His Holiness, jumbling together two passages of Scripture entirely separate and distinct, said:

"In the garden of Olives, on the night before Christ's crucifixion, the multitude with Judas came to him. And they said, 'Art thou a king?' and he answered, 'I am.' And they went back and fell on the ground." Certainly this is no small tax on the credulity of those who so loudly proclaim the Pope infallible, especially and pre-eminently in interpreting Scripture. This argument is only exceeded by that of Pope Boniface IV., who employed his infallibility in establishing this proposition: MONKS ARE ANGELS.

 Major Premise: All animals with six wings are angels.
 Minor Premise: Monks have six wings, viz., the cowl, two; the arms, two; the legs, two.
 Ergo: Monks are angels.

Quod erat demonstrandum.

PART III.

Popery the Foe of Liberty.

PERSECUTION IN ITALY.

CHAPTER I.

PERSECUTION.

TYRANTS, the more effectually to secure power, have ever professed supreme regard for man's highest interests. It was under the plea of extending Grecian learning, the proudest gift of human genius, that Alexander burned villages, sacked cities, and trampled upon rights dear as life itself. Under the cloak of unrivalled regard to the unity of God, Mohammed established, what had otherwise been impossible, a despotism as cruel as the most heartless fatalism could devise.

What others secured by reiterated protestations of devotion to one single principle, Rome attained by seizing upon the Gospel. The religion of Jesus, the fountain of all true liberty, personal and national, civil and religious, was so obscured by error as to become, in the hands of those claiming sole right to impart religious instruction, a most powerful engine of Satanic cruelty. When, therefore, all other agencies had failed in crushing the spirit of freedom, the Romish Church, in the sacred name of religion, a religion proclaiming good will to men, solemnly inaugurated a system of persecution unparalleled in the annals of the most blood-thirsty Paganism.

Popery, in her noonday of glory, unblushingly denied to those rejecting her dogmas even the right of inheriting property, of collecting moneys justly due them, and of bequeathing even the savings of poverty to their own children.* Is not this a fulfilment, to the very letter, of that ancient prediction, " He caused .... that no man might buy or sell, save he that had the mark, or the name of the beast, or the number of his name?" † For the single offence of rejecting Papal supremacy, the true followers of Christ were subjected to every species of annoyance which diabolical malignity could invent. With the design of tempting, or forcing men, from worldly considerations, to yield unquestioned obedience, treachery, deception, and cunning were freely resorted to, and in some instances with such success as to rivet the detested system of Popery upon people who loathed the very name.

When even these agencies, powerful as they were,

---

* The Council of Constance anathematized "all who should enter into contracts or engage in commerce with *heretics.*" In a decree of Pope Alexander III., this sentence occurs : " We therefore subject to a *curse* both themselves and their defenders and harborers, and under a *curse* we prohibit all persons from admitting them into their houses, or receiving them upon their lands, or cherishing them, *or exercising any trade with them.*" Frederick II., in an edict against " the enemies of the faith," orders " their goods to be confiscated, their children to be disinherited, *and their memory and their children to be held infamous forever.*"

† Rev. xiii. 17.

proved ineffectual, others more potent still were speedily devised. The Inquisition, or, where the establishment of this was impossible, holy wars relentlessly waged against heretics, it was hoped, would bring all men within the pale of Mother Church. The employment of such agencies was clearly foretold. "And it was given unto him to make war with the saints and to overcome them." "And he had power . . . . to cause that as many as would not worship the image of the beast should be killed." "I saw the woman drunken with the blood of the saints and with the blood of the martyrs of Jesus." *

That the Papacy makes persecution an essential of religion—although the Rev. James Kent Stone, Rome's latest conquest, in his "Invitation Heeded," ridicules the assertion—is certainly susceptible of clear proof. In its defence arguments are drawn, by their most eminent theologians, from Scripture, from the opinions of emperors, from the laws of the Church, from the testimony of the fathers (that inexhaustible treasury of unanswerable reasoning!), and from experience. That death is the proper penalty of presuming to disobey His Infallibility, is, we are told, the teaching of reason as well as the dictate of piety. Heretics, unless destroyed, will contaminate the righteous. By tortures inflicted on the few, however, the eternal salvation of the many may be secured. Nay, even to the deluded

---

* Rev. xiii. 7, 15; xvii. 6.

infidels themselves it is a mercy; it sends them to hell before they shall increase the torments of perdition.*

Nor was the defence of a doctrine so essential as the right of the Church to persecute, left to the ingenious, though possibly fallible reasoning of bishops and cardinals. Even Popes, infallible vicars, in the exercise of sovereign authority, undertook the laudable task of hounding on crazed fanatics to murder men, women, and even defenceless children, in the name of the meek, loving, forgiving Jesus. Urban II. issued a bull declaring: "No one is to be deemed a murderer who, burning with zeal for the interests of Mother Church, shall kill excommunicated persons." In 1825, Pope Leo XII. suspended his plenary indulgence on "the extirpation of heretics." Can immutability change? Can infallibility err? Has any Pope of the last thousand years disapproved of persecution? Has Pius IX. abrogated one solitary law against heretics?

Even Councils, not provincial—the authority of these, Papists might possibly call in question—but general Councils, and of these not less than five, have enjoined

---

* "The blood of heretics," says the Rhemish annotators, "is no more the blood of saints than the blood of thieves, man-killers, and other malefactors, for the shedding of which, by order of justice, no commonwealth shall answer."—Rev. xvii. 6.

Bellarmine says: "Heretics condemned by the Church may be punished by temporal penalties, and even with death."

Thomas Aquinas affirms: "Heretics may not only be excommunicated, but justly killed."

Bossuet declares: "No illusion can be more dangerous than making toleration a mark of the true Church."

or sanctioned the extermination of heretics, giving their voice for death as the proper punishment of what they choose to denominate heresy. Surely the Romish Church, if the declarations of her priests, bishops, cardinals, Popes, and Councils prove anything, is the deliberate defender of persecution, even to death, for opinion's sake. Every priest, therefore, in taking oath " to hold and teach all that the sacred canons and general Councils have delivered, declared, and defended," swears to believe and to teach Rome's right to torture and burn heretics, that is, Protestants.*

Even kings " were compelled by Church censures to endeavor, in good faith, according to their power, to destroy all heretics marked by the Church, out of the lands of their jurisdiction." Four Councils, the Third Lateran, the Fourth Lateran, Constance, and Trent, endorsed this order.† That the woman, Mother of Harlots, sitting upon a scarlet colored beast, and drunken with the blood of the martyrs, should be aided in her work of death by the civil authority, was plainly foretold: " These ten horns which thou sawest, are ten kings. . . . . These have one mind, and shall

---

* In the oath commonly administered to bishops occur these words: "Schismatics and rebels to our Lord, the Pope, and his successors, I will, to the utmost of my power, persecute and destroy."

† Frederick II., loyal son of Popish arrogance, issued an edict, asserting the divine right of kings " to wield the material sword . . . . against the enemies of the faith, for the extirpation of heretical pravity." "We shall not suffer," he adds, " the wretches, who infect the world with their doctrines, to live."

give their power and strength unto the beast."—Rev. xvii. 3, 13.

And with terrible energy did Rome vindicate her much-vaunted right to persecute. The holy Inquisition, Satan's masterpiece, with St. Dominic, a raving fanatic, for its first general, Innocent III. for its founder, a powerful order of monks for its defenders, and kings for the executioners of its fiendish penalties, became an engine of unexampled cruelty, sending terror into every land, suspicion into every home, and anguish into almost every heart. Neither age, nor sex, position nor past services, were guarantees of security. A word jestingly spoken, or neglect in bowing to the consecrated wafer (the elevated bran-god), or a look of contempt cast upon a begging friar, might prove the occasion of imprisonment and torture. Personal resentment, or even suspicion, especially where the parties suspected were wealthy, might lead to arrest. Even ladies, in many instances, were torn from endeared husbands, or doting parents, because lust inflamed their fiendish persecutors.*

Having made certain, through spies,† that the person whom they determined to arrest was at home, the offi-

---

* When the French, on entering Aragon (1706), threw open the doors of the Inquisition, sixty young women were found, the harem of the Inquisitor General.—Gavin's "Master-Key to Popery."

† In Spain alone, 18,000 were employed, whose business it was, with Satanic cunning, to insinuate themselves into every company, speak against the Pope and the Church—thus beguiling the unwary—and drag the suspected before the holy Inquisition.

cers of the inquisition, at the dead hour of midnight, knocked at the door. To the question, "Who is there?" a voice from the darkness responds, "*The holy Inquisition.*" Terror opens the door, and the daughter, the son, the wife, or the husband, seized by ruffians, is carried away to the cells of a dungeon, the remaining members of the family not daring to complain, scarcely to disclose their grief. Theirs is a sorrow unknown except to him whose eye never slumbers, who counts the tears of suffering innocence.

These officers, the better to fit them for their fiendish business, were earnestly admonished not to allow nature to get the better of grace. In some instances they were actually ordered to arrest their own near relatives, that by conquering human weakness they might prove themselves worthy of the favor of Holy Mother. Fiendish heartlessness! Adamantine cruelty!

The accused were never confronted with the acccuser. They were ordered to confess; refusing, torture was applied to extort an acknowledgment of guilt. If to save themselves from present anguish, they confess to doubts in regard to the real presence, papal supremacy, priestly absolution, the worship of images, the invocation of saints, the existence of purgatory, or the doctrine of infallibility, they sentence themselves to martyrdom; refusing to confess—perhaps because conscious of no crime—they are tortured to the extent of human endurance, and then bleeding, lacerated and trembling, are thrust into a loathsome dungeon to pine in solitude, unrelieved, unpitied, friendless, dying a hundred deaths in one. Were ever laws devised more evidently contrary to the plainest dictates of equity?

These punishments, inflicted in an underground apartment denominated the "Hall of Torture," were of every species which fiendish ingenuity could invent. Of the unfortunate victims of Papal fury, some were suffocated by water poured into the stomach; others, with cords fastened around the wrists behind the back, and heavy weights suspended from the feet, were drawn up to great heights, and then let fall to within a few feet of the floor, dislocating every joint; some were slowly roasted in closed iron pans; of some, the feet smeared with oil were roasted to a crisp; of others, the hands were crushed in clamps, or the bodies pierced with needles. The *Auto da fè* periodically closed the horrid tragedy. On a Sabbath morning, day sacred to him whose essential attribute is love, numbers of these lacerated beings were led forth—and in the name of Christianity!—to the place of burning. The heart, sickening at the recital of such deeds of hellish cruelty, and recalling the names of such worthy martyrs as Wycliffe, Huss, Ridley, Latimer, Cranmer, and thousands of others, joins, with a holy fervor of devotion, in the prayer of the redeemed souls ceaselessly ascending from under the altar of the Almighty: "How long, O Lord, holy and true, dost thou not judge and avenge our blood on them that dwell on the earth?"—Rev. vi. 10.

Having found, after centuries of trial, that the

Inquisition and the Crusades were powerless in crushing the pure religion of Jesus, that, in fact, "the blood of the martyrs became the seed of the Church," Rome endeavored, in the language of Scripture, to wear out the saints of the Most High. In place of death she substituted every species of annoyance which malignant hatred inspired of Satan could invent. Comparatively few however were induced to betray the Lord. "Herein is the faith and patience of the Saints."

When the number of those denying the Pope's supremacy became, in any country, too great to be killed by the Inquisition, holy wars were advocated. With the cross, symbol of love, on their banners, the Papal legions went forth in cold blood to butcher men, women, and children. For the mortal sin of presuming to employ the faculties God gave them, they must be utterly destroyed. In these Crusades the Romish Church actually gloried, and does still glory, feeling no remorse for the massacre of thousands, no shame for the extinction of kingdoms and people.

Armed with a bull of indulgence, the Papal emissaries went forth to preach the Crusade. Everywhere they exclaimed, "Who will rise up against the evil doers? Who will stand up against the workers of iniquity? If you have any zeal for the faith, any concern for the glory of God, any desire to reap the rich benefits of Papal indulgence, receive the sign of the cross, join the army of Immanuel, lend your aid in purging the nations, and extending the holy Catholic religion."

These crusades were waged not against those guilty of great sins, but against those whose only crime was a refusal to acknowledge the sovereignty of Rome's arrogant bishop. This was the deep-seated error which roused such unequalled fury. Those communities which failed to recognize the proud pontiff enthroned in the eternal city as Christ's Vicar on earth, must pay the penalty. The sword, and fire, and death, must proclaim that the rights of property and the comforts of home belong alone to those who permit His Holiness to think for them.

By way of extenuating the guilt of the Crusaders, modern Papists, though ardent advocates of Papal immutability and of the infallibility dogma, remind us that civilization had then made but little progress. These crusades, say they, are justly chargeable, not to Romanism, but to the barbarism of the times. Who instigated those wholesale butcheries? Infallible Popes. Who lauded those unparalleled atrocities which for centuries disgraced humanity? Infallible Popes. Does infallibility need the light of civilization's dim taper? Erring Protestants might, with some show of candor, advance such a plea, but for Papists, it is a betrayal of doctrines vital to their system. Have they shown any sorrow for the past? Have they expressed repentance for the slaughter of unoffending Christians? Have they abandoned the right to persecute? Deceive ourselves as we may, Popery is the same unblushing monster of cruelty, unchanged, and unchangeable. Pharisee-like, while promising liberty of conscience, she is continuously engaged in honoring, applauding, and even canonizing those whose only title to fame consists in the horrid cruelties practised towards the innocent followers of Jesus.

The blood-thirsty vengeance of the Popes against the infidels of the Holy Land, what pencil shall do justice to that scene of horror? Crusades, carried on with infernal fury for more than a century, caused the death of 2,000,000. Followers of Christ the Turks were not; but did butcheries convert them? Did they and their children learn to love that Saviour in whose name they were slaughtered? Can we even hope that in the moment of death on the hard-fought battle-field, many, even one, turning a tearful eye towards the ensigns of the hated foe, sought mercy from him whose cross emblazoned that blood-stained banner? The blood of these clings to the skirts of Romanism.

In the indictment against Popery, another specification is the deliberate massacre of 300,000 Waldenses and Albigenses. Against these true successors of the Apostolic Church, who, even on the concession of their murderers, were abstemious, laborious, devout and holy, Pope Innocent III. raised an army of 500,000. These blood-hounds of cruelty were let loose with intense delight upon those whose only crime was the belief, publicly and fearlessly expressed, that Rome was the "Babylonish Harlot" of the Apocalypse. Even Count Raimond, their Catholic sovereign, because tardy in the work of utterly exterminating his loyal subjects, was publicly anathematized in all the churches. Trembling under excommunication, the Count took solemn oath to pursue the Albigenses with fire and sword, sparing neither age nor sex, until they bowed to Papal authority. Rome, however, not content with even such abject subserviency, ordered him to strip naked and submit to penance. Nine times was he driven around the grave of the Monk Castelnau, and beaten with rods upon the bare back.

In the taking of Beziers, the Pope's legate, when asked how the soldiers should distinguish the Catholics from the heretics, shouted: "Kill all; the Lord will know his own." When the demon had completed his work, the city, swept by fire, was the blackened sepulchre of 60,000.

Bearing the standard of the cross, and singing "Glory to God," the army of the Crusaders, under the bloody Montfort, entered Menerbe. Pointing to a prepared pile of dry wood, the legate roared: "Be converted, or mount this pile." The merciful flames soon released the faithful from the relentless fury of their persecutors.

The persecutions in the valleys of Loyse and Frassiniere were cruel beyond description. Christians, after receiving the most solemn assurances of protection, were thrust into burning barns, suffocated in caves, led forth by scores and beheaded.

And the Waldenses of Calabria were subjected to barbarities no less incredible. Their children, forcibly taken from them, were placed in monasteries to be educated in the detested system of Popery. Large numbers of truly devout Christians, encumbered not unfrequently with the aged, and even with helpless babes, were driven to the mountains, there to meet death in every conceivable aspect of horror: some were starved, some frozen, some buried alive in the drifting snows, some

> "Slain by the bloody Piedmontese that rolled
> Mother with infant down the rocks."

But why proceed further? To recount Popery's cruelties, even a tithe of them, is impossible. Her history is echoed in the carnage of the battle-field, in the sighs of suffering innocence, in the unmeasured anguish of widowhood. Her pathway upon the earth is but too plainly visible, marked in blood, the blood of fifty millions of earth's noblest. Of this martyred host who can conceive the agonies? Can language convey any adequate conception of the sufferings of the Moors in Spain, the Jews in the various Catholic countries they have inhabited, the Christians in Bohemia, Portugal, Britain, and Holland?* Known alone to God are the sufferings of his chosen ones. In his book of remembrance are recorded the tears, the sighs, the sorrows of Christ's struggling Church.

To relate the intrigues, deceptions and atrocities by

---

* In the last-mentioned country, the Duke of Alva boasted that in the short space of six months he had caused the death of 18,000 Protestants.

which Rome succeeded in crushing out Protestantism in poor, down-trodden Ireland, we shall make no attempt. They are part of her history written in blood, —only other illustrations of the same intolerance.

In France, "with infinite joy"—if human joy can be infinite—Popery shed the blood of the saints. Passing by the butcheries of Orange and Vassey, the heart sickens in recounting the incidents of the Bartholomew massacre. On that day, recalled by Protestants only with shuddering horror, the demon of Popish cruelty went forth by royal command, to gorge himself with blood. The poor Huguenots, assembled in Paris under the pretext of a marriage between the Protestant king of Navarre and the sister of Charles IX., were attacked by hired assassins at midnight, and, notwithstanding the pledges of protection repeatedly and solemnly given (the occasion of their presence, and their defenceless condition) were slain in such numbers that the streets ran blood to the river. The dead bodies, dragged over the rough pavements, were thrown into the Seine. Even the king himself, from a window in his palace, viewed with seemingly intense delight the work of death going forward in the court beneath. Above the groans of the dying, and the curses of the soldiers, his voice could be distinctly heard, shouting, "Slay them, slay them." Even those pressing into his immediate presence to implore mercy and plead his pledged protection, received this as their only answer, *death from his hand.* In one week, according to Davilla, 10,000 were slain in Paris alone. And the slaughter in the capital was the signal for rekindling the fires of persecution throughout the entire empire. In nearly all the provinces the scenes of Paris were re-enacted; at Lyons, at Orleans, at Toulouse, at Meaux, at Bordeaux. In these massacres 30,000 perished.

And upon this sea of blood—heaven forgive them—the Pope, the Church, and the king delighted to look. Standing over the dead body of Admiral Coligny, whom by assurances of friendship he had drawn within his grasp, Charles exclaimed: "The smell of a dead enemy is agreeable." To the Pope he sent a special messenger: "Tell him," said Charles,—"tell him, the Seine flows on more majestically after receiving the dead bodies of the heretics." "The king's heart," exclaimed one of Rome's proud cardinals, "must have been filled with a sudden inspiration from God when he gave orders for the slaughter of the heretics." And then—as if the Papacy must needs put on the scarlet robe—the Pope and the cardinals, entering one of Rome's grandest cathedrals, returned solemn thanks to God, the God of mercy; thanks for the slaughter of Christians! thanks for the cold-blooded murder of thousands of unoffending followers of Jesus!

The record of these events, like that of the revolution in later times, France would now gladly bury in oblivion. They are spots on her history, however, which ages of tears can never efface. And that Papists of the present day ardently desire to reverse the testimony of history, or obliterate these unpleasant facts, is but too plain from the futile efforts repeatedly put forth, as in the "Invitation Heeded," the *Catholic World*, the *Freeman's Journal and Catholic Register*, to prove that the Pope and the cardinals were grossly imposed upon. Deceived by *Charles' special messenger* into returning thanks for the murder of heretics, instead of expressing gratitude to God for the overthrow of those rebelling against civil authority! Certainly such a defence is well worthy the system it seeks to shield.

MIRACLE OF THE CUT THROAT. *Page* 163

CHAPTER II.

POPERY THE ENEMY OF CIVIL LIBERTY.

THAT the Romish Church is nothing less than a conspiracy against liberty, personal and national, civil and religious, we firmly believe. Being the twin sister of despotism, she ever has been, and is now, most bitterly hostile to freedom of conscience, freedom of the press, education of the masses, distribution of the Bible, in fact to everything which Republicans are accustomed to regard as the basis and the safeguard of popular government. Accordingly she is industriously engaged, even now, and in this Republic, in undermining, insidiously but surely, the beauteous temple of liberty, whose foundations were laid in the blood of persecuted Protestants. Her system, in accordance with its time-honored principles, is producing hostility to our free institutions.

The Papal Church is the foe of our system of common schools. This scheme of popular education, the most successful agency ever devised for inculcating those moral principles which are indispensable to the continuance of self government, is the object of enmity as unrelenting as it is universal. Every available agency is employed to shake the confidence of our people in its equity, wisdom and efficiency. First, it was said, the public schools are sectarian. The Protestant Bible is used. That their hostility is not so much against our version as against the Bible itself, the basis of public morality, the most essential part of true education, the palladium of civil liberty, is conclusively proved by their unwillingness to circulate even their own version, *the Douay Bible.* Popery has always maintained that "the Bible is not a book to be in the hands of the people." "Who will not say," exclaims a recent advocate of Romanism, "that the uncommon beauty and marvellous English of the Protestant Bible is one of the great strongholds of heresy in this country?" "We ask," says Bishop Lynch, of New Orleans, "that the public schools be cleansed from this peace-destroying monstrosity—Bible reading." The Bishop of Bologna, in an advisory letter to Paul III., said: "She (the Catholic Church) is persuaded that this is the book which, above all others, raises such storms and tempests. And that truly, if any one read it, ... he will see . . . . that the doctrine which she preaches is altogether different and sometimes contrary to that contained in the Bible."

Since the council held in Baltimore in the spring of '52, Rome's efforts have been put forth to secure a distribution of the school fund. The demand is general, open, persistent. In New York, Philadelphia, St. Louis, Cincinnati, Chicago, Newark,—in all our large towns and cities,—they have erected commodious school houses, employed nuns and priests as teachers, and petitioned for a *pro ratâ* share of the school money. The *Tablet*, a Catholic paper of New York, argues, March 14, 1868, as follows:

"The reason why the Catholics cannot, with a good conscience, send their children to the public schools, is that the public schools are really sectarian. The State is practically anti-Catholic, and its schools are necessarily controlled and managed by sectarians, who are hostile to the Catholic religion and seek its destruction. The reason why the sectarians want the children of Catholics brought up in the public schools is because they believe that if so brought up they will lose their Catholicity, and become sectarians or infidels. This, and this alone, is the reason why they are unwilling that Catholics should have their quota of the public moneys to support separate schools . . . . . It is idle to talk to sectarians, no matter of what name or hue, of justice or of the rights of conscience; and yet we cannot forbear to say that there is a manifest injustice in taxing us to support schools to which we cannot in conscience send our children . . . . . What religious liberty is there in this?"

Again, in March, 1870, it exclaims:

"No, gentlemen, that will not do, and there is no help but in dividing the public schools, or in abandoning the system altogether."

The *Freeman's Journal* once said:

"What we Roman Catholics must do now, is to get our children out of *this devouring fire*. At any cost and any sacrifice, we must deliver the children over whom we have control *from these pits of destruction*, which lie invitingly in their way, under the name of public or district schools." *

---

* In the year 1868, the Pope, in an allocution containing a violent assertion of Papal power, severely denounces the King of Austria for

Not only the press, but public lecturers are employed to bring this movement into favor. The most barefaced falsehoods are palmed off upon the credulous public. We are told that our political institutions are of Roman Catholic origin; that Protestantism is crumbling to pieces; that religion, beyond the pale of the Catholic Church, is "*machinery, formalism, and mummery;*" that infidels are the originators of our school system. Our common schools are denominated "*public soup-houses, where our children take their wooden spoons.*" "*Every such school,*" it is asserted, "*is an insult to the religion and virtue of our people.*" * "The prototype of our school system," said another Roman Catholic orator, "is seen *in the institutions of Paganism.* Unless the system be modified, and put the *Christian* (Catholic) school upon the same ground as the *Godless school* (Protestant), it requires but little sagacity to perceive its speedy and utter destruction."

To accede to this demand would destroy our entire system of popular education. Upon no principle, bear-

---

sanctioning a law "which decrees that religious teaching in the public schools must be placed in the hands of members of each separate confession, that any religious society may open private or special schools for the youth of its faith." This law, His Infallibility solemnly pronounces "abominable," "in flagrant contradiction with the doctrines of the Catholic religion; with its venerable rights, its authority, and its divine institution; with our power, and that of the Apostolic See." Consistency, that jewel! What Popery condemns in Austria, she clamors for in America.

* Editor *Freeman's Journal*, 1853.

ing even the semblance of justice, can money be given to one class and withheld from another. If Catholics may claim their share of the school fund, so also may Jews, Infidels, Rationalists, Buddhists, and every denomination of Christians. To divide the fund among all the claimants would utterly destroy the efficiency of the system, leaving our children to be educated in small schools under incompetent teachers. And what shall we say of the logic of these self-lauded champions of religious liberty? Must we believe that our government, because it knows no state religion, is therefore purely atheistic? And what is atheism but a system of religious negations? Shall then the Government establish atheistic schools? No, to this the Catholics object. Shall it provide for the separate instruction of each sect? Shall it sanction, encourage, and aid schools opened for the incoming horde of Chinese Pagans? Shall it disburse funds to German Rationalists to teach that the stories of the Bible, however sacred they may be to Christians, are no more worthy of credence than the myths of Hesiod? Shall it support schools in which Protestant Irish, by recounting the soul-inspiring incidents of the Battle of the Boyne, shall rekindle the dying embers of hostility to Popery? This Papists would never endure. Even if this Republic should succeed in divesting itself of everything bearing relations to religion, Catholics would certainly complain. They would clamor for the introduction of Catholic instruction. Unless, therefore, we are prepared to abolish the entire system, giving over all efforts at popular education, our only motto must be, "NO SURRENDER."

And none certainly have just cause of complaint. A system liberal and equitable—as much so as any ever devised—opens the school-room to all. Any class is of course at perfect liberty to educate its children in separate schools. To that no one has ever objected. If, however, a disaffected portion of the community have a right to destroy an organization in which the vast majority are deeply interested, then evidently government itself is impossible. Rome's hostility to our public school system shows, therefore, the determined antagonism of Papacy to liberal institutions.

That we do Romanists no injustice in assuming that the exclusion of the Bible from the public schools would not long satisfy them, is susceptible of clear proof. Already the question is entering upon a new stage. They loudly affirm that without Catholic instruction the schools are *irreligious, infidel, godless*. Their oft-repeated assertion is that to *the Church* belongs the exclusive right to educate the young. One day they affirm, "it is contrary to the genius of our republican government for the majority to dictate to the minority, especially in matters of faith;" the next they shout, "we, the minority, have the God-given right to coerce the majority: the organization and control of all educational agencies belong by divine right to us." The *Tablet* contains the following:

"The organization of the schools, their entire internal arrangement and management, the choice and regulation of studies, and the selection, appointment, and dismissal of teachers, *belong exclusively to the spiritual authority.*"

The *Boston Advertiser* affirms:

"Catholics would not be satisfied with the public schools, even if the Protestant Bible and every vestige of religious teaching were banished from them."

The *Catholic Telegraph* of Cincinnati declares:

"It will be a glorious day for the Catholics in this country, when under the blows of justice and morality, our school system will be shivered to pieces. *Until then modern Paganism will triumph.*"

The *Freeman's Journal* speaks as follows:

"*Let the public school system go to where it came from—the devil.* We want Christian schools, and *the State cannot tell us what Christianity is.*" Dec. 11, 1869.

"Resolved, That the public or common school system, in New York city, is *a swindle on the people, an outrage on justice, a foul disgrace in matter of morals, and that it imports for the State Legislature to abolish it forthwith.*"

"There can be no sound political progress—no permanence in the State, where for any length of time children shall be trained in schools without (the Roman) religion."

"This country has no other hope, politically or morally, except *in the vast and controlling extension of the Catholic religion.*"

It is idle to discuss the question of excluding the Bible from our public schools, when evidently those making the demand would not be satisfied if it were granted. Unless, therefore, we are prepared not merely to exclude the Bible and all Protestant text books, but to substitute Catholic instruction in their stead, we might as well abandon all efforts to satisfy the complainants. Do they expect we will sell our birthright? —and for what?—a mess of mummeries? The Constitution of the United States provides as follows: "Religion, morality and knowledge being necessary to a good government and the happiness of mankind, schools and the means of education shall forever be encouraged." What religion? Christianity. What form of Christianity? Protestantism, the parent of constitutional liberty. And who are they who demand the sacrifice of our public school system? Are they the sons of our Protestant forefathers? Are they not foreigners from the priest-ridden countries of Europe? They who owe all they have acquired in the past, all they enjoy in the present, all they hope for in the future, to our free institutions, employ the very liberty we accord them in endeavoring to overturn our liberties.

The Catholics, withdrawing their children, especially in the large cities, from the public schools, and failing to obtain a portion of the fund, began to solicit assistance from Legislatures and Common Councils. With what success these appeals were made, the appropriations of the city and State of New York too plainly show. In 1863, the year of the New York riots, the Common Council donated $78,000 to Roman Catholic institutions. During the year ending Sept. 30, 1866, the Sate of New York paid to Roman Catholic orphan asylums and schools $45,674. In addition to this a special donation of $87,000 was made to the " Society for the Protection of Destitute Roman Catholic Orphan Children." The entire contribution to the Papal Church this year reached $124,174. The Protestant sects received during the same year $2,367. Shall the State support the Catholic religion? Shall it tax its citizens for the purpose of inculcating doctrines subversive of Republican government? It would be difficult to conceive of injustice greater than this.

In 1867, by enactment of the Legislature of New York, $110 was appropriated to every ward of "The Society for the Protection of Roman Catholic Orphan Children." For this purpose $80,000 was raised by tax on the city and county of New York. The city leased, in 1846, to the Roman Catholic Orphan Asylum, two entire blocks on Fifth Avenue, for ninety-nine years, at one dollar per year.* Over the entire country the

---

* Moneys voted from the Public Treasury of the city of New York for ten years·

A. D.	Totals.	Roman Catholic Institutions.	Protestant, Charitable, Jewish, Public, and all other Religious Institutions.
1860	$5,430.00		$5,430.00
1861	31,560.80	$18,791.27	12,769.53
1862	45,253.49	9,153.63	36,099.86
1863	91,522.11	78,000.00	13,522.11
1864	87,094.40	73,000.00	14,094.40
1865	63,552.66	40,000.00	23,552.66
1866	47,407.02	21,607.24	25,799.78
1867	133,100.40	120,000.00	13,100.40
1868	153,296.98	124,424.60	28,872.38
1869	528,742.47	412,062.26	116,680.21
Ten Years	1,186,960.33	897,039.00	289,921.33

same spirit prevails. Even in the far west, Idaho and Colorado each appropriated $50,000 for Catholic schools.

Catholic consciences, so tender about the tax for public schools, silence their throbbings long enough to allow the acceptance of taxes paid by Protestants to schools intensely sectarian. Hands that would be defiled by touching Protestant Bibles, handle Protestant money with impunity. And they want even more than our money. A bill introduced into the New York Legislature by the party bidding for Catholic votes, and earnestly advocated, proposes a fine of one hundred dollars on any institution, public or private, incorporated or not incorporated, and upon any Protestant guardian, presuming to impart religious instruction to a Roman Catholic child. The faith of the drunken, houseless, shiftless father shall determine the belief of even the child that eats the bread of Protestant charity. Having stolen from our State treasuries large sums for the support of their schools, asylums, and hospitals, why not at once enact a law compelling us to support their poor, and instruct their children in the tenets of Catholicism? As it would be a good speculation, conscience need not make them linger. They who have stolen the chickens might as well take the coop.

And the schools, aided by these munificent donations, are maintained for the express purpose of inculcating the doctrines of the Roman Catholic Church. In the report (1866) of the "Society for the Protection of Roman Catholic Orphan Children," this is expressly affirmed. The *Freeman's Journal* once said: "This subject (the school question) contains in it the whole question of the progress and triumphs of the Catholic Church in the next generation in this country." Their schools are strictly sectarian. The Catechism is taught. The children cross themselves before a crucifix. Bowing before an image of the Virgin they repeat, "*Hail, Mary, full of grace, our Lord is with thee, pray for us sinners now and in the hour of death.*" In one of their reading books, "Duty of a Christian towards God," occur these words: "We sin by irreverence in profaning churches, the relics of the saints, the images, the holy water, and other such things. . . . . . The use of images is exceedingly beneficial. . . . . . It is good and useful to invoke them (the saints) that we may obtain from God those graces of which we stand in need. . . . . . A true child of Mary will say every day some prayers in her honor." In the Cathechism published by Sadlier & Co., N. Y., and taught in their schools, the second commandment, "Thou shalt not make unto thee any graven image," etc., is entirely suppressed. In another text-book we find the following: "What is baptism?" "It is a sacrament which regenerates us in Jesus Christ by giving us the spiritual life of grace, and which makes us the children of God and of the Church." "Does baptism efface sin?" "Yes: in children it effaces original sin; and in adults, besides original sin, it effaces all the actual sin which they may have committed before being baptized." "Is baptism necessary for salvation?" "Yes: it is so necessary for the salvation of men, that even children cannot be saved without receiving it." "Of whom is this (the Devil's party) composed?" "Of all the wicked, Pagans, Jews, infidels, heretics, and all bad Christians." In a "Synopsis of Moral Theology," prepared for theological students, this question occurs: "Are heretics rightly punished with death?" "St. Thomas says Yes, because forgers of money, and disturbers of the State are justly punished with death; *therefore also heretics, who are forgers of the faith, are justly punished with death.*" The dogma of Infallibility, and the doctrine of Purgatory are also taught. In one of the Catechisms now in use it is asked, "Can the Church err in what she teaches?" "No, she cannot err in matters of faith." "What do you mean by purgatory?" "A middle state of souls suffering for a time on account of their sins." "Are all the souls in purgatory helped by our prayers?" "Yes, they are."

Verily, only a Jesuit can see the justice in taxing Protestants for the purpose of making munificent donations—$400,000 in a single city in a single year—to schools in which such instructions are given. And while receiving the gift, they complain piteously of our injustice in denying them the right of converting our common schools into nurseries of Papal superstition.

Catholics by their crouching subserviency to a foreign despot are disqualified from becoming good Republican citizens. Bound by solemn obligations to the only Sovereign whom they can in conscience recognize, loyalty, if indeed it be loyalty, is suspended on the will of the Pope. And he, Peter's successor, can, says the canon law, dispense with oaths and vows of allegiance, even the most sacred. That this arrogant ruler must of necessity, if faithful to the principles of his Church, claim sovereignty even in temporal affairs over Republicans, even in this country, can be proved beyond contradiction from assertions of eminent Papal writers, from the acts of the Popes, from canon law, and from the decrees of at least eight general Councils.* He wears the triple crown surmounted by the cross. He denominates himself, "*Lord of all the earth.*" Did ever assumption equal this? All other claims of authority are mere moonshine—a pleasing delusion. When the claims of our country come in collision with his—he being judge—the Catholic must obey the latter on pain

---

* "The spiritual power must rule the temporal, by all means and expedients, when necessary."—Bellarmine.

"It is the duty of the Roman Catholic Church to compel heretics, by corporal punishment, to submit to her faith."—Dens' Theology (a Catholic text-book).

"A Roman Pontiff can absolve persons even from oaths of allegiance."—Can. Authoritatis 2, caus. 15, quest. 6, pt. 2.

"All things defined by the canons and general Councils, and especially by the Synod of Trent (these declare the Pope an absolute temporal Sovereign), I undoubtedly receive and profess; and all things contrary to them I reject and curse. And this Catholic faith I will teach and enforce on my dependents and flock."—From the oath administered to priests.

of mortal sin, perjury.* Can such slaves ever become good citizens in a free Republic?

And this claim, so resolutely maintained in the past, is adhered to in the present. The Syllabus of 1864, which contains ten general charges, supported by eighty specifications, denominated *"damnable heresies,"* denounces all the leading ideas of Republicanism, in fact, of modern civilization. It is an indictment of all Protestant educational agencies, of marriage by civil contract, of the independence of Church and State, of freedom of the press, of Bible societies, of the functions of modern legislation, of Democratic forms of government, and of the existing relations between the governed and the governing classes. In a letter addressed to Prosper Gueranger, an ardent defender of the Infallibility dogma, the Pope says: "This madness (Gallicanism) reaches such a height that they undertake to reform

---

* The Bishop's oath contains the following : "To the extent of my power, *I will observe the Pope's commands* (in temporal as well as spiritual things, for so the Pope explains the oath) ; *and I will make others observe them : and I will persecute all heretics and all rebels to my Lord the Pope.*"

The famous bull against the two sons of wrath begins : "The authority given to St. Peter and his successors, by the immense power of the Eternal King, excels all the powers of earthly kings and princes. It passes uncontrollable sentence upon them all ; . . . . it takes most severe vengeance of them, casting them down from their thrones though ever so puissant, and tumbling them down to the lowest parts of the earth as the ministers of aspiring Lucifer."

"He who prefers a king to a priest, does prefer **the creature to the** Creator."—Morn. Exer. on Popery, p. 67.

even the divine constitution of the Church, and to *adapt it to the modern forms of civil government.*"

Evident and well authenticated as is Rome's claim to temporal power over her subjects, and her consequent inherent hostility to Republicanism, Jesuits, with an effrontery that Satan himself might covet, peremptorily deny it. They pretend to love our form of government, to laud our liberty, and to wish for us a future of success.

"Timeo Danaos et dona ferentes."

Father Hecker—founder of the community of Paulist Fathers, New York, whose special mission it is to bring the steam printing-press to bear upon the spread of the Catholic religion in the United States, and who furnish most of the literary matter for the Publication Society, including tracts, the articles in the *Catholic World*, and volumes for Sunday schools—in a lecture delivered in Horticultural Hall, Philadelphia (Jan. 19, 1871), entitled "The Church and the Republic," boldly affirms, in the face of all history, that Protestantism is essentially hostile to Republicanism, and Catholicism its unwearied friend. His only argument, laboriously drawn out to nearly an hour's length, is summed up in this syllogism:

Protestants teach that man is totally depraved. (Untrue.)

They who believe in total depravity are incapable of self-government. (Untrue.)

∴ Protestants are enemies of Republicanism. (Doubly untrue.)

And what shall we think of the propriety, to say nothing of the honesty, of affirming that Catholicism is the firm friend, the only true friend of Republican forms of government, and of making this assertion at the very time when all Catholics are clamorously shouting that Pius IX. shall be reinstated in temporal power against the will, formally and emphatically expressed, of those whom he proposes to govern? When every Catholic city in the United States, almost every Catholic church, is ringing with protests against what they choose to denominate the robbery of St. Peter, and every means, fair and foul, is employed to induce the Governments of Europe, and even the United States, to demand that the worst despotism which modern times has known, shall be resurrected and forced upon an unwilling people,—at this very time, Father Hecker dares to stand before an audience of American freemen, and affirm, "We Catholics are the truest, the best, the only firm friends of civil liberty, which is the gift of our Church to the world."

Popery's hostility to free institutions is manifested in ways almost innumerable. A priest some months ago peremptorily refused to give testimony in a St. Louis court, on the ground that by the authority of the Pope, the priesthood was under no obligation to obey the civil law.* In the city of Boston a man, be-

---

* "A priest cannot be forced to give testimony before a secular judge."—Taberna, vol. ii. p. 288.

"The rebellion of priests is not treason, for they are not subject to civil government."—Emmanuel Sa.

lieved to be a murderer by ninety-nine in every hundred who heard the evidence, was recently acquitted, because, on one trial, two jurors, on the next, one, obstinately refused to unite with the rest in conviction, and apparently, and in the opinion of the lawyers and judges, simply because they belonged to the same brotherhood, the immutable, infallible Church of Rome. During our recent struggle in breaking the chains of slavery—a struggle involving the question of national existence—the Catholics, true to their time-honored principles, proved themselves hostile to our Government. We speak advisedly. We know they boast much of their loyalty. It is indeed true that in the first year of the war many enlisted. Rome had not yet spoken. Carried along by the irresistible tide of patriotism they enthusiastically joined in the cry, "Secession is treason, and must be punished." In the second year of the war, however, Archbishop Hughes visited Europe. Almost the first intimation we had of his presence at the Vatican was the acknowledgment by the Pope of the independence of the Confederate States. A written benediction was forwarded to Jefferson Davis, addressing him as "Illustrious and Honorable President."

Very soon enlistments among the Irish ceased almost entirely. Desertions became frequent. The entire Catholic population became intensely hostile to the

---

"A common priest is as much better than a king, as a man is better than a beast."—Demoulin.

Government. Banded together, they declared, in language not to be mistaken, their determination to resist the draft. Riots were by no means infrequent, and would no doubt have been more numerous but for the apparent hopelessness of the effort to resist the will of the American people. Who inspired this fiendish malevolence? Who instigated outrages like those in New York? Was the Pope's temporal power unfelt on this continent? Were we not furnished with illustrations frequent and painful that the first allegiance of our Catholic citizens is due to their spiritual sovereign in Rome?

And the assassination of President Lincoln, how strangely is it connected with Rome's hostility to our Republican Government. The deed was planned in the home of a devout Catholic. It was associated in its inception with the prayers and hopes of the Romish Church. One of the prominent actors, aided in his escape by our Catholic enemies in Canada, found refuge in a convent, and afterwards became a soldier in the army of Pius IX. These and other circumstances—all possibly purely fortuitous—taken in connection with the known principles of Romanism and the well-established fact that Catholics, during the last years of the war, were intensely disloyal, certainly reflect little honor on Popery's ability to inspire devotion to civil liberty. If, as St. Liguori says, "*Although a thing may be against God, nevertheless, on account of the virtue of obedience, the subject who does that thing, does not sin,*" certainly it is reasonable to believe that Papists prefer the favor of the Pope, even if purchased by unwarrantable means, to the empty gratitude of their adopted country. The editor of the *Catholic Quarterly*, waxing bold, once said: "Protestants are not to inquire whether the Catholic Church is hostile to civil and religious liberty or not; but whether that Church is founded in divine right. If the Papacy be founded in divine right, it is supreme over whatever is founded only in human right, and then *your institutions should be made to harmonize with it, and not it with your institutions . . . . Liberty of conscience is unknown among Catholics. The word liberty should be banished from the domain of religion.* It is neither more nor less than a fiction to say that a man has the right to choose his own religion."

Popery, to borrow a figure from Augustine, is the proud and gorgeous city of superstition, set over against the Church of God, which it attacks with all the forces which bigotry and malice can invent; or to change the figure, it is a vast political engine, employed in the effort to crush out the liberties of the human race. *The Catholic World* (endorsed by the highest dignitaries of Rome, including the Pope himself), in the leading article of July, 1870, entitled "The Catholic of the Nineteenth Century," asserts in unmistakable language the supreme duty of the Papists to obey the commands of the Pope, and seek, in every way, and especially by means of the ballot, to render the Papal policy effective in this country. Its first assertion,

"The Catholic, like the Church, is one and the same in all ages," is followed by the still more arrogant affirmation, the Roman Catholic religion is, "with reference to time as well as eternity," "absolutely perfect," "as perfect as God." This is the basis of the obligation, felt by every "dutiful subject," "to vindicate with property, liberty and life," the supremacy of the head of the Church. If the Pope's authority and that of any civil government "come in conflict upon any vital point," the Papist is to do, "in the nineteenth century, precisely as he did in the first, second, or the third." Legislation is valid only when in harmony with Catholicism, "the organic law;" all other is "unjust, cruel, tyrannical, false, vain, unstable, and weak, and *not entitled to respect or obedience*." This has one transcendent virtue, clearness. And how is our legislation to be brought into harmony with "the organic law infallibly announced?" By "the mild and peaceful influence of the ballot, directed by instructed Catholic conscience." And how shall Romanists know which way to vote? "The Catholic Church is the medium and channel through which the will of God is expressed." His will is announced to men "from the chair of St. Peter." To what extent must this devotion to Popery be carried? "We do not hesitate to affirm that in performing our duties as citizens, electors, and public officers, we should always and under all circumstances *act simply as Catholics*." "The Catholic armed with his vote becomes the champion of faith, law, order, social and political morality, and Christian civilization." By the ballot he must place "the regulation and control of marriage" where it "exclusively belongs," in the hands of the Romish priesthood. And the rightful control of marriage "implies, by necessity, the Catholic view of all the relations and obligations growing out of it; the education of the young, the custody of foundlings and orphans, and all measures of correction and reformation applicable to youthful offenders and disturbers of the peace of society."

Another victory to be achieved by Catholic votes is the destruction of " a godless system of education," or—which is the same thing—an uncatholic system, and the substitution of the perfect system of that Church which " flatly contradicts the assumption on the part of the State of the prerogative of education." Nor is this the only arduous task laid on the Catholic voters of the nineteenth century. They are to legislate all existing evils out of the world and into eternal oblivion; red-republicanism, Fourierism, communism, free love, Mormonism, mesmerism, phrenology, spiritism, sentimental philanthropy, sensuality, poverty, and woman's rights. They propose to vote all men into holiness; if not, certainly into servitude. And then, too, over us Protestants, who freely accord them the privilege of denouncing severally and collectively every institution considered essential to civil liberty, they hope by the omnipotent power of the ballot to erect " a censorship of ideas, and the right to examine and approve or disapprove all books, publications, writings, and utterances intended for public instruction, enlightenment or entertainment, and the supervision of places of amusement." Champions of liberty! Gladly would we add more quotations from an article, all of which so well deserves the serious consideration of every lover of his country. Want of space forbids. With one, showing the kind of republicanism which the author loves, we close:— "The temporal government of the head of the Church is to-day (July, 1870) the best in the world." His subjects evidently thought otherwise.

Catholics are strangely consistent friends of liberty, if we may judge from the riots in New York, July 12th, 1870, the anniversary of the Battle of the Boyne, when unoffending Orangemen peacefully celebrating the day commemorative of the victory of William of Orange over James II., and the consequent ascendancy of the Protestant religion, were attacked; some killed and many wounded. And the Catholic papers of the city—where for many long years Catholics have been permitted uninterruptedly to form processions on Sundays, and to celebrate St. Patrick's and other days, blocking up the streets, excluding Protestants from their own sanctuaries, and making every demonstration calculated to exasperate them—argue, with surprising unanimity, that "this miserable faction ought not to be allowed to madden this nation by their annual celebration." Have Protestants no rights which Catholics need respect?

NEW YORK RIOT, 1871.

It was left, however, for the year 1871, to witness a still more emphatic illustration of the intense devotion felt by our Catholic fellow-citizens to the doctrine of popular liberty. The Orangemen of New York having resolved to celebrate, notwithstanding the riotous proceedings of last year, the anniversary of the defeat of their enemies, nearly two centuries ago, the Roman Catholics announced their determination to suppress a public parade. The city authorities, quailing before the threats of those whose united vote, uniformly cast in the interest of political Romanism, elects to office or consigns to oblivion, surrendered and forbade the procession. "It is given out," said the superintendent of police, at the dictation of the Mayor, "that armed preparations for defence have been made by the parading lodges." Was it not first announced, however, that armed preparations had been made for an attack? Is Protestantism destitute of even the right to prepare for self-defence? Must we set it down as a fixed fact that when Catholics object to a procession, and arm for its suppression, it may not occur? And for such liberty New York—its wealth mostly in the hands of Protestants—pays $50,000,000 a year. Another pretext was, that processions in the streets are not matters of right, but merely of toleration. This important legal fact it seems was allowed to sleep in the ponderous tomes of the City Hall till a band of desperadoes chose to announce their determined purpose of preventing the Orange parade. Why was not this decision proclaimed prior to the overwhelming processions of St. Patrick's day? Why are Catholic parades allowed both in the least frequented and the most important business streets of the city? If the circumstances had been reversed, and Orangemen had threatened a riot if Roman Catholics were permitted to celebrate the honors of Ireland's patron-saint, who does not know that the city officers would have thundered their determination to defend the inalienable rights of American Citizens? Not less absurd is the pretext, as flimsy as it is specious, that foreign events and feuds are not to be allowed the opportunity of perpetuating their memory on American soil. Were not the Germans permitted, in their boisterous rejoicings over a united fatherland, to flaunt their banners in the very faces of the deeply humiliated and bitterly exasperated Frenchmen?

So intense and wide-spread was the popular indignation—showing that Protestants though submissive are not slaves—that the Governor issued a circular, pledging protection to the much-abused Protestant Irish, promising them the support of the strong arm of the State. The 12th of July, accordingly, witnessed an inspiring scene, the State in her majesty affirming that every class of its citizens, whether Orangemen, Germans, Frenchmen, Chinese, or Hottentots, whether two or ten thousand, should be defended in their rights; that a frenzied mob, though composed of infuriated Romanists, must respect the fundamental principle of American liberty, or take the consequences. The bigoted intolerance of their enemies thus thrust a small but heroic band of Orangemen into a prominence which they had otherwise in all probability never attained; securing for them the warm sympathy of every true patriot. These accidental representatives of a principle ever dear to the American people were escorted—all honor to the Governor of New York—by the militia and police, the superintendent joyously redeeming himself from the deep infamy to which political trickery had so nearly consigned him. Yet, notwithstanding the armed escort, an attack with clubs, brick-bats and firearms was made, necessitating a return fire from the defenders of law and order, and leaving more than a score of dead bodies, and over two hundred wounded, to mark the scene of Popery's ardent devotion to liberty. Eighth avenue and Twenty-third street witnessed the inculcation of a lesson which it is earnestly hoped will be long remembered alike by Protestants and Catholics; by the former as evincing the spirit of Popery, by the latter as an indication, in fact an emphatic declaration, that Protestants, at least in their own land, will resolutely defend the principles of Republican Government.

We are told, however, that not Romanists, but Hibernians, a class of persons only nominally Catholics, are responsible for the riot and its accompanying horrors; that the priests, foreseeing the dangers, urged their congregations not to interfere with the proposed procession; that Archbishop McCloskey exhorted his flock " to make no counter demonstration of any kind."

He referred, however, with exceeding bitterness to the Orangemen, and expressed it as his deep conviction that the parade ought not to be permitted. It is undeniably true that Catholics, with scarcely a dissenting voice, said, with an emphasis not to be mistaken, "Protestants as a body shall not parade in the streets of New York." And the entire Catholic press of New York—the *Tablet* alone excepted—studiedly ignored the bare existence of Protestant rights. Among the headings of their leading editorials, after the riot, were the following: "GOVERNOR HOFFMAN'S Bloody Procession!" "Is JOHN T. HOFFMAN, Governor of the State of New York, a Murderer?" "HOFFMAN'S Holocaust!" "HOFFMAN'S Massacre!" "Our Orange Governor!" etc.*

The psychological explanation of such hearty devotion to liberty we scarcely know how to make. We would sooner attempt to explain how some men— "midway from nothing to the Deity"—succeed in con-

---

* "We call upon the friends of the murdered citizens, by every duty which they owe to society and to themselves, to raise this issue at the proper tribunals of the country, and impeach Gov. Hoffman before a jury of his peers to answer to a charge of murder."—*The Irish People.*

"Gov. Hoffman is answerable for the whole of it, and—we say it with pain—is guilty of every drop of blood shed that day."—*The Irish Citizen.*

"Let the cry of the orphan, whose home he has left desolate, blast him! And let the hot tear of the widow, whose heart he has made sore, rot him in his pride of place and imperious despotism!

"The greatest mistake made in the whole massacre business seems

vincing themselves that they are atheists, notwithstanding the entire class have so far signally failed in persuading the world that a genuine consistent atheist has ever existed. Possibly we might conceive an explanation of the singular phenomenon that human beings, possessed of bodies, living on the earth, eating bread, and drinking laudanum-negus, can reason themselves into the belief that they are really idealists, believing that the entire material universe, with its myriad forms of life, is a mere phantom, a conception of their own brain. Nor is it, perhaps, entirely impossible to imagine how some may dream themselves into the belief that God is everything, and everything God; that this impersonal, unconscious Deity sighs in the wind, smiles in the sunbeam, glitters in the dewdrop, rustles in the leaf, moans in the ocean, speaks in the thunder; that each person is part and parcel of God, a visible manifestation of the Invisible, one conscious drop of the unconscious ocean of being, existing for a brief moment between two vast eternities, a past and a

---

to be that Mayor HALL did not arrest JOHN T. HOFFMAN for interfering with the peace of the city."—*The Irish World.*

"The 'sober second thought' of the people, lately so excited, will consign JOHN T. HOFFMAN to the obscurity from which he has arisen by luckier manœuvrings."—*Freeman's Journal.*

The Society, formed on the day of the riot, in Hibernia Hall, "by the unanimous decision of all patriotic Irish soldiers present," and which, it was affirmed, should prove "no delusion," among others of similar import, unanimously passed the following resolution :—"That we call upon all Irishmen in these States to form themselves into a combination for self-protection."

17

future; coming, we know not whence; going, we know not whither, a troubled thought in the dream of half-sleeping nature; sinking, like the ripple on the ocean, upon the heaving bosom of emotionless Infinitude. We might even venture a defence, or at least an apology, of the custom prevalent in Siam, of exposing the mother, for one month after the delivery of a child, on a cushionless bench before a roasting fire. Nay, we might even undertake to explain the couvade—a custom widely prevalent in the thirteenth century, and even now, Max Muller informs us, extant among the Mau-tze; according to which the father of a new-born child, as soon as its mother regains her accustomed strength, goes to bed, and there, fed on gruel, tapioca, and that quintessence of insipidness, panada, receives the congratulations of his friends. Even this custom, ridiculous as it is, and which prompted Sir Hudibras to say,—

> "Chineese go to bed,
> And lie-in in their ladies' stead,"

is susceptible of an explanation at least semi-rational. But how to explain the idiosyncrasies of our Irish fellow-citizens, how to reconcile their conduct with their oft reiterated protestations of devotion to civil liberty, we know not. Call that liberty which has naught of liberty save its name, which has all of despotism save its manliness! Such faith as that which prompts Catholics to denominate Popery the stanch defender of freedom—if it be faith—we have seldom, if indeed ever, found, certainly not among Protestant Americans, scarcely among the Communists of Paris, or the enlightened citizens of Terra del Fuego.

And what interpretation shall be given to this sad, this long-drawn wail of the Papal Church, in all parts of the United States, over the Pope's loss of temporal power?* As he and the Catholic Episcopate have declared the civil sovereignty indispensably necessary to the due exercise of his rightful spiritual supremacy, these liberty-loving Americans—having escaped from the cruel oppression of Catholic governments to proclaim themselves the stanch friends of liberty—are holding meetings, in cathedrals, in public squares, forming processions, making speeches, and signing protests against—what?—against that cruel despotism which has for centuries disgraced the "States of the Church?" No; against the liberation of a people who have been long hoping and struggling for freedom, and who have been kept down, only by foreign bayonets in the hands of Catholics, by the ill-fated Napoleon, and the misguided Papal Zouaves.

And these protests—"full of sound and fury, signifying nothing," reiterating for the thousandth time

---

* The Archbishop of Baltimore, in a plea with Catholic ladies, affirms :—"Their Father in Christ, like St. Peter, is in chains, robbed of the very necessaries of life, reduced to the very verge of want, and almost—starvation, and wholly at the mercies of his enemies, who are also the enemies of Christ, and of all religion, and all virtue." To call this a liberal draft upon an excited imagination is too mild, too charitable entirely.

the infamous falsehood, "The Church in chains," "Peter in prison," and entirely ignoring the rights of the people who have deliberately chosen Italian unity —all claim temporal power for the Pope; many, sanctioned by office-hunting politicians, even denying the validity of any plebiscitum against the Pope's sovereign rights, even when fairly and freely taken.* Certainly these lengthy and carefully prepared documents—now crowding the pages of every Catholic paper, and making them, which is evidently needless, even more intensely political than ever before—may be legitimately denominated, The solemn Protest of American Papists against Republican forms of Government, against the Liberties of the People.

What is to be the end of all this bluster and war of words? If the Catholic papers are to be believed, there is to be no rest—movements creating sentiment, sentiment distilling into purpose, purpose developing into action, war in Italy, crusades from America, havoc and bloodshed—till the Vicar of Christ is again on his throne.†

---

* In the Philadelphia protest, read at a meeting which, according to the *Freeman's Journal*, numbered 30,000, this language occurs:— "We do not believe that the 'States of the Church' ever did, or now do, desire Italian unity; *but even if they did, they had no right to demand it.*"

The same thing is affirmed in the *Catholic World*, Nov., 1870, p. 284.

† See *Freeman's Journal*, Dec. 10th, 17th, 24th, and 31st, 1870, etc.

"If there is nothing but a stupid grunt in response to the call of God, then there will be in this land of ours either a bloody persecution or an infamous apostasy."—*Freeman's Journal*, Feb. 11, 1871.

All over Europe men are volunteering to join the crusade against popular government. Funds are pouring into the Pope's treasury. The faithful, even in democratic America, are asked to contribute. And the response has been such as to inspire bishops and archbishops, and even the despondent Pope himself, with new energy and fresh hopes. In Baltimore, at the Pontifical Jubilee, (the twenty-fifth anniversary of the accession of Pius IX. to the Papal throne,) that "beam from the immortal throne of St. Peter," that "jewel fit to be placed in the Tiara," when, according to Catholic authority, "twenty thousand, by receiving communion for Our Holy Father, promised to do all in their power to effect his restoration," sixty men, dressed in the uniform of the Papal Zouave, knelt by the communion rails in St. James, "not as an idle pageant, not for mere form's sake, but to proclaim what they and the Catholic Church will do when the time comes. By this they have given pledge of their espousal of the cause of the captive Pontiff." * *St. Peter*, a new Catholic paper of New York, says :—" To say it (the crusade)

---

* "This is not an act of transitory fervor, or the enthusiasm of the hour. By this act the Catholics of the United States of America have taken their stand with those of Europe and Canada. The fervor and enthusiasm of the hour will settle down into permanent and determined resolve, and by union with all parts of Christendom take a tangible and defined purpose. It is what the Pope predicted in saying that if union of action, resulting from identity of thought and feeling, be amongst Catholics, the gates of hell shall not prevail."
—Correspondence of *Freeman's Journal*, July 8, 1871.

is not necessary, is equivalent to denying the necessary right of self-defence. Catholics have, by degrees, seen themselves despoiled by the revolution of their most precious rights. We have been patient, but we will not be slaves. What form the new crusade may take we know not; but a crusade there truly will be to deliver the Sepulchre of Peter and the Catholic world."

And the methods employed in securing funds for this and similar holy purposes are indeed worthy the inventive genius of St. Dominic. Among others, all shrewd, the raffle for the Pope's sacred snuff-box strikes the infidel world as characteristically ingenious. The Prisoner Pope, "the most august of the poor," gave, March 17, 1871, to Dr. Giovanni Acquiderni, President of the upper council of the association of the Catholic youth of Italy, "his gold snuff-box, exquisitively carved with two symbolic lambs in the midst of flowers and foliage," to be disposed of for the benefit of Holy Mother Church. Dr. Acquiderni, "anxious speedily to fulfil the sacred desire of the octogenarian Father and Pontiff," opened a general subscription of offerings of one franc each. All good Catholics in the United States were earnestly exhorted to contribute twenty cents, and thereby secure a chance of one day possessing this sacred souvenir. They were assured—lest possibly lack of confidence might lessen the subscription—that "at the completion of the Pontifical Jubilee, Dr. Acquiderni will have an urn prepared containing as many tickets as there may be franc offerings, and in

DRAWING THE CHANCES FOR THE SNUFF-BOX OF PIUS IX.

the presence of a Notary Public, proceed to the extraction of the fortunate name that will indicate the new possessor of the snuff-box of Pope Pius IX., which will be immediately sent to the address marked after his signature in the subscription list."

What Patrick or Bridget was the fortunate drawer of this matchless prize, the uninitiated have not yet learned. Infallibility—if it is important the world should know—will no doubt inform us, explaining, perchance, at the same time the full import of those two symbolic lambs, symbols of a world-wide crusade.

As Protestants we have no fears. If Popery, in defying the common conscience of humanity, resisting the spirit of the age, and challenging the scorn of its own most liberal-minded men, wishes to commit suicide, let it go on.

Already Catholics, "standing afar off," in Ireland, England, Germany, Oregon, Washington, New York, Philadelphia, in every country and city, are mournfully exclaiming, "Alas, alas! that great city, that mighty city, for in one hour is thy judgment come."

Nor has Romanism shown less hostility to another principle of our national life, the separation of Church and State. This, which Protestants have ever viewed as one of the defences of civil liberty, has been and now is the object of incessant attack. Almost every Pope for the last thousand years has pronounced it a "damnable heresy." Schleigel, a member of the Leopold Foundation, in lecturing to the crowned heads of Europe with the design of showing the mutual supports which Popery and monarchy lend to and receive from each other, said :—" Church and State must always be united, and it is essential to the existence of each that a Pope be at the head of the one, and an Emperor at the head of the other . . . . Protestantism and Republicanism is the cause and source of all the discords, and disorders and wars of Europe." (Vol. iii. Lect. 17, p. 286.) Again :—" The real nursery of all these destructive principles, the revolutionary schools of France and the rest of Europe, has been North America." This Antichrist, the union of Church and State, even the Pope St. Gregory himself being witness, was cradled in Rome.

Of Popery's opposition to the freedom of the press, the free circulation of the Bible, and liberty of conscience, we have no time to speak. These may find a place in our next Chapter. Our task, in proving Romanism hostile to Republicanism, is completed. Further proof is needless. It must certainly be evident to every one of our fellow-citizens that where the principles and spirit of Popery attain full power, Republicanism must soon perish, and over her grave, the grave of man's hopes for this life, the lordly priest, representative of civil and ecclesiastical despotism, shall exultingly shout, "THUS ALWAYS: POPERY ALONE HAS PERMANENCY."

CHAPTER III.

THE PAPACY A FOE TO RELIGIOUS LIBERTY.

WE presume it is already manifest to every unbiassed reader that Romanism is a necessary and determined enemy of all liberty, civil and religious. Her cardinal principle takes away the right of private judgment, denying the subject the privilege of even obeying the clear teachings of conscience, thus forbidding him to use the very faculties God has given him, and for the proper exercise of which he alone is accountable. The people must receive their opinions from, and rely implicitly upon the priests; these are under the spiritual authority of bishops, and these under the Pope. Hence he alone has the right to think,—he alone has liberty: his is absolute. The people have an existence merely for the good of Christ's vicegerent on earth, who owns them soul and body, life and property.

Rome—certainly none will deny—proves herself an enemy of religious liberty by condemning the use of the Bible. The Council of Trent declared:—" It is manifest from experience that if the Holy Bible, translated into the vulgar tongue, be indiscriminately allowed to every one, the rashness of men will cause more evil than good to arise from it." Accordingly they condemn its use, and do everything in their power to prevent people from reading it. Societies for its publication and distribution have been repeatedly condemned by the Pope. Surely an enemy of the Bible is an enemy of all liberty—personal and national.

And this hostility to the inspiring cause of all true liberty is unmistakably evinced even in the full-orbed light of this nineteenth century, and in this Protestant country, which owes its greatness to the unfettered Word of God. A warfare, bitter, unrelenting, almost fiendish, has been waged for years against its reading in our common schools. Even in their own schools, though catechisms and crucifixes and rosaries are abundant, the Bible, even their own version, is a rare book.

With separate organizations for almost everything, the Romish Church has no society for the distribution of God's will to men. In fact, they have never yet published, in the vernacular, *an authorized edition, without note or comment.** Here is an extract from the version in general use:—" Images, pictures or representations, even in the house of God and in the very sanctuary, so far from being forbidden, are expressly

---

* St. Liguori says:—" The Scriptures, and books of controversy, may not be permitted in the vernacular tongue, as also they cannot be read without permission." Cardinal Bellarmine declares:—" The Catholic Church forbids the reading of the Scriptures by all, without choice, or the public reading or singing of them in vulgar tongues, as it is decreed in the Council of Trent."

authorized by the Word of God." (Comment on Second Commandment.)

And even the burning of Bibles is not yet one of the lost arts; and the immutable Church seems loath to allow it to become such. In the year 1842 (Oct. 27), at Champlain, N. Y., according to a statement prepared and published by four respectable citizens appointed for that purpose, a pile of Bibles, brought from the priest's house, was set on fire, and in open day, and in the presence of many spectators, *burned to ashes.* And the last year witnessed in unhappy Popery-cursed Spain a similar "act of faith," accompanied by various Catholic ceremonies, and a tremendous philippic against the execrable heretics.

Liguori, one of Rome's canonized saints, author of the "Glories of Mary," and of a standard text-book on Moral Theology, exclaims with holy horror:—"How many simple girls, because they have learned to read, have lost their souls." The *Freeman's Journal* once said:—"The Bible Society is the deepest scheme ever laid by Satan in order to delude the human family, and bring them down to his eternal possession." Bishop Spotswood affirmed:—"I would rather a half of the people of this nation should be brought to the stake and burned, than one man should read the Bible and form his judgments from its contents."

Catholicism is opposed to freedom of conscience. The Protestant Church holds—in fact the true Church in all ages has held—that God alone is Lord of the conscience, that this right He will not share with another, and that man should allow no miserable, arrogant human tyrant to usurp the throne of his Maker. Romanism, however, resembles all false religions in claiming the right to rule over the individual conscience; utterly denying its adherents the privilege of having any opinions except according to rules prescribed by an infallible Church. One of the recent Popes declared that "liberty of conscience is an absurd and dangerous maxim; or rather the ravings of delirium." A bishop in the Council of Trent said, with the concurrence and approbation of the holy (?) fathers: —" Laymen have nothing to do but to hear and submit." The New York *Tablet* recently informed its readers:—" There is no difference of opinion on this subject (the temporal power of the Pope), *for we do not allow any difference on such questions. The decrees of the Church forbid it.*" Father Farrel, of St. Joseph's Church, New York, for the mortal sin of having written (Jan. 12, 1871) an exceedingly mild approval of a public meeting in favor of Italian Unity, was peremptorily ordered by Archbishop McCloskey—three holy fathers, the council summoned to try the case, and several politicians demanding the order—to retract his liberal ideas, that every people had a right to choose its own rulers, or immediately withdraw from the Church. So then there is only one mind, only one conscience in the Catholic Church. Priests are simply mirrors, to reflect the opinions and aims of His Infallibility, Pope Pius IX. What freedom can men retain after thus yielding the right of private judgment—after surrendering conscience? Very appropriately does one born in Catholicity, educated in her doctrines, and still in the enjoyment of her services, ask:—" How long is this enlightened spirit of the nineteenth century to continue pandering to such narrow bigotry and prejudice as this?"

Romanism shows itself an enemy of religious liberty, by opposing the freedom of the press. Protestantism courts the light, loves the truth, and invites discussion, believing that error is inherently weak, and cannot present arguments which will sway the enlightened conscience of the educated masses. It is willing that the two should enter the lists, well assured that the former will gain an easy victory. Of the freedom of the press, it is, therefore, the stanch defendant; it has nothing to fear from discussion; everything to hope. On the other hand, of this liberty the Pope is a deadly foe. He denominates it *" that fatal licence of which we cannot entertain too much horror."* Weak, indeed, must be the cause which dares not undertake its own defence; corrupt must be the Church that endeavors to shut out the light of God; insecure must be the foundations of a system of religion which dreads, and, as far as lies in its power, prohibits public discussion. And assuredly this hatred of a free press is thoroughly antagonistic to the spirit of the age.

Nor are Papists less hostile to another support of

religious liberty, the education of the masses. Rome detests the very term, *popular* education. Her maxim is, "Ignorance is the mother of devotion and order." Accordingly, we nowhere find in Catholic countries good public school systems. They are the glory of Protestant lands. In this respect compare Spain with England; France with Prussia; Lower Canada with New England; Ireland with Scotland. In Protestant countries the people are intelligent, thrifty, industrious, moral; in Roman Catholic nations the masses are poor, degraded, ignorant, vicious. In Canada East, it is said, not more than one in ten can read; in Italy not one in fifty. In Ireland there reigns, even in this day, the ignorance, superstition and brutality of the dark ages. In Spain, out of a population of less than sixteen millions, according to the last census, more than twelve millions can neither read nor write. Certainly none will deny that such ignorance endangers civil and religious liberty.

In face of these, and countless similar facts which might be adduced, how astounding the frequent assertions of the Papal literature of the present day! The *Catholic World*, a monthly magazine published in New York, actually has the hardihood to affirm[*] that Catholicism has ever shown itself the guardian of civilization, the friend of liberty, the advocate of Republican forms of government; that it fosters science, encourages education, and places no shackles on reason. And the

---

[*] June, 1870.

same periodical denounces, in unmeasured terms, the civilization of the present day, defends the Crusades, advocates the dogma of Infallibility, asserts and reasserts the immutability of the Church, fights our common school system, and is ready to deluge Italy in blood to secure the restoration of the Pope to temporal power.* Does warmth of devotion to the cause of Republicanism such as this enkindle a flame on liberty's altar? Do we broil our beefsteak by the glowing fires of an arctic iceberg? Shall we intrust the cause we love to the hands of its enemies?

Protestantism, now as ever, boldly presents itself to the world, challenging the fullest investigation; demanding an unfettered press, an open Bible, a free platform, an untrammelled conscience, liberal education, full discussion and fair play, having faith to believe that truth will ultimately triumph. Romanism fetters the limbs of freedom, represses independence of thought, trammels conscience, cuts the nerve of individual energy, and saps the foundations of all true liberty. Father Farrel presumes to breathe the hope that Italy may be free, and is summarily decapitated. A German writes "Janus," an unanswerable refutation of Papal infallibility; his work is placed in the list of condemned books, and Papists forbidden to read it. Hyacinthe conscientiously endeavors to bring the Church of his

---

* See especially June and August, 1870.

love into harmony with the spirit of the age, to extract the molar teeth from the growling despot, and is excommunicated. E. Ffoulkes candidly writes his impressions of Romanism; he is excommunicated and his book condemned. Thus Popery treats her own sons.

Without religious liberty, to which Romanism has ever shown herself an enemy, civil liberty is manifestly impossible. To establish the most perfect system of Republicanism in Spain, or Ireland, would be to cast pearls before swine. Despotism, government by brute force, is the only government fitted, or in fact possible, to those who, having sold reason and conscience, are ignorant, prejudiced, superstitious, passionate, brutal. Thus the Roman Catholic Church is at once a school and an engine of despotism. So long as it retains sway, promulgating its doctrines, civil liberty is a boon beyond the reach of its subjects, nay, would in fact be, as it once proved in France, and may again soon, their greatest curse. What Catholic countries need is education, virtue and individual self-restraint, at once fitting for, and bringing after them, true, lasting, heaven-bestowed freedom.

With an apt quotation from Gattini, the noted Italian, we close this chapter:—" Civilization asks what share the Papacy has taken in its work. Is it the press? Is it electricity? Is it steam? Is it chemical analysis? Is it free trade? Is it self-government? Is it the principle of nationality? Is it the proclamation of the rights of man? Of the liberty of conscience? Of all this the Papacy is the negation."*

---

* Father Hyacinthe, in a letter addressed to Bishops, urging reforms, says:—"The result, if these documents (the Encyclical and Syllabus) were treated seriously, would be to establish a radical incompatibility between the duty of a faithful Catholic and the duty of an impartial student and free citizen."

CHAPTER IV.

POPERY AND MORALITY.

THE author of the "Invitation Heeded" entitles one of his chapters, "The Church the Guardian of Morals." Whatever effect his argument may have had upon others, there is one whom it has signally failed in convincing. With even increased boldness, we now affirm that Popery is unfriendly to morality. We do not affirm that Romanists are enemies of private and public morals; nor deny that many are extremely exemplary, patterns of goodness; nor even assert that they knowingly advocate a system which is far less efficient than Protestantism in wedding its adherents to a life of morality. We make the assertion, however, without the fear of refutation, that Romanism, as a system, has failed in reforming the morals of the masses. It has been frequently said in certain quarters that Protestantism is a failure, what then shall be said of Popery? As a moral educator, her failure is deplorable. Compare Mexico and South America with the United States; Italy with New England; Spain with Scotland; the Protestant counties of Ireland with those mostly Popish; Ulster with Tipperary.

In Roman Catholic Belgium there are, we are officially informed, eighteen murders to a million of the population; in France thirty-one; in Bavaria thirty-two; In Italy fifty-two; in Protestant England four. The illegitimate births in Brussels are thirty-five in the hundred; in Paris thirty-three; in Vienna fifty-one; in England five. In Chicago, according to the report of the Superintendent of Police, the Irish, who are about one-tenth of the entire population, supplied, in the year 1867, one hundred and seventy-four more offenders than all the other nationalities together. During the month in which the report was rendered (September), one in eight of the Catholic voters reported at the police court. Are Papists worse in Chicago than in the other cities of the Union? The *Irish Republic* says, "No."

The *Westminster Gazette*, a Roman Catholic journal, recently made the following acknowledgment:—" The neglected children of London are chiefly our children, and the lowest of every class, whether thieves or drunkards, are Catholics."

The Pope's own city, it is well known, has been in the past, and is now, extremely immoral. His Holiness, Alexander VI., for eleven years the occupant of the Papal chair, the anointed head of the so-called true Church, the pretended successor of Peter, gave a splendid entertainment to fifty public prostitutes in the halls of the Holy Vatican. And in our own day no caricatures are so much enjoyed in Rome as those at the expense of the priesthood; no stories are too astounding to be believed, if against priests and cardinals; no cry is so emphatic and frequent as this :—" Down with the priests." When those claiming sanctity, wearing the honors of the Church, careful in the observance of her forms, and zealous in extending her influence, are, many of them, openly or secretly immoral, what is to be expected from the lower classes? If, according to one of their own historians, Baronius, " He was usually called a good Pope, who did not excel in wickedness the worst of the human kind;" if moral character is not an essential qualification of a legitimate priest, but spiritual blessings of incalculable value may be pronounced by the tongue that an hour before, in a drunken revel, cursed its Maker; if grace flows through an unbroken succession direct from Peter, unimpeded in its blessed flow, as it streams from the jewelled fingers of a mitered monster of iniquity, *then assuredly* unbridled wickedness is excusable in the laity. Can they see any beauty in such holiness that they should desire it? To what organized iniquity do these remarkable words refer—" MOTHER OF HARLOTS AND ABOMINATIONS OF THE EARTH?"

That profanity should prevail in Catholic countries none need wonder. The Popes have set examples that may challenge the blasphemous ingenuity of the most hardened reprobate.* Cursing—solemnly and deliber-

---

* Take the cursing and excommunication of the Pope's alum-maker as a specimen :—" May God the Father curse him! May God the Son curse him! May the Holy Ghost curse him! May the Holy

ately done, but cursing none the less—seems to be one of the functions of their office. The Bull of Excommunication, dated Oct. 12, 1869, pronounces damnation upon all apostates and heretics, thus separating not only from the Church on earth, but from the Church in heaven, eight hundred millions of the human race, cutting them off, as Romanism affirms, from all rational hope of salvation. Even this, alas! does not exhaust his power of cursing. He fulminates a particular anathema against all who knowingly possess or read any book condemned by himself or his predecessors.

Cross curse him! May the Holy and Eternal Virgin Mary curse him! May St. Michael curse him! May John the Baptist curse him! May St. Peter, and St. Paul, and St. Andrew, and all the Apostles curse him! May all the martyrs and confessors curse him! May all the saints from the beginning of time to everlasting curse him! May he be cursed in the house, and in the fields! May he be cursed while living, and while dying! May he be cursed in sitting, in standing, in lying, in walking, in working, in eating, in drinking! May he be cursed in all the powers of his body, within and without! May he be cursed in the hair of his head, in his temples, his eyebrows, his forehead, his cheeks, and his jaw-bones, his nostrils, his teeth, his lips, his throat, his shoulders, his arms, his wrists, his hands, his breast, his stomach, his reins, . . . his legs, his feet, his joints, his nails! May he be cursed from the crown of his head to the sole of his foot! May heaven and all the powers therein rise against him to *damn* him, unless he repent and make satisfaction! Amen."—Spelman's Glossary, p. 206. If this poor man is not suffering in the deepest pit of hell, it's not the Pope's fault. He was well cursed. If there is any hope, even the faintest, then the righteous indignation, the foaming fulminations of an infallible Pope, are harmless; then we more fortunate heretics may safely despise the feeble anathemas pronounced against us.

As the interdicted list contains books in most of the cultivated languages, both ancient and modern, and upon almost every subject—Science, History, Religion, Morals, Metaphysics, and Literature, including most of our standard classics—down go the hopes of by far the greater number of educated Papists the world over. And then too, all who impede the work of the Church, directly or indirectly, especially such as subject priests to trial before civil courts—which even Catholic nations are now doing—are honored with a special malediction, sealing the fate of many millions more. That only a select few may escape a sound cursing, other classes also are pronounced anathema, all members of secret societies—Free Masons, Odd Fellows, Orangemen, and even his own dear children, Ribbonmen and Fenians. Still further to narrow the number of the elect, a curse is pronounced upon all who hold converse with excommunicated persons, upon all guilty of simony, and upon all ecclesiastics presuming to grant absolution to excommunicants, except in the article of death. The whole immense power of the keys is exerted, it would seem, in peopling the regions of the lost. "*The Infallible teacher of faith and morals,*" "*the only mouth-piece of divine mercy,*" damns more than four-fifths of the human family.

Nor is the character of Rome's stanch adherents, the Jesuits, any less worthy of reprehension. Having taken one of the most solemn oaths ever administered of unflinching fidelity to the interests of "Mother Church," they are thenceforth dead to every sentiment of virtue, to every motive of honor, to every feeling of humanity, unless these are means for the accomplishment of their deep-seated schemes of Popish aggrandizement. They have no love of morality, no fear of God before their eyes, no chord of sympathy with suffering humanity; they are simply, and almost solely, unprincipled, unreasoning, but shrewd, energetic, untiring devotion to Rome. Inheriting from their illiterate founder, Ignatius Loyola, a fanaticism the blindest conceivable—and for that very reason the most intense possible—they have been during all the years of their existence one of the greatest curses Europe has been called upon to endure.*

Some, perhaps, may be inclined to account for the increased prevalence of crime in Roman Catholic countries, by assigning other causes than the influence of the Romish Church. But certainly human nature is the same in all lands; and while external influences and modifying circumstances may indeed in some

---

* The Parliament of France, in ordering their expulsion from the Empire (1762), set forth their moral character as follows:—" The consequences of their doctrines destroy the law of nature ; break all bonds of civil society ; authorize lying, theft, perjury, the utmost uncleanness, murder and all sins! Their doctrines root out all sentiments of humanity ; excite rebellion ; root out all religion ; and substitute all sorts of superstition, blasphemy, irreligion and idolatry."

Lord Macaulay says :—" It was alleged, and not without foundation, that the ardent public spirit which made the Jesuit regardless of his ease, of his liberty, and of his life, made him also regardless of truth and of mercy ; that no means which could promote the interests of his religion seemed to him unlawful, and that by these interests he

measure affect the state of morals, it is inconceivable that these should universally operate, in all climates and in all ages, to the evident greater deterioration of lands under the rule of the Pope. The conclusion is irresistible, that these gross immoralities are the result, the natural fruit of Rome's teaching. The whole system tends to produce exactly this state of things. When men believe that the favor of heaven can be purchased for a few paltry dimes, why should they endeavor to secure it by a life of self-denying virtue? Why follow the despised, humble and meanly-attired Jesus, in the narrow way, with few companions, when taught from early infancy to believe that the gay, the worldly, and even the immoral, being within the Church, are sure of entering the bliss of heaven? With no just sense of the heinousness of sin as a violation of divine law; with no fear of the righteous indignation of Almighty God, in fact, with conscience thoroughly debauched by the teachings of the priest, what shall

---

too often meant the interests of his society. It was alleged that, in the most atrocious plots recorded in history, his agency could be distinctly traced; that, constant only in attachment to the fraternity to which he belonged, he was in some countries the most dangerous enemy of freedom, and in others the most dangerous enemy of order. . . . Instead of toiling to elevate human nature to the noble standard fixed by Divine precept and example, he had lowered the standard till it was beneath the average level of human nature. . . . In truth, if society continued to hold together, if life and property enjoyed any security, it was *because common sense and common humanity restrained men from doing what the Society of Jesus assured them they might with a safe conscience do.*"—Vol. i., chap. 6.

restrain them from the commission of any crimes they may desire to commit? Could any system be devised better fitted to spread vice, disorder and crimes; to dissolve the bonds of society? If men were left without any religion, it is believed that even the natural conscience, unenlightened by divine revelation, would prompt to a purer code of morals than that of Rome.

Another powerful agent in producing these abounding immoralities, there can be no doubt, is the *confessional*. The influence of this can be only bad, both on the minds of those who recount all their sins to the confessor, and on the mind of the priest. The heart of Father Confessor is a receptacle for all the villanies and immoralities of an entire congregation. If these do not corrupt even one who holds his office under the authority of St. Peter, he must be more than human. But, alas! we have innumerable evidences all around us that priests are men of like passions with others. Defiled in mind by becoming familiar with forms of sin, the listener becomes the tempted; the tempted becomes the tempter.

And the maxims laid down for the direction of confessors in the discharge of their duties with the faithful are worthy a passing notice. "After a son has robbed his father, as a compensation, the confessor need not enforce restitution, if he has taken no more than the just recompense of his labor." "Servants may steal from their masters as much as they judge their labor is worth more than the wages they receive." * There would seem to be some virtue in doing the deed *secretly*.† Are we to infer that Papists, like the ancient Spartans, deem theft honorable, if so adroitly done as to escape detection? And how convenient the standard by which to determine how much may be taken without sin—as much as the Catholic judges his or her services worth more than the wages received. Some servants, under such instruction, learn to set a very high estimate on their labors. Not only may servants steal from their employers, but wives may from their husbands. "A woman may take the property of her husband to supply her spiritual wants, and to act as other women act."

According to the moral theology of Liguori, " To strike a clergyman is sacrilege;" but, " It is lawful for a person to sell poison to one who, he believes, will use it for bad purposes, provided the seller cannot refrain from selling it without losing his customer." It is likewise lawful to keep a concubine, to shelter prostitutes, to rent them a house, and to carry messages between them and their gallants. " In case of doubt whether a thing which is commanded be against the command-

---

* See Molina, vol. ii. p. 1150.

† The Catechism approved by French Bishops—their catechisms, like their prayer-books, are unnumbered—asks, " Is one always guilty of robbery when he takes the property of another? No. It might happen that he whose goods he takes has no right to object. For instance, *when he takes in secret of his neighbor by way of compensation.*"

ment of God, the subject is bound to obey the command of his superior." The same high authority assures us that gambling, betting, disobedience of parents, gluttony, vain-glory, hypocrisy, opening another's letters, babbling, scurrility, and the ordination of drunkards and debauchees to the priesthood, are lawful under certain circumstances. Condemning the Wycliffites for opposing simony, he makes an excuse for its prevalence in the Romish Church. "A voluntary confession to a priest," he affirms, "is a sign of contrition."

For the practical carrying out of their cherished principle, "The end justifies the means," the injured Catholic may read, " If a calumniator will not cease to publish calumnies against you, you may fitly kill him, not publicly, but secretly, to avoid scandal." Again:— " It is lawful to kill an accuser, whose testimony may jeopard your life and honor." And to make this code of infamous morals as convenient as possible, it is further affirmed:—" In all the above cases, when a man has a right to kill any person, another may do it for him, if affection move the murderer."

We know it may indeed be said, these precepts are not widely known, nor generally practised; they are only found in Rome's books; they are merely a portion of the legacy of the dark ages, and to hold Rome to account for them is, in every sense, and to the highest degree, unfair. No, not unfair; for immutability changes not, and a Church which assumes the right to place its ban on every immoral issue from the press, to tell the world what to believe, what to read, and now to act, and has gone to the most distant publishing houses of the civilized world to drag thence for condemnation the principles of Protestantism, might surely take the trouble to expunge these and similar teachings from books written by her own sons, and once sanctioned.

The practice of the Popes in dispensing with oaths, obligations and contracts, and absolving subjects from allegiance to their lawful sovereigns in cases where kings rebel against the authority of Rome, has had no little influence in producing immoralities. It is a principle with Rome that "no faith is to be kept with heretics." *

And this dogma of Roman Infallibility has on several occasions been practically interpreted. John Huss was conducted to the Council of Constance, under the solemn pledge of protection from the Emperor. The Council, however, condemned the reformer as a heretic,

---

* Gregory IX. decreed :—"Be it known to all who are under the dominion of heretics, that they are set free from every tie of fealty and duty to them; all oaths and solemn agreement to the contrary notwithstanding." Pope Innocent VIII., in his bull against the Waldenses, gave his nuncio full authority "to absolve all who are bound by contract to assign and pay anything to them." Gregory VII., in a solemn council held at Rome, enacted :—"We, following the statutes of our predecessors, do, by our Apostolic authority, absolve all those from their oath of fidelity who are bound to excommunicate persons, either by duty or oath, and we loose them from every tie of obedience." Martin V. says :—"Be assured thou sinnest mortally, if thou keep thy faith with heretics."

and ordered him to be burned at the stake. In vain the Emperor interposed, pleading his pledged word of honor. It was solemnly decreed:—" The person who has given the safe conduct to come thither shall not, in this case, be obliged to keep his promise, by whatever tie he may have been engaged;" and poor Huss perished in the flames! Did ever ingenuity in devising rules of casuistry excel this? It is only equalled by the treachery of Judas. And even he, without attempting a defence of faithlessness, exclaimed, in the bitterness of remorse, "I have sinned." But Rome, to this day, has never expressed the slightest regret in having—not merely on this occasion, but on hundreds of others—deliberately broken faith, and consigned to the rack, the dungeon, or the flames those whose only crime was, that they loved Christ, the Bible, and a pure Christianity more than the Scarlet Mother on the seven hills of Rome.

In remembrance of such deeds, it is with a sense of holy satisfaction that the follower of Jesus reads, "Her sins have reached unto heaven, and God hath remembered her iniquities." And the prayer of the devout soul is, "Come, Lord Jesus, come quickly;" vindicate truth and justice; let the angel's voice be heard above the waves of earth's turmoil, saying, "Is fallen, is fallen, Babylon the great."

Did space permit we might easily prove that unblushing atheism is a natural fruit of Popery. In every Catholic country of the present day the more intelligent classes are either infidel or atheistic. Without pausing to ascertain whether Popery is condemned or taught in Scripture, but presuming it is all it claims to be, the only form of religion having the sanction of the Bible, they deliberately reject God's Word as a guide to morality, holiness and happiness. To receive as a boon from our Father in heaven a book which, it is believed, wrongly indeed, yet firmly believed, sanctions such enormities, is justly considered a slander on the Creator. Accordingly, they look upon it as a cunningly devised fable, admirably adapted to bind the fetters of despotism on an ignorant people, precisely fitted to uphold and enrich an arrogant priesthood, but no guide to the sin-burdened soul on the way to eternal favor with God. Some, however, of the educated in Romish countries, perhaps the greater number, do not pause short of atheism. In rejecting a system of religion which cannot command even common respect, they, alas! reject also the triune God, who, although worthy the devout homage of every heart, is so dishonored by those who profess to serve him, as to be despised by those outside the Church claiming to be his. By the excesses of Popery they are drawn away from the Bible and God, and driven into atheism. Consciously or unconsciously they have reasoned, if this be the true religion of the true God (and they who claim talent, knowledge and piety so affirm), then we deliberately prefer to believe there is no God. The atheism, which, in the bloody excesses of the French Revolution, disgraced humanity, was the legitimate offspring of Romanism.

With the testimony of Coleridge as to the ruinous moral effects of Popery, we close :—" When I contemplate the whole system of Romanism as it affects the great principles of morality, the terra firma, as it were, of our humanity; then trace its operations on the sources and conditions of human strength and well being; and lastly, consider its woeful influence on the innocence and sanctity of the female mind and imagination; on the faith and happiness, the gentle fragrancy and unnoticed ever-present verdure of domestic life, I can with difficulty avoid applying to it the Rabbi's fable of the fratricide, Cain—*that the firm earth trembled wherever he trod, and the grass turned black beneath his feet.*"

CHAPTER V.

POPERY UNCHANGED.

IN some respects Popery has indeed changed, notwithstanding her boasted claim of immutability. Pius IX., the world's "infallible teacher in faith and morals," though the successor of Gregory VII., would find exceeding great difficulty in forcing a modern Henry IV. to stand in the court of his palace, hungry and shoeless, humbly pleading during three successive days from morning till night—the Holy Father meanwhile enjoying the society of an intelligent, beautiful, honored countess, his illegitimately endeared friend— for the superlative privilege of kissing the toe of him, *"appointed of heaven to pull down the pride of kings."* Popery, so far as regards the respect it is able to command, has greatly changed since the twelfth century, when kings considered themselves honored in being permitted to lead by the bridle rein the sacred horse, or even the holy mule, that bore Christ's Vicar. Now his Holiness begs the favors he no longer can command, soliciting Peter's pence from those despising his anathemas; impotently imploring the support of bishops who scorn his holy indignation. Urban VIII. condemned as "perverse in the highest degree" the doctrine of the earth's revolution. His successors, with as much grace as possible, have silently yielded to the inevitable. Now this little orb is allowed to revolve, no one, not even an infallible Pope, objecting. Formerly, and even now in countries purely popish, agencies for disseminating religious literature must incur anathema; now, as the press is a powerful agent in moulding public sentiment, the Catholic Publication Society of New York, organized with the sanction of the Pope for the express purpose of combating Protestantism with its own weapons, is issuing tracts and pamphlets which in Italy would even now, as in former times, be considered unfriendly to the sacred prerogatives of God's vicegerent on earth.

Whilst in methods of exhibiting her temper, Rome has changed somewhat—endeavoring to put old wine into new bottles—it is undeniably true that in reality she is the same, unprincipled monster; in dogma unaltered, in spirit unbroken, unsubdued, untameable. "Those," says Hallam, "who know what Rome has once been, are best able to appreciate what she is." "It is most true," says Charles Butler, "that Roman Catholics believe the doctrines of their Church unchangeable; it is a tenet of their creed that what their faith ever has been, such it was from the beginning, such it is now, and such it ever will be." What else could be expected from a Church claiming infallibility? To alter its dogmas, or to condemn the cruel practices of the past, would be to overturn the foundation on which it rests.

Hence we search in vain in the Encyclical Letters of the present for the slightest intimation that Popery has changed its character or purposes. Has one single decree been revoked? one solitary regret expressed for the atrocities which have made her name a synonym for cruelty? Does any doctrine once held by the Church now lack strenuous defenders? All the superstitious and idolatrous practices of the past find advocates in the present,—the adoration of the host, the invocation of saints, the granting of indulgences, the worship of the Virgin, the veneration of relics, absolution by the priest, the cursing of "all heretics, be they kings or subjects," and detestation of "Protestantism, that damnable heresy of long standing."

Patient waiting for a return of strength, or of a favorable opportunity, is not change of nature. The sleeping lion, with wounded paws and broken teeth, is a lion still. In most countries Romanism does indeed lack the power to execute its fiendish designs; and even in those nations almost exclusively Roman Catholic, it would be the acme of human folly to insult the untrammelled conscience of Christendom; but its principles, doctrines and spirit are in no respect changed for the better. It is simply restrained by a public sentiment which it despises and does all in its power to break down, which, however, it dares not so far disregard as to re-enact the untold horrors of the Inquisition. This would be its certain destruction. And yet, even in republican America, it is in spirit the same despotism it was in Europe. Of individual liberty, of education, of the general diffusion of gospel truth, and of government by the people, it is the same uncompromising foe it has always been.

Is the Romish Church less eager for power now than during her past history? Certainly not. Never were greater exertions made to retain the influence it has, and to recover what it has lost. The Jesuit order, which has been revived and inspired with new energy, is straining every nerve to enlarge its numbers and secure a controlling influence in legislation, especially in these United States, with the hope of ultimately bringing them under Papal domination. True to their principles —deceitful always—they laud the liberty of our country while forging the weapons for its destruction. Warmed into life by our self-denying kindness, like the fabled serpent, they are distilling deadly poison into the bosom to which they owe existence itself.

Is Rome less avaricious now than in the ages past? No. Her system which, it would seem, must have been devised for the express purpose of procuring money—each of her seven sacraments is a market, every spiritual blessing has a price—is as admirably adapted to this end, and as efficiently operated now as heretofore. And so perfect is the machinery of this iniquitous system of collecting revenues, and so successfully is it driven, that Catholicism has impoverished every country in which it has held sway. Spain pays annually out of her penury fifty millions to the Romish Church. Ireland's poverty is traceable directly to Popery. Even from our own land large sums are annually exported to the treasury of the Pope,—last year three millions, this year all that can possibly be raised for " Peter in prison."

Is Romanism less intolerant than formerly? The hope is vain. Her ever memorable words are: " The good must tolerate the evil, when it is so strong that it cannot be redressed without danger and disturbance to the whole Church, ... otherwise, where ill men, be they heretics or other malefactors, may be punished without disturbance and hazard of the good, they may and ought, by public authority, either spiritual or temporal, to be chastised or executed." * Is this less than an open declaration of determination to persecute even unto death so soon as they can obtain the power? We exist merely by tolerance, being mercifully allowed to retain our own cherished doctrines and worship God in the way that to us seems according to Scripture, simply because Rome has granted us present indulgence. But the right to chastise us with rods of iron, Holy Mother has not yielded. Her loyal sons defend every act of persecution, even all her past enormities. The Crusades are lauded. Even the Inquisition is unblushingly defended and even applauded. It is declared: " It saved society from a danger only second to that from which it was preserved by the Crusaders." Rome is represented as the one " place on earth where error has never been permitted to have a foothold." Protestantism is de-

---

* Rhemish Testament, Matt. xiii. 6.

clared to be "a gigantic rebellion against the Church of God." Accordingly, Rome establishes " the Congregation of the Inquisition" to " protect the souls of her children from the fatal pestilence of heresy and umbelief." "Protestantism is everywhere the intruder—the innovator." By the right of prior occupation, " in a special manner she claims this land." And whilst they have the right to persecute and silence us, we have scarcely the right to protest, for " Protestantism tolerating every error can make no exception against the truth." Sublime arrogance!

With a candor that is truly refreshing, considering whence it proceeds, the Jesuits, Rome's sworn adherents —who by intrigue and perjury and diabolical malignity have sown discord everywhere, and been thirty nine times expelled from the different countries of Europe— whilst claiming full liberty to extend the principles of their Church unmolested and even unchallenged, yet unequivocally deny that they have abandoned the right to persecute. Did ever audacity equal this? It amounts to saying that constitutional liberty must warm them into vigor, that they may have the power to inflict upon it a deadly wound. *The Shepherd of the Valley*, a Catholic paper published in St. Louis, with the approbation of the archbishop, says:

"The Catholic who says that the Church is not intolerant, belies the sacred spouse of Christ. The Christian who professes to be tolerant himself, is dishonest, ill-instructed, or both!"

"We say that the temporal punishment of heresy *is a mere ques-*

tion of expediency. Where we abstain from persecuting them (the Protestants), they are well aware that it is *merely because we cannot do so; or think that by doing so we should injure the cause that we wish to serve.* .... If the Catholics ever gain—which they surely will do—an immense numerical majority, *religious freedom in this country is at an end.* So say our enemies, so we believe."

"Heresy and unbelief are crimes, that's the whole of the matter; and where the Catholic religion is an essential part of the laws of the land, *they are punished as other crimes.*" *

The *Freeman's Journal* a few years since treated its readers to the following :—

"A Catholic temporal Government would be guided in its treatment of Protestants and other recusants, *solely by the rules of expediency.* .... Religious liberty, in the sense of liberty possessed by every one to choose his own religion, is one of the most wicked delusions ever foisted upon this age by the father of all deceit. The very word liberty, except in the sense of permission to do certain definite acts, ought to be banished from the domain of religion."

"*None but an atheist can uphold the principles of religious liberty.* Short of atheism, the theory of religious liberty is the most palpable of untruths. Shall I therefore fall in with this abominable delusion and foster the notion of my fellow countrymen, that they have a right to deny the truth of God, in the hope that I may throw dust in their eyes, and get them to tolerate my creed as one of the many forms of theological opinion prevalent in these latter days?"

"Shall I hold out hopes to him that I will not meddle with his creed, if he will not meddle with mine? Shall I lead him to think that religion is a matter of private opinion, and tempt him to forget that *he has no more right to his religious views than he has to my purse, or my house, or my life-blood? No! Catholicism is the most intolerant of creeds. It is intolerance itself*—for it is truth itself.

---

* Editorial, April 10, 1852.

We might as rationally maintain that a sane man has a right to believe that two and two do not make four, as this theory of religious liberty. Its impiety is only equalled by its absurdity."

A Papal bull annually "excommunicates and curses—on the part of God Almighty, the Father, Son and Holy Ghost—all heretics, under whatever name they may be classed." To such anathemas we may reply in the language of David to Shimei, "It may be the Lord will look on our affliction, and requite us good for their cursing."

The text-books now studied in their theological seminaries are well calculated to keep alive the spirit of persecution. Dr. Den, in his "System of Theology," a standard with Papists, affirms: "Protestants are by baptism and by blood under the power of the Romish Church. So far from granting toleration to Protestants, it is the duty of the Roman Catholic Church to exterminate their religion." Again, "It is the duty of the Roman Catholic Church to compel Protestants to submit to her faith." The Rhemish Testament, in its commentary on Matthew xviii. 17, declares: "Heretics therefore, because they will not hear the Church, be no better, nor no otherwise to be esteemed of Catholics, than heathen men and publicans were esteemed among the Jews." Again, 2 Cor. vi. 14 : "Generally here is forbidden conversation and dealing with all heretics, but especially in prayers and meetings at their schismatical service." Once again: "Protestants ought by public authority, either spiritual or temporal, to be chastised or executed." In exposition of these words, "drunken with the blood of the saints," these Rhemish annotators say: "The Protestants foolishly expound it of Rome, for that there they put heretics to death, and allow of their punishment in other countries; but their blood is not called the blood of saints, no more than the blood of thieves, man-killers, and other malefactors, for the shedding of which by order of justice no commonwealth shall answer." Liguori, in his "Moral Theology," a work very highly prized in their theological seminaries, says: "As the Church has the right of compelling parents to hold to the faith, so she has the power of taking their children from them." Canon XII. of the recent Œcumenical Council affirms:—"If any think that Christ, our Lord and King, has only given to his Church a power to guide, *by advice and permission*, but not ordain by laws, *to compel and force* by anterior judgments, and *salutary inflictions*, those who thus separate themselves, let them be anathema." Surely, in language at least, Rome is no less intolerant than in the centuries past. And doctrines such as these are taught to youth in this land of Protestant liberty!

And Rome's actions, as well as her teachings, unmistakably evince the same unchanged spirit. Jewish parents in Rome employ a Catholic nurse. Their infant son is clandestinely baptized by a Popish priest. Henceforth it is the child of the Church. Stolen from the home of its parents—who in vain demand the God-given right to their child—immured in a monastery, carefully instructed in the doctrines of Popery, the Jewish dog, transmuted into a priest, Mortara, at manhood enters the world thanking God that His true church is a baby-stealer. Raffaele Ciocci, honorary librarian of a Papal college in Rome, is entrapped by Jesuits into a monastery. Infallibility, carefully instructing him in the mysteries of Romanism, designs him for a missionary to distant lands steeped in the ignorance of Protestantism. Becoming, through the instrumentality of God's blessed word, a determined enemy of the Papacy, death is decreed against him. With Jesuitical hypocrisy, under the cloak of friendship, a poisoned beverage is handed him. Saved by a timely antidote, he seeks release from the iron grasp of his inhuman persecutors by appealing to the Pope. This only rendering his situation doubly more intolerable, he finally consents to sign a recantation in the hope of effecting an escape. Landing, in the year 1842, on the shores of free England, he is watched and dogged by Franciscans and Jesuits, and every available means employed to entangle him again in the cruel snares of Romanism. In his revelations of the Man of Sin, Ciocci has conclusively proved that Popery in this nineteenth century is the same uncompromising foe of the Gospel, the same bitter persecutor, unchanged and unchangeable.

We must content ourselves with a mere reference to most of the recent cases of Popish intolerance. Protestants, and especially American Protestants, ought not to forget the cruel persecutions of the unhappy inhabitants of Lower Valais, Switzerland, where, in 1843, the Jesuits after innumerable iniquitous proceedings, signalized their triumph by the passage of a law prohibiting all Protestant worship, public and social; forbidding God's people to meet for the reading of his Word even in their own houses. And in what language shall we characterize the banishment, in 1837, of 400 Protestants from one of the States of Austria on the simple charge of refusing Papal supremacy?—or the imprisonment, in 1843, of Dr. Kally, a Scottish physician, on the island of Madeira?—or the sentence of death pronounced against one of his converts, Maria Joaquina, for "maintaining that veneration should not be given to images, denying the real presence of Christ in the sacred host, and blaspheming the Most Holy Virgin, Mother of God?" And assuredly every lover of liberty will bear in sad remembrance the history of the lengthy imprisonment, cruelty and protracted sufferings of the Madiai family; the studied persecution, arrest, impoverishment, imprisonment, and sufferings of Matamoros in a loathsome cell —where in sickness he was refused a physician and even medicine; his condemnation to the galleys for nine years on the testimony of suborned witnesses; his banishment from Spain, to which his throbbing heart and enfeebled voice would fain have proclaimed, "Salvation is of the Lord," and his triumphant death in Switzerland, whither he had gone in the faint hope of sending some message of life to his endeared countrymen enslaved by the superstitions of Rome. Even our own land within a few years, for aught we know, may have given a martyr to the truth. Bishop Reese of Michigan, charged with ecclesiastical error, entered Rome in response to the citation of the Pope. So far as the world knows, he entered eternity the day he stepped within the magic circle of the heartless Inquisition.

Until the present year—and for the change no thanks to Popery—Protestant worship was prohibited in Rome. Did ever intolerance equal this? While allowed in England, and the United States to hold their services, build churches, found monasteries, establish theological seminaries, collect enormous sums of money for transmission to the Pope, and foment insurrection and rebellion against the Governments whose protection they claim, they will not permit Protestant worship even in a private house where they have the power to prevent it. The foreign resident who dares to join with his countrymen in worshipping God according to the forms of worship to which he has been attached from youth, places himself "in the power of the Inquisition, both for arrest and imprisonment," and is earnestly advised, unless he courts exile or a dungeon, "never again to repeat these illegal acts." *

Another fact evincing the present spirit of Popery claims attention. A full regiment of Canadians, a few years since, proffered their services to aid in upholding the temporal power of the Pope. The spirit of Peter

---

* See Letter from Joseph Severn, British Consul at Rome, to Rev. James Lewis, dated Dec. 29, 1866.

the Hermit still lives. From every Catholic pulpit in Canada appeals were made for aid for Pius IX. in his embarrassments. With every Catholic newspaper office a recruiting station, and with a central committee to secure unity of action, volunteers offered themselves in greater numbers than were needed. On the day of their departure an address was delivered by Archbishop McCloskey:—"You are going to stand with others like you, as a rampart of defence and a tower of strength around the presence of your Holy Father, to protect his safety and defend his rights." Defend his rights; his right to steal the children of heretics, to imprison Protestants, to prevent all forms of worship except Popish, to fetter freedom, to curse the institutions of modern liberty, to trample on the dearest hopes of the Italian people, and keep them, though longing for escape, in the grossest ignorance, under the severest despotism, in the most abject poverty!

The Archbishop continues:

"They (Catholics in the United States) are as strongly devoted to the sustenance and maintenance of the temporal power of the Holy Father as Catholics in any part of the world; and if it should be necessary to prove it by acts they are ready to do so. . . If that policy (non-interference) should ever change to a sympathy with the Italians as against the Holy Father, then Catholics must be prepared to show their readiness by acts as well as words, to give their lives, if necessary, for their Holy Father."

This first crusade failed. And now, forsooth, the tocsin is sounding a grander, a world-wide crusade. From all the nations that on earth do dwell, the faith-

BLESSING THE PAPAL ZOUAVES.

ful, for multitude like the swarms of flies in Egypt of old, are to meet at some designated spot, proceed to Italy, wipe out the rebellious sons of Holy Mother, and restore Pius IX. to the throne from which he has been ejected by the almost unanimous voice of his own people. *Festinate.* "Whom the gods design to destroy, they first make mad." In this holy work the Catholics of these United States—those ardent friends of popular Government, who so loudly proclaim that every nation, even every State has the right to the choice of its own government—are expected, and are preparing, by firing their enthusiasm by volumes of wordy protests—they have all turned Protestants at last—to take a prominent part, the highest seat in the synagogue of war.

We have authority stamped with the signet of infallibility for asserting that the first allegiance of the Catholic of the United States is due not to our Government, but to the Pope. We are explicitly told that we are protecting an organization which holds itself ready at any time to obey the commands of a foreign despot.*

---

* The *Tablet*, in a recent issue, asks:—"Is the American idea higher than this Church idea? No Catholic can pretend it; for to him the Church idea is divine, and nothing is, or can be, higher than God, who is Supreme Creator, proprietor and Lord of all things, visible and invisible. If, then, between the Church or Catholic idea, and the American idea, there should happen to be a collision, which should give way, the lower or higher? The Catholic idea being supreme, must be the law, the universal standard of right and wrong,

Certainly, on the question of intolerance and detestation of civil and religious liberty, none can charge Rome with vacillation. If language and actions express the determination of the will, and the desire of the heart, we may certainly be excused for believing the assertion of our Catholic friends :—" IF THE CATHOLICS EVER GAIN AN IMMENSE NUMERICAL MAJORITY, RELIGIOUS FREEDOM IN THIS COUNTRY IS AT AN END."

Since Popery is an outgrowth of the depraved heart, may we not expect that it will remain essentially unchanged, so long as human nature remains unaltered? Are we not taught in Nebuchadnezzar's dream, and Daniel's vision, and Paul's prophecy, that this giant evil shall afflict the world until the dawn of the millennium? *

By gradually undermining the foundations of a simple faith in the unadulterated Gospel, Popery established itself as the desperate and malignant foe of all that is life-giving in the spiritual religion of Christ, all

---

of truth and falsehood, and consequently all ideas, whether Celtic or Saxon, English or American, that contradict it, or do not accord with it, are to be rejected as false and wrong, as repugnant to the supreme law of God, even to God himself, and not to be entertained for a moment."

* " But the judgment shall sit, and they shall take away his dominion *to consume and to destroy it unto the end.*"—Dan. vii. 26.

"And then shall that Wicked be revealed, whom the Lord shall consume with the spirit of his mouth, and *shall destroy with the brightness of his coming.*" " *Unto the end,*" " *shall destroy with the brightness of his coming.*" The best Commentators say, till Christ's Second Advent.—2 Thes. ii. 8.

that is ennobling in the liberty it inspires. And how otherwise than by gradual destruction can the doctrines and superstitions of millions of human beings be utterly consumed? Their overthrow "in an hour" would not produce in the hearts of the enslaved instantaneous detestation of these follies and errors. Rome's temporal power is indeed gone, perhaps forever, but her spiritual despotism is still complete, and may continue nearly or quite the same for centuries. So long as there are those who are willing to be victims of spiritual thraldom, there will no doubt be those who are ready to enslave them. Consume the hated organization to-day, and to-morrow another, phœnix-like, will spring from its ashes. Love of power, and preference of the forms of devotion to the spirit, will no doubt continue—calling for the unceasing labors of God's people—till the river of time issues into the ocean of eternity.

We may, therefore, expect in the future what we have witnessed in the past—an unceasing struggle. Many complications may arise. Often victory may seem to perch on the banners of the enemy. Many hopes will be crushed, the hearts of God's people "failing them for fear, and for looking after those things that are coming upon the earth." Since, however, we have witnessed in the last three centuries the gradual decay of Popery, may we not confidently rejoice in the hope that He who delights to write on the page of history the evidence of his far-reaching designs will, in his own time, strike the final blow, causing this gigantic system of falsehood to dissolve like mist before the rising sun? Ours is the task of hoping, laboring, praying, till even in Rome spiritual liberty shall dawn on civil,

"Like another morning risen on mid-noon."

"How long, O Lord our God,
 Holy, and true and good,
 Wilt Thou not judge Thy suffering Church,
 Her sighs, and tears, and blood?"

THE END.

OTHER TITLES AVAILABLE THROUGH THE BOOK TREE • CALL FOR OUR FREE CATALOG

TRIUMPH OF THE HUMAN SPIRIT: The Greatest Achievements of the Human Soul and How Its Power Can Change Your Life by Paul Tice. A triumph of the human spirit happens when we know we are right about something, put our heart into achieving its goal, and then succeed. There is no better feeling. People throughout history have triumphed while fighting for the highest ideal of all – spiritual truth. Some of these people and movements failed, other times they changed the course of history. Those who failed only did so on a physical level, when they were eliminated through violence. Their spirit lives on. This book not only documents the history of spiritual giants, it shows you how you can achieve your own spiritual triumph. Various exercises will strengthen your soul and reveal its hidden power. In today's world we are free to explore the truth without fear of being tortured or executed. As a result, the rewards are great. You will discover your true spiritual power with this work and will be able to tap into it. This is the perfect book for all those who believe in spiritual freedom and have a passion for the truth. (1999) • 295 pages • 6 x 9 • trade paperback • $19.95 • ISBN 1-885395-57-4

PAST SHOCK: The Origin of Religion and Its Impact on the Human Soul by Jack Barranger. Introduction by Paul Tice. Twenty years ago, Alvin Toffler coined the term "future shock" – a syndrome in which people are overwhelmed by the future. *Past Shock* suggests that events which happened thousands of years ago very strongly impact humanity today. This book reveals incredible observations on our inherited "slave chip" programming and how w've been conditioned to remain spiritually ignorant. Barranger exposes what he calls the "pretender gods," advanced beings who were not divine, but had advanced knowledge of scientific principles which included genetic engineering. Our advanced science of today has unraveled their secrets, and people like Barranger have the knowledge and courage to expose exactly how we were manipulated. Readers will learn about our past conditioning, and how to overcome the "slave chip" mentality to begin living life as it was meant to be, as a spiritually fulfilled being. (1998) • 126 pages • 6 x 9 • trade paperback • $12.95 • ISBN 1-885395-08-6

GOD GAMES: What Do You Do Forever? by Neil Freer. Introduction by Zecharia Sitchin. This new book by the author of Breaking the Godspell clearly outlines the entire human evolutionary scenario. While Sitchin has delineated what happened to humankind in the remote past based on ancient texts, Freer outlines the implications for the future. We are all creating the next step we need to take as we evolve from a genetically engineered species into something far beyond what we could ever imagine. We can now play our own "god games." We are convinced that great thinkers in the future will look back on this book, in particular, as being the one which opened the door to a new paradigm now developing. Neil Freer is a brilliant philosopher who recognizes the complete picture today, and is far ahead of all others who wonder what really makes us tick, and where it is that we are going. This book will make readers think in new and different ways. (1998) • 310 pages • 6 x 9 • trade paperback • $19.95 • ISBN 1-885395-26-4

OF HEAVEN AND EARTH: Essays Presented at the First Sitchin Studies Day. Edited by Zecharia Sitchin. Zecharia Sitchin's previous books have sold millions around the world. This book contains further information on his incredible theories about the origins of mankind and the intervention by intelligences beyond the Earth. This book offers the complete proceedings of the first Sitchin Studies Day. Sitchin's keynote address opens the book, followed by six other prominent speakers whose work has been influenced by Sitchin. The other contributors include two university professors, a clergyman, a UFO expert, a philosopher, and a novelist – who joined Zecharia Sitchin to describe how his findings and conclusions have affected what they teach and preach. They all seem to agree that the myths of ancient peoples were actual events as opposed to being figments of imaginations. Another point of agreement is in Sitchin's work being the early part of a new paradigm – one that is already beginning to shake the very foundations of religion, archaeology and our society in general. (1996) • 164 pages • 5 1/2 x 8 1/2 • trade paperback • $14.95 • ISBN 1-885395-17-5

FLYING SERPENTS AND DRAGONS: The Story of Mankind's Reptilian Past, By R.A. Boulay. Revised and expanded edition. This highly original work deals a shattering blow to all our preconceived notions about our past and human origins. Worldwide legends refer to giant flying lizards and dragons which came to this planet and founded the ancient civilizations of Mesopotamia, Egypt, India and China. Who were these reptilian creatures? This book provides the answers to many of the riddles of history such as what was the real reason for man's creation, why did Adam lose his chance at immortality in the Garden of Eden, who were the Nefilim who descended from heaven and mated with human women, why the serpent take such a bum rap in history, why didn't Adam and Eve wear clothes in Eden, what were the "crystals" or "stones" that the ancient gods fought over, why did the ancient Sumerians call their major gods USHUMGAL, which means literally "great fiery, flying serpent," what was the role of the gigantic stone platform at Baalbek, and what were the "boats of heaven" in ancient Egypt and the "sky chariots" of the Bible? (1997, 1999) • 276 pages • 5 1/2 x 8 1/2 • trade paperback • $19.95 • ISBN 1-885395-25-6

Call for our FREE BOOK TREE CATALOG with over 1100 titles. Order from your local bookstore, or we accept Visa, MC, AmEx, or send check or money order (in USD) for the total amount plus 4.50 shipping for 1-3 books (and .50¢ thereafter). The Book Tree • PO Box 724 • Escondido, CA 92033 • (760) 489-5079 • Visit www.thebooktree.com • Call today (800) 700-TREE

www.ingramcontent.com/pod-product-compliance
Lightning Source LLC
Chambersburg PA
CBHW030433190426
43202CB00035B/46